William Arnold Stevens, Alvah Hovey, Justin Almerin Smith

Commentary on the epistle to the Ephesians

Vol. 3

William Arnold Stevens, Alvah Hovey, Justin Almerin Smith

Commentary on the epistle to the Ephesians
Vol. 3

ISBN/EAN: 9783337731045

Printed in Europe, USA, Canada, Australia, Japan

Cover: Foto ©Lupo / pixelio.de

More available books at **www.hansebooks.com**

AN

AMERICAN COMMENTARY

ON THE

NEW TESTAMENT.

EDITED BY

ALVAH HOVEY, D.D., LL.D.

PHILADELPHIA.
AMERICAN BAPTIST PUBLICATION SOCIETY,
1420 CHESTNUT STREET.

COMMENTARY

ON THE

EPISTLE TO THE EPHESIANS.

BY
JUSTIN A. SMITH, D. D.

PHILADELPHIA:
AMERICAN BAPTIST PUBLICATION SOCIETY,
1420 Chestnut Street.

Entered, according to Act of Congress, in the year 1890, by the
AMERICAN BAPTIST PUBLICATION SOCIETY,
in the Office of the Librarian of Congress, at Washington.

INTRODUCTION TO THE EPISTLE TO THE EPHESIANS.

I. THE EPISTLES OF THE CAPTIVITY.

Four of the epistles of Paul, owing to the circumstances under which they were written, are sometimes grouped in a general mention of them, as "Epistles of the Captivity." These are the epistles to the Ephesians, the Colossians, the Philippians, and to Philemon. In three of these the writer speaks of himself, expressly, as being at the time of writing a prisoner: three times in that to the Ephesians (3 : 1 ; 4 : 1 ; 6 : 20), once to the Colossians (4 : 18), and once to Philemon. (1 : 1.) Allusions in the letter to the Philippians imply the same fact, as respects the condition of the writer. In one place (1 : 13), he speaks of his "*bonds*," as having become manifest in Christ throughout the whole Prætorian guard" (Revised Version, "Prætorium," in the margin); while in another (4 : 22) where he mentions "Cæsar's household," we are made to understand by his "bonds," not only imprisonment, but imprisonment where his influence was felt in the Imperial Court; in other words, at Rome. The four epistles afford evidence, also, of having been written so nearly at the same time as to have been sent, three of them at least, to those for whom they were intended by the same persons ; to the Ephesians by Tychicus (6 : 21, 22), to the Colossians by Tychicus and Onesimus (4 : 7-9), to Philemon by Onesimus again. Although the Epistle to the Philippians was sent by another hand, that of Epaphroditus, still the evident condition of the writer is so much the same as in the other cases, that its composition under the same circumstances seems the only right conclusion.

That this imprisonment was at Rome is matter of general agreement among writers upon these epistles, although some attempt has been made to show that it was at Cesarea, and during the time of Paul's waiting in that city, pending the arrival of the new Procurator, Porcius Festus. The effort to establish this, however, is a forced one, and in the opinion of good judges, far from successful. One can hardly help sympathizing, indeed, with the "surprise" of Archdeacon Farrar ("Life and Work of St. Paul," p. 591, note), that such a critic as Meyer should accept this view. The mention of "Cæsar's household," from converts in which Paul sends greetings to the Philippians, and by which can in no way, though one German critic, Bottger, strangely argues for this, be intended the palace of Herod in Cesarea ; the presence with him of such brethren as Tychicus, Onesimus, Marcus, Epaphras, and Jesus Justus, who are nowhere spoken of as with him at Cesarea, and very unlikely to have been so ; the desire expressed by him in one place that he might have utterance given him so as to open his mouth boldly, to make known the mystery of the gospel (Eph. 6 : 19), implying opportunity for such utterance like that allowed him at Rome, but not so far as appears in the city of his earlier imprisonment :—in fact, what may be termed "the local coloring" in all four of these epistles is such as to compel the conclusion that only a decided tendency toward what Farrar calls "hypercritical ingenuity" could make one satisfied with any other theory of location for the imprisonment during which they were written than that which places it in the imperial city itself.

Of the duration of this imprisonment, and of the occupation of the illustrious prisoner while it lasted, we learn from the concluding words of the "Acts": "And Paul dwelt two whole years in his own hired house, and received all that came unto him, preaching the kingdom of God, and teaching those things which concern the Lord Jesus Christ, no man forbidding him." As to the date of his arrival in Rome, and so that at which his two years of captivity began, we are to note that his departure from Cesarea occurred upon the arrival in that city of Porcius Festus "in Felix's room" as Procurator of Judea. This has been shown to be in the year A. D. 60 (Wiesler, quoted by Rev. G. Lloyd Davies). In the autumn of that year those who were to conduct Paul to Rome, as a prisoner, sailed with him from Cesarea. In the spring of the following year, A. D. 61, he arrived in Rome, and the two years of his imprisonment began, closing, it is thought, in the spring of the year A. D. 63. At this point, our certain knowledge of him ceases, save that mention is made by writers such as Clemens, "the disciple and companion of Paul," by the "Canon of Muratori," and by Eusebius, of his release from this imprisonment, his subsequent missionary journeys "to the boundary of the West," and his martyrdom under Nero. It was during this latter period, supposed to be within the dates A. D. 63 and A. D. 68, that the two epistles to Timothy and the Epistle to Titus were written; the second to Timothy being last of all these productions of the Great Apostle. (See Hackett's "Commentary on the Acts" in this series, p. 325.)

These four epistles of the Captivity, with the study of one of which we are to be occupied in the pages following this introduction, derive from the circumstances under which they were written an individuality quite as marked as one discovers in their contents. The author of them is not now, as in the case of so many other of these remarkable productions, actively pursuing his missionary journey from city to city, or amidst the activities and anxieties of his daily ministry at Corinth or Athens or Philippi. We picture him in the hired lodgings at Rome, which he had been permitted to occupy, instead of any one of the prisons there, such as that which tradition assigns to him in his second imprisonment, and from which he went forth to his death. He enjoys, it is true, a measure of freedom not commonly allowed to prisoners, yet is in one way never permitted, by night or by day, to forget the fact of his real condition. The hand with which these letters were written wore, during the whole two years of his captivity, a chain, the other end of which was fastened to the left hand of the soldier who guarded him. This unwelcome attendance was never under any circumstances intermitted, and the fact of it lends genuine pathos to those places in his letter to the Ephesians, where, in speaking of himself as "the prisoner of Jesus Christ," or, "prisoner in the Lord," he uses the Greek word ὁ δέσμιος, which means, "one bound with a chain."

Apart from this, we find the tedium of his captivity relieved in ways which almost surprise us. The "Cæsar" to whom he had "appealed" was that Nero whose name in history is the synonym of brutal tyranny. This bad man had not yet arrived at that extreme in degrading personal vices and utterly heartless cruelty which he was soon to reach, but he was well on the way thither. He had recently put to death his own mother, Agrippina; he had become otherwise a terror and a horror to those nearest his person; he had dismissed from his counsels the only reputable men who had remained there, his teacher, the philosophical Seneca, and the Prætorian Prefect Burrus, and had surrendered himself wholly to the guidance of a man almost as despicable as himself, Tigillinus. What Rome was under such a "Cæsar" it is not difficult to imagine. That one like Paul should have passed these two years of his captivity there in such vicinity to the court as to win converts in the imperial household itself, and still with so little of molestation, and so much freedom of opportunity for "teaching the things which concern the Lord Jesus Christ," seems remarkable. And the more so as it was by command of this same emperor that, a few years later, he was to suffer a martyr's death.

However we account for it all, on the ground of Nero's preoccupation with other things, or want of knowledge of either the apostle or the causes of his imprisonment, or general indifference at the time to matters of religion, we can at least see in it a divine ordering of events so as that the church of later ages should not miss that treasure of spiritual instruction and stimulus and comfort which these Epistles of the Captivity supply. His own sense of something like this, the apostle intimates where he speaks of himself as "the prisoner of Jesus Christ" (3 : 1)—not Nero's, but Christ's; and with a mission even in this regard as distinct, as clear, as inspiring as when called into Macedonia, or when standing before his audience on Mars Hill at Athens.

Of this we become the more conscious as we study these epistles themselves, especially the two of them which so remarkably resemble each other, and which differ in some respects so widely from all other of Paul's writings—those to the Ephesians and the Colossians. With the former of these we are now to be concerned in the pages which follow.

II. EPHESUS AND THE CHURCH IN THAT CITY.

Next to Jerusalem and Antioch, Ephesus holds the most conspicuous place in the very earliest annals of Christianity. As the scene of Paul's labors during "the space of three years;" as the site of the most important of those "seven churches of Asia," to which John wrote from Patmos; as the centre of Asian Christianity during all the early centuries, as it had long been for the same wide and populous region the centre of Pagan power, and culture, and corruption, Ephesus, after Jerusalem and Antioch had lost the prominence in Christian progress which they originally enjoyed, long held a place second only to Rome itself.

Of the city, as Paul found it, Farrar says ("Life and Work of St. Paul," p. 356): "It was more Hellenic than Antioch, more Oriental than Corinth, more populous than Athens, more wealthy and more refined than Thessalonica, more skeptical and more superstitious than Ancyra or Pessinus." That temple of Diana, which was the chief ornament of the city, was also the chief centre of every manner of corruption. "Just as the mediæval sanctuaries," says Farrar, "attracted all the scum and villainy, all the cheats and debtors and murderers of the country round, and inevitably pauperized and degraded the entire vicinity—just as the squalor of the lower purlieus of Westminster to this day is accounted for by the direct affiliation to the crime and wretchedness which sheltered itself from punishment or persecution under the shadow of the Abbey—so the vicinity of the great temple of Diana reeked with the congregated pollutions of Asia." The temple enjoyed what was termed the right of asylum, where criminals of every class found shelter against arrest or punishment, a circumstance which, while it enhanced the fame of this celebrated shrine, was a source of active moral contagion of the worst kind.

Paul appears to have been drawn to this city as the centre of his own labors for a considerable period, partly by its leading position among the cities of Asia Minor, partly by the fact that he found "a great door and effectual open to" him there (1 Cor. 16 : 9),

6 INTRODUCTION TO THE EPISTLE TO THE EPHESIANS.

although at the same time there were "many adversaries." A stronghold of the most corrupting forms of Paganism, it was at the same time a centre of commerce, of literature, and of learning, with a name famous in the history of Grecian art and Grecian philosophy. Finding some there imperfectly instructed, and knowing only the baptism of John, yet favorably disposed to Christianity, he had, in these, first-fruits of his own labor in the Lord. With these twelve as fellow-laborers, he began preaching, first in the synagogue of the Jews, then "in the school of one Tyrannus," while the attestations of divine power in the working of miracles gave his word great effect. "So mightily grew the word of God and prevailed." The storm of opposition which subsequently arose, and the circumstances of peril amidst which his own work in Ephesus came to an end, naturally helped to invest his recollection of this period in his ministry with interest, and to keep alive sympathy and concern on behalf of the church he had planted there.

Of this the Epistle to the Ephesians affords example and illustration. He seeks to fortify them in knowledge and conviction of those Christian truths which are at once most fundamental and most inspiring. To this he adds warnings and injunctions in regard to duties of the Christian life in various relations, put in a form to suggest how fully he had in mind the peculiar surroundings and exposures of those to whom he wrote. It is a notable fact that the vivid and impressive picture of the Christian soldier clad in "the whole armor of God," which has so often been studied and applied in connection with the perils to which believers are exposed in a world abounding in temptation, occurs in this Epistle, addressed to a church whose liabilities in that regard were so peculiar. From all these circumstances the message "to the angel of the church in Ephesus" from John in Patmos (Rev. 2 : 17), first of these addresses to the seven churches, draws a peculiarity of interest which may prepare us for a more interested study also of the Epistle now before us.

III. AUTHORSHIP OF THE EPISTLE.

That a question as to the authorship of this Epistle should have arisen amongst critics may well seem remarkable. Either it must have been written by "Paul, an apostle," who is announced as its author in the opening words, or it is a forgery. If a forgery, it is certainly a most surprising one. Imitation of an author's style is comparatively easy, especially when there are characteristic peculiarities or mannerisms; although actual success, even in such cases, is one of the rarest incidents in literary history. In the present case, the question as to style is the least difficult of all. The strange thing would be, as Farrar observes in writing upon the subject, that one whose purpose was "to deceive the church and the world," should have "poured forth truths so exalted, and moral teaching so pure and profound." This, too, we may add, with so many indications of the deepest sincerity, and at times such intensity of emotion. Added to this is the fact that no critic has attempted to suggest any real author other than the apostle, or to explain how it could be that a man in that age capable of writing an epistle second to none in the indications it affords of the highest intellectual and spiritual gifts, yet was never so conspicuous in any other way as to be known even by his name.

The two critics whose denial of Paul's authorship of this Epistle has attracted most attention are De Wette and Baur. The chief grounds urged by the former may be thus stated. 1. The resemblances noticed between this Epistle and that to the Colossians, suggesting, as is urged, the likelihood of the former being partly a copy and partly an imitation of the latter. To which it may be replied, that the differences between the two

INTRODUCTION TO THE EPISTLE TO THE EPHESIANS.

are quite as noticeable as the resemblances, while these differences exist in the case of those peculiarities which are most characteristic of each; also, that there can be nothing remarkable in the fact that, written so nearly at the same time and under the same circumstances, there should be in these two epistles occasional use of the same phraseology, or even here and there almost identity in both thought and expression. 2. The second of De Wette's grounds of objection is what is claimed as unlike Paul, in the diction, and even in the teaching of the Epistle. It is certainly a hard measure for an author if he can claim proprietorship in his own work neither because in it he is like, nor because he is unlike himself. The two points of objection are certainly not consistent each with the other, and may be treated as rendering us the service of mutually supplying all the really needed answer to either.

Baur, in what he has to say upon the subject, dwells much upon certain words and allusions in the Epistle which he interprets as having reference to Gnostic and other heresies that appeared only after the death of this apostle. Such words and allusions are very few in number, and by no means necessarily refer to heresies of any kind, although in the Epistle to the Colossians such reference is more evident. But even if the fact be as supposed, any resemblances in words or phrases used to those customary later in heretical writers may, as Eadie suggests, as well be due to imitations of Scripture phraseology on the part of these writers, which, indeed, is known to have been their practice. "The Gnosticism of the second century," says Dr. Eadie, "was not wholly unchristian, either in idea or in nomenclature, but it took from Scripture whatever in thought or expression suited its specious theosophy, and borrowed such materials to a large extent from the New Testament. Such a procedure may be plainly proved. The same process has been repeated in various forms, and in more recent times, in Germany itself. The inference is not," he adds, "as these critics hold, that the epistles to Colosse and Ephesus are the product of Gnosticism in array against Ebionitism, but only that the Gnostic sophists gilded their speculations with biblical phraseology."

It is surely unnecessary for us to occupy more space than we have now done with this example of a method in criticism whose achievements have been so futile, and whose real claim to attention, never great, is now scarcely appreciable. It would be difficult to name any one of the writings of the Great Apostle which in its substance, and diction, and spiritual tone offers less opportunity for such a theory of authorship as these critics have proposed, than the Epistle to the Ephesians. It should be added that until these late years the Pauline authorship of the Epistle was never questioned in any quarter, the testimony of primitive Christianity in that regard being absolutely unanimous.

IV. TO WHOM ADDRESSED.

In two very ancient manuscripts, the Sinaitic and the Vatican, both belonging to the middle of the fourth century, and in one other of much later date, the first verse in the Epistle is found with the words "in Ephesus" ($\dot{\varepsilon}\nu\ \dot{\varepsilon}\phi\dot{\varepsilon}\sigma\psi$, in the Greek) omitted. Passages occur, also, in certain of the oldest Christian writers which by some critics are interpreted as implying that in the copies of the Epistle used by them, these two words are not found. Others read these passages differently, and at most the sense, in so far as this point is concerned, is doubtful. Upon the other hand, in the second of the two manuscripts just named, the Vatican, the words ($\dot{\varepsilon}\nu\ \dot{\varepsilon}\phi\dot{\varepsilon}\sigma\psi$) are given in the margin, perhaps as suggesting that they ought to be supplied in the text, while in the Sinaitic manuscript a similar marginal entry appears, though considerably later in date than the manuscript. The Alexandrian manuscript, belonging to the fifth century, has the words in the text itself. The same is true of all the old versions, while such writers as Ignatius, Irenæus, Clement of Alexandria,—all of them writing before the close of the second century,—Tertullian, Cyprian; all of these, save the first, certainly, and Ignatius himself probably, quote or otherwise speak of the Epistle as written to the Ephesians.

The two ancient writers whose authority is by some critics quoted as against the received theory that the Epistle was addressed to the church in Ephesus, are Origen and Basil the Great. The single passage taken from each of these writers is an example of the fanciful interpretations so frequent in both, and especially Origen. We may quote these passages as translated by Eadie, in the introduction to his "Commentary on the Ephesians." That in Origen is as follows: "We found the phrase 'to the saints that are,' occurring only in the case of the Ephesians, and we inquire what its meaning may be. Observe, then, whether, as He who revealed His name to Moses in Exodus calls His name I AM, so they who are partakers of the I AM are those who be, being called out of non-existence into existence—for God, as Paul himself says, chose the things that are not that he might destroy the things that are."

Basil has a similar conceit in the passage quoted from him. Paul, he says, "in writing to the Ephesians, . . . calls them in a special sense THOSE WHO ARE, saying, To the saints WHO ARE (τοῖς οὖσι), and the faithful in Christ Jesus. For thus those before us have transmitted it, and we have found it in the ancient copies."

A very great deal of critical ingenuity has been expended upon these two passages. Considering them without any attempt of that kind, we find these points, at least, very evident: 1. That both Origen and Basil represent the Epistle as written "to the Ephesians," since they both speak of it in that way. 2. That the meaning they seek to find in such an expression as "the saints that are," is wholly fanciful, and has no place in the present argument. 3. That how much is imported by their testimony to the presence or absence of the words in dispute in ancient copies of the Epistle is wholly uncertain. Even supposing that copies existed in which the words were wanting, that might be accounted for otherwise than upon the theory that Paul himself did not place them in the Epistle as written by himself, while the fact that both Origen and Basil nevertheless treat the Epistle as written to the Ephesians, shows that they themselves were aware of sufficiently good reasons why it ought to be regarded as so written and addressed.

Those who maintain that the Epistle was not intended for the Church in Ephesus, nor written expressly to that church, assume to find an argument in the fact that the Epistle does not have near its close those salutations and other expressions of Christian affection addressed to individuals, which are noticed in other of Paul's letters to churches. This is thought to be remarkable in view of Paul's peculiar relations to the Ephesian Church, as one founded under his own personal ministry, and whose love for it was so touchingly shown in his parting interview with the elders of this church at Troas, while on his way "bound in the Spirit to Jerusalem," knowing that "bonds and afflictions abided him there." It is hence inferred that whatever may have been the destination of this Epistle, that destination can not have been Ephesus, at least Ephesus exclusively. Upon this we may observe: 1. That the salutations and greetings in question are found in letters of Paul to churches which cannot have been, as a body, known to him as the Ephesian Church was, and such salutations were, therefore, naturally sent to those amongst them whom he did thus know, and whom he had personal reasons for remembering in this way. Such is the case with the Epistle to the Romans, the first to the Corinthians, and that to the Colos-

INTRODUCTION TO THE EPISTLE TO THE EPHESIANS. 9

sians. 2. These personal salutations, however, are not so common as those who urge this argument would imply. In First and Second Thessalonians, in the second to the Corinthians, in Galatians, the salutation is wholly general, just as we find it here in Ephesians, the closing verses of which have very warm expressions of Christian attachment, although addressed to the church as such, rather than to individuals. 3. It is easy to see why, in a case like this church at Ephesus, Paul should not single out individuals for express affectionate mention. The entire membership were in a like relationship with him as the minister by whom they had been made to know the gospel and to accept it with all its precious hopes. Even if he had no reason to fear that jealousies might be awakened by special messages to individuals, he would doubtless feel in himself that whatever message of affection he had for one he had for all. The whole Epistle is, in fact (4), pervaded by a tone of personal interest, and seems so much suggested by what he thoroughly knew of those to whom he was writing, that from its first word to its last, it might very properly be regarded as expressing to each member of the Ephesian Church, and to all of them, his love for them as his spiritual children, and his desire for their welfare in all things.

We shall not think it necessary, in view of all, to dwell upon the theory proposed by some and advocated by such writers as Conybeare and Howson, and others, that the Epistle probably had originally the form of a circular letter, being intended for several churches, including Ephesus; that it was sent by Tychicus in a form to be addressed to either the church at Ephesus, the church at Laodicea, or at Philadelphia as delivered by him, and that this may account for the appearance of the words in Ephesus ($\mathit{\dot{\epsilon}\nu\ \dot{\epsilon}\phi\acute{\epsilon}\sigma\omega}$) in some, its omission in others, and also for what seems to have been a statement of the heresiarch Marcion, that the Epistle was really written to the Laodiceans. There seems to be no occasion for what appears so much like an evasion of the difficulty, and for which there is no real support.

The sum of all may perhaps be thus stated: One very ancient manuscript, and all of later date save one, contain the words in question. All the ancient versions, including the Syriac and the Latin, have them. All of the most ancient Christian writers, including Origen and Basil themselves, speak of the Epistle as written to the Ephesians, while only these two make any allusion to copies of manuscripts in which the words did not appear. The internal evidence found in the general tenor and spirit of the Epistle justifies the view that it was written to the Ephesians, and to them was addressed, as in the case of other churches named, as this one is, in the opening words. Of recent critics and commentators who upon grounds like these just indicated regard the words "in Ephesus" ($\mathit{\dot{\epsilon}\nu\ \dot{\epsilon}\phi\acute{\epsilon}\sigma\omega}$) as belonging to the original text, we name Meyer, Davidson, Stuart, Alexander, Alford, and Eadie. Ellicott, although he regards the Epistle as written to the Ephesians and so addressed, thinks it very probable that it was intended also for other churches in the neighborhood of that metropolitan city, and was for this reason made more general in form than was usual with this apostle. This is not to view it as a circular letter in any proper sense, and may probably be accepted as the correct view. The words ($\mathit{\dot{\epsilon}\nu\ \dot{\epsilon}\phi\acute{\epsilon}\sigma\omega}$) Ellicott "retains as genuine."

V. PECULIARITIES OF STYLE.

It is agreed among writers on this Epistle who accept it as genuine, that the Epistle to the Ephesians excels all other writings of this apostle alike in the comprehensiveness of its doctrinal content and in the sublimity of its style. Alford speaks of it as made, in this way, "by far the most difficult of all the writings of St. Paul." Elsewhere he adds: "As in the Epistles to the Romans, Galatians, and Colossians, the difficulties lie for the most part at or near the surface, a certain degree of study will master, not indeed the mysteries of redemption which are treated of, but the contextual coherence and the course of the argument; or, if not so, will at least serve to point out to every reader where the hard texts lie, and to bring out into relief each point with which he has to deal; whereas here the difficulties lie altogether beneath the surface, are not discernible by the cursory reader, who finds all very straightforward and simple." The student of this Epistle, he says further on, "must not expect to go over his ground rapidly; must not be disappointed if the week's end finds him still on the same paragraph or even on the same verse, weighing and judging."

The two Epistles, to the Ephesians and Colossians, are often compared with each other, and between them there are indeed marked resemblances. Evidently, they were both written very nearly at the same time, and in much the same state of mind and feeling. They are dissimilar, however, through differences both in the purpose of the writing and in the circumstances of those addressed. In writing to the Colossians, Paul appears to have a distinct purpose to gain; a correction of certain speculative tendencies beginning there to appear, more especially a tendency to exaggeration of certain outward observances, such as superstitious distinctions of meats and drinks, feast days, "new moons and Sabbaths"; these being partly remnants of heathen, partly of Judaic, notions of what is essential to religion. In contrast with all this, he sets before them the Lord Jesus Christ, in whom all fullness dwells, and in whom they are to find summed up all the great and precious realities of faith. Thus, in the doctrinal part of the Epistle he dwells upon the person of Christ as "the image of the invisible God," as he in whom all things were created, as head over all things to the church, and as the substance and fulfillment of all types; while to him all manner of outward observance is intended to lead us in faith, and hope, and obedience. It may be true, also, as some think, that incipient heresies of another sort had appeared at Colosse, germs of the later Gnosticism; that to these things the writer refers where he warns against those who would "beguile" them "with enticing words," or "spoil them through philosophy and vain deceit." The purpose of the Colossian Epistle, at all events, is distinctively practical, although in seeking to realize this purpose, the writer touches upon some of the loftiest teachings of the Christian faith.

It is thought by many, and is probably the fact, that the Epistle to the Colossians was written first of the two. In the writing of it, thought and feeling are kindled to a flame. Calling to mind, then, those in another city of Asia Minor, amongst whom he had passed longer periods of personal ministry than in any other case, cherishing toward them a measure of affectionate confidence which encouraged the opening to them of all his mind and all his heart, he resumes his pen in a letter to them, in which, setting forth from those more elementary teachings which he had given to them in his personal ministry, he leads them out in a wider range of revealed truth than he had attempted, either in this case, or in that of any other church. It is "the mystery of Christ" (ch. 3 : 4) in a very special sense, with which he deals; a revelation of the mind, and purpose, and act of God in the great plan of human redemption in no other instance so fully set forth.

The style partakes very much of the nature of the subject. Something of the same peculiarity appears also in the letter to the Colossians, and is due there to much the same cause. No one writes in this manner who is not completely carried away by his theme. There is no attempt, at least in the doctrinal portion of the Epistle, at anything like a concise and orderly construction of the sentences. In repeated instances (as in 2 : 1-4 and 3 : 1-14), a thought is taken up and the thread of it immediately dropped, while another, though a related thought, comes in, parenthetically, and commands attention, till further on, though with very little of orderly readjustment, the first one is resumed. Profound truth, as related to purposes of God in the eternity past, and the person and office of Christ in the great work of redemption, is put in the form of rapid statement, suggesting to the cursory reader, as Alford intimates, scarcely more than a hint of the immensity of the conception or the wide-reaching relations of the doctrine implied. We find, as Dr. Hodge says, "clause linked with clause," as one thought suggests another which cannot wait for utterance, till the writer "is forced to stop and begin his sentences anew." To appreciate the reason of this, we must see the writer of the Epistle in his forced comparative seclusion, and realize how the fervor of his soul, which had been wont to find such ample expression in the ceaseless labors of his ministry from city to city and from continent to continent, is now limited to such casual opportunities as transient visitors might afford him, and to communications, like this, with those in distant cities, whose spiritual welfare was still with him a constant desire and prayer. Meditating thus upon the great themes of his ministry, his soul is filled with them, and when he takes his pen to write the rush of thought and feeling carries him away. It is quite possible, besides, that the peculiarity of style here mentioned is occasioned in a degree by the fact that he writes with a chained hand, the guarding soldier seated near, and perhaps with other things in the surroundings to make deliberate and careful composition a matter of difficulty.

The Epistle to the Ephesians becomes thus a somewhat striking example of the manner in which inspiration not only allows, but uses, peculiarity of character and temperament in the writer, and as well the influences of time and place. It is possible that under no other circumstances would the apostle have found his mind led forth into such a field of inspired meditation or have gained such conceptions of the kingdom of God in its relation to God's own redeemed people. The language he uses has in consequence a peculiar intensity. Five times in the Epistle and twice in the same chapter he employs a phrase (τοῖς ἐπουρανίοις) which it seems impossible to render adequately from the Greek into English. It is imperfectly translated "in the heavenly places"; or, as by some writers, though with a meaning too vague, "the heavenlies"; and in which it almost seems as if the distinction of earthly and heavenly had faded away, so that when he speaks of what is now in possession, it were already heaven begun, even by himself, "the prisoner of Jesus Christ"; or, as if in other connections of the same phrase, the temporal were already lost in the spiritual. We find him also with great frequency using such intense expressions as "the riches of the glory of his inheritance in the saints"; "God, who is rich in mercy"; "exceeding riches of his grace"; "grant you according to the riches of his glory"—the Greek word, (πλοῦτος or πλούσιος), meaning "riches," "wealth," "fullness," "plenitude," becoming thus with him a favorite one for expressing his sense of the wonderful kindness of God to redeemed men. The word for "grace" (χάρις) occurs thirteen times; and may, as Farrar says, be considered "the keynote of the Epistle." The word for "mystery" occurs five times; in no other Epistle more than twice. Another significant peculiarity is the frequent occurrence of compounds with the Greek preposition for "with" (σύν), expressing participation, or community of possession. We find it in such words and phrases as "made alive," or "*quickened together with Christ*," "*raised up together*" with him, "made us *sit together* in heavenly places with Christ," "*fellow-citizens* with the saints," "*builded together* for an habitation of God through the Spirit," "*fellow-heirs*," "*fellow-members* of the body," "*fellow-partakers* of the promise"—all of which represent a leading thought in the Epistle, which is the union of all believers in a common faith, and hope, and calling, and especially their oneness in Christ.

In a word, we may say that while this Epistle has qualities of style common to this apostle's writings, it has characteristics of its own, due in part to the subject, and in part to the conditions under which it was produced. It should be added, however, that neither the glow of feeling inspired by the subject, nor the peculiar circumstances of the writer, is allowed to mar the logical connection of the general argument, or lessen the force with which all is made to bear upon the special purpose in writing.

VI. SUBSTANCE OF THE EPISTLE IN A GENERAL VIEW.

Although the Epistle to the Ephesians deals so much with doctrine, it is still not a doctrinal treatise, but an Epistle, with the characteristics proper to such. That personal element which gives to epistolary writing its distinctive quality, pervades it, in spite of the fact that direct personal mention, or even express allusion, is less frequent than in most of Paul's letters to the churches. About the middle of the fourth chapter, the apostle turns directly to those whom up to that point he has addressed more in the form of general instruction, and from thence on to the end of the Epistle appeals to them in counsel and exhortation, covering the various relations of the Christian life, doubtless with adaptations to what both he and they knew of their peculiar circumstances. Indeed, he had twice before seemed about to break off the strain of high doctrinal exhortation upon which he had entered at the outset of the Epistle, and to begin upon that more practical appeal. The third chapter opens with, "For this cause I Paul, the prisoner of Jesus Christ, to you Gentiles," seeming as if some matter more directly personal were to follow.

Then the fourth chapter itself begins, "I therefore, I the prisoner in the Lord, beseech you that ye walk worthy of the vocation wherewith ye are called," passing away, however, as before, from that more personal theme to dwell upon the divine provision made in this behalf. With the seventeenth verse of this fourth chapter he enters fully upon that which he has clearly had in view all along, making it evident that this "knowledge in the mystery of Christ" which he had been unfolding, is just intended to make faith more ample, and life more pure and true.

It is, perhaps, not too much to say that the theme of the Epistle, and the writer's method in treating it, are both implied in the third and fourth verses of the first chapter: "Blessed be the God and Father of our Lord Jesus Christ, who hath blessed us with every spiritual blessing in the heavenly places in Christ: even as he chose us in him before the foundation of the world, that we should be holy and without blemish before him in love." The three first chapters of the Epistle, and the fourth as far as the seventeenth verse, are an expansion of the doctrinal thought in these two verses; while what follows from the middle of the fourth chapter to the end is devoted to showing how the great motive to holy and blameless conduct in all life's relations, so brought to view, should prompt and rule each Christian believer.

As linking, so to speak, these two main divisions of the whole theme, we have what is contained in verses 3-16 in chapter 4. It is there shown that in the gracious provision made, there is adaptation to the peculiar needs of men in this world. When the Redeemer, his ministry and suffering ended, went up on high, leading captivity captive, he received gifts for men. It was included in the functions of his great office as Redeemer that he should be also in a certain living relation with his redeemed people; not only should impartations of spiritual life flow to them through him, but it was his to endow them, as the church bought with his own blood, his "body," with ordinances and offices suited to promote in every way their personal growth and their efficiency as instruments of grace and salvation to the world. Thus, in some sense, we have, along with the doctrine of Redemption, the doctrine of the Church, the purpose of both being, as said at the beginning, "that we should be holy and without blemish before him in love." Alike the doctrine of redemption and the doctrine of the church are set forth in a way to some extent peculiar to this Epistle. We have, indeed, the church elsewhere spoken of as "the body of Christ," and offices in the church, with the duties appropriate to each, are in other places named with much more of detail than is attempted here. But in this fourth chapter of our Epistle, the church—not simply nor chiefly the local church, but the church in its largest spiritual sense—is put in a relation with Christ peculiar to this one of all Paul's epistles. The sixteenth verse of the chapter, very difficult of precise exposition, is a wonderful representation of the absolute dependence of each individual Christian, and of the whole spiritual body as such, upon "him who is the head, even Christ." Then what appears of the ultimate unity of this spiritual body is found, as we dwell upon it, to have a wonderful scope of meaning. What is said in ver. 14 of troubled agitations under opposing winds of doctrine, while it has an application to each individual church and each individual Christian, looks in its largest meaning beyond all that is individual and special; it forecasts centuries of stormy division among those claiming to be the followers of the one Lord, anticipating, indeed, all that which for us is now history, and that which for those living after us may be history again. In ver. 13, however, we have foreshadowed that for which we have a right to look in this kingdom of God among men—a coming at last to "the unity of faith, and of the knowledge of the Son of God, the measure of the stature of the fullness of Christ." However it may be elsewhere in the world, in the kingdom of God division struggles ever toward unity, and the time will come when unity, and no longer division, shall be the law of that kingdom. Foretokens of that final issue already appear.

This doctrine of the church may be said to stand as the corollary of that doctrine of redemption which occupies so much of the whole space in this Epistle. As already intimated, this doctrine as unfolded, has its ground in what is said in the fourth verse of the first chapter: "According as he hath chosen us in him before the foundation of the world." What is said more than this is concerned entirely with the fulfillment of that gracious election, so truly divine in its motive, and so complete in its operation. All that we realize in redemption comes to us just in the fulfillment of that purpose. But what is peculiar in the view the apostle here takes of a subject which in other ways he treats of in other epistles, is intimated in the ninth and tenth verses of the same chapter, where we are told how God has "made known unto us the mystery of his will, according to the good pleasure which he purposed in him [that is, in Christ] unto a dispensation of the fullness of times, *to sum up all things in Christ*, the things in the heaven, and things upon the earth." This is the central thought of all which is said here upon this great theme of human redemption—" to sum up all things in Christ." The writer returns to it again and again. It is in reference to it, chiefly, that he makes those Gentile Christians at Ephesus so fully aware of "the grace of God" shown to them, in that the full treasure of this gracious provision had been made as free to them as to God's covenant people themselves. It is also what lends peculiar significance to that which is said of the ultimate unity of the church. It is to be unity *in him*. Christ is one day to fully and gloriously appear before the universe of men and angels in that transcendant personality which belongs to him as the Redeemer of men and the Head over all things to the church. That is the thought which there, in his Roman prison, has seized upon and fired the whole soul of the writer of this Epistle, and the thought which imparts to what he here says such intensity of feeling and such dignity of utterance. In proportion as we realize this, and in proportion as we enter into the substance and spirit of what we find here written, shall we feel the force of the appeal based upon this view of what our redemption imports, that we do indeed "walk worthy of the calling wherewith we have been called."

VII. ANALYSIS OF THE EPISTLE MORE IN DETAIL.

It is quite surely to be gathered from the tenor of this Epistle, that the church in Ephesus was chiefly composed of Gentile converts. There were also Jews, as may be inferred from the fact that Paul's own preaching there had been at first in "the synagogue." Yet, as the narrative in Acts (19 : 8, 9) seems to imply, he found his own countrymen less accessible than the Gentile population, and so he left the synagogue, and we then find him reasoning daily in the school of one Tyrannus. Whatever may have been the relative proportion of Jews and Gentiles in the church, it is to the latter that he seems to address himself chiefly in this Epistle—a fact to be borne in mind in the study of it. His desire evidently is to strongly impress these Gentile believers, (1) with the general truth, that salvation, whether of Jew or Gentile, is a work of divine grace, executing a divine purpose ; (2) with the truth that the whole scheme of redemption, whether as respects its original purpose, its method, or its result, centers wholly in Christ ; and, (3) with the truth that they, as Gentiles, were under an especial obligation of gratitude for this grace, since the opening to them of this door of mercy was the receiving of them to all that special favor which had once been given to God's covenant people, with every middle wall of partition now broken down. In the light of these considerations the practical lessons and appeals in the closing chapters of the Epistle are pressed home.

The general doctrine of the divine purpose of redemption, and the election of a redeemed people, chosen in Christ before the foundation of the world, occupies the first fourteen verses of the first chapter. This is followed to the end of the chapter by expressions of thanksgiving in behalf of those addressed, that in the grace of redemption they had been made participants, with the prayer that they might be enabled, by divine help, to enter into the full realization and experience of the grace so manifested ; especially realizing how pre-eminent in all is the place filled by him who is the Redeemer.

With a view to impress this truth more strongly, in the opening verses of the second chapter (ver. 1-2), he reminds them of the condition in which the grace of God had found them, the same essentially (ver. 3, 10) as that in which those to whom the gospel first came had been found, while in the "quickening" of the new birth both Jew and Gentile had experienced a like blessing and a common joy. Then in the remainder of the chapter he dwells upon the spiritual union into which Jew and Gentile are brought, in the experience of the same grace, of a common faith and a common hope.

In chapter 3 this of which he had been speaking is dwelt upon as that "mystery of Christ" which had been hidden through ages, adumbrated in types and divinely foreshadowed in prophecy, yet now clearly and fully revealed. He speaks of himself (ver. 7-9) as having been specially "made a minister" of that revelation, more particularly as it affected the Gentiles themselves. Following this, again, with an earnest prayer that they might come into rich and full possession of this blessing, and especially might come to know the love of Christ which passeth knowledge.

Chapter 4, as far as to the seventeenth verse, is occupied with that communion of saints into which believers, Jew and Gentile, are brought. They have "one Lord, one faith, one baptism, one God and Father of all." They are in all their wide dispersion, all their long succession, from age to age, "one body," with Christ as the Head, from whom proceeds to every member and through all channels of spiritual vitality, the one life. To promote this unity, with growth to the stature of the fullness of Christ, and to endow them for their world-wide ministry, are given to them, as gifts of the ascended Lord, apostles and prophets, pastors and teachers, and evangelists.

The weighty inference from all comes out in the seventeenth verse: "This I say, therefore, and testify in the Lord [a solemn adjuration], that ye henceforth walk not as other Gentiles walk." To the end of the chapter this appeal is set down in a vivid contrast of that which these Ephesian Christians had all about them, in a great and rich and wicked heathen city, with that which was to be expected of them as having "put on the new man, which after God is created in righteousness and true holiness."

The fifth chapter, and the sixth as far as the eleventh verse, deal with those several relations of life in which it is required that the spirit and law of the Christian profession shall thus be fulfilled. It is noticeable how in all these relations, of husband and wife, of parent and child, of master and servant, there is constant reference to that which he has so copiously set forth in earlier parts of the Epistle. This is not a mere morality which he enjoins. It is as "children of light" that we are to observe these things, walking in the new light shed upon the path of each redeemed one. It is as "filled with the Spirit," and as ourselves spiritual, that we utterly repudiate all "fellowship with the unfruitful works of darkness." It is as seeing in Christ and the church a symbol of that most sacred of all human relations, upon which it is sacrilege for any to lay unholy hands, or to treat it with levity, that husbands and wives are to have mutual regard for what this relation implies. It is with that "first commandment with promise," ever in mind, that children are to reverence their parents, while parents are to rear their children "in the nurture and admonition of the Lord." Servants are to render the service expected of them as "unto Christ," while masters are to remember that they also have a Master, even one in heaven, with whom is no respect of person. What a different thing from mere morality do the ethics of Christianity become in the handling of this Epistle!

Then at the eleventh verse comes the "Finally, my brethren." What a masterly picture is here given us of the Christian soldier, wrestling against principalities, against powers, against the rulers of the darkness of this world, "clad in the whole armour of God!" What a word is that in which he represents the whole idea of the steadfast Christian, faithful unto death—"*Stand!*" Called with such a calling, chosen for such a mission and such a destiny, God's redeemed one, fronting the world's wickedness, and the world's temptations,—what a noble picture he gives us of the steadfast Christian! Writing from his Roman prison, every word is enforced by his own heroic example; while in his closing words he becomes again tender and loving and prayerful, reaching out in his sympathies to all Christian believers throughout the world and throughout the ages: "Grace be with all them that love our Lord Jesus Christ in sincerity. Amen."

THE EPISTLE TO THE EPHESIANS.

CHAPTER I.

PAUL, an apostle of Jesus Christ by the will of God, to the saints which are at Ephesus, and to the faithful in Christ Jesus:

1 PAUL, an apostle of Christ Jesus through the will of God, to the saints who are ¹ at Ephesus, and the

1 Some very ancient authorities omit *at Ephesus*.

Ch. 1: 1, 2. THE SALUTATION.

1. Paul, an apostle of Jesus Christ. Of the authors of these apostolical communications to churches, to individuals, or to "the faithful" in general, Paul and Peter alone name themselves as apostles. James styles himself simply "the servant of Jesus Christ"; Jude employs the same form of personal introduction, while John, save in his first epistle, where no form of the kind is employed, is "The Elder." The difference in this particular may be without significance save in the case of Paul, whose relation to the apostleship was peculiar by reason of the fact that he was not of the original twelve, and who had found occasion, especially in writing to the Galatians, to claim with emphasis his right of recognition in this regard. He opens each of his epistles, accordingly, save those to the Philippians and the Thessalonians, with the same formula as here, more or less varied. We find also, in repeated instances, as in First and Second Corinthians, the Colossians, in Second Timothy, and here, the accompanying phrase, **by the will of God,** while in First Timothy this becomes, "according to the commandment of God our Saviour and Christ Jesus, our hope." The still more emphatic form used at the opening of Galatians is especially deserving of notice. Sometimes, too, in the body of the Epistle, mention is made of the writer's official position in this particular, as in Rom. 11: 13; 1 Cor. 9: 1; 2 Cor. 12: 12; 1 Tim. 2: 7. Of this peculiarity we need only say that it was very essential to the purpose of his mission that his full apostleship should have due recognition, as being "through the will of God" in his special call, not less than as if he had been of those who "companied with" the original apostles, from the beginning. **To the saints which are at Ephesus.** As to the question whether this Epistle shall be viewed as addressed originally to the Ephesian Church, or to them in association with other churches in their neighborhood, we refer the reader to the "Introduction." Assuming the correctness of the conclusion there stated, we find no necessity for treating the text here as if, in the form of a circular letter, it must read, "to those who are saints," etc. The Epistle was undoubtedly sent to the church at Ephesus, as one of those to be addressed, and probably, from the importance of that city and the position of the church as founded by Paul himself and the scene of his labors for three eventful years, that to which it was first of all communicated. The word 'saints' is in the epistles, especially of Paul, used so often as to suggest that it may then have been well nigh as commonly employed to designate believers in Christ, as the word "Christian" is now. This latter word occurs but three times in the New Testament, and only once as used by an apostle (1 Peter 4: 16), "if any man suffer as a Christian," the two other instances of its use being in the Acts (11: 26; 26: 28), and in both cases by persons who were themselves not Christians. The mediæval sense of the word "saints" must not be allowed to confuse its meaning here. It means simply consecrated persons; those given to the Lord as offerings of the sanctuary were anciently made, and in the same sense "holy" (ἅγιοι), save that, as will be noticed more fully hereafter, the character proper to such personal consecration is implied. **And to the faithful in Christ Jesus.** The Greek word for 'faithful,' Ellicott thinks, is "not here, in its general and classical sense, *qui fidem præstat*," equivalent to fidelity, "but its particular and theological sense, *qui fidem habet*," faith itself in exercise: "a meaning," he adds, "which it indisputably bears in several passages in the New Testament." Upon the other hand, Thayer, in his "Lexicon of the New Testament," instances numerous places where the word is employed

2 Grace be to you, and peace, from God our Father, and *from* the Lord Jesus Christ.

3 Blessed *be* the God and Father of our Lord Jesus Christ, who hath blessed us with all spiritual blessings in heavenly *places* in Christ:

2 faithful in Christ Jesus: Grace to you and peace from God our Father and the Lord Jesus Christ.

3 Blessed *be* ¹ the God and Father of our Lord Jesus Christ, who hath blessed us with every spirit-

¹ *Or, God and the Father.*

---

in the sense of "trusty," "faithful," one of them in this same Epistle (6 : 21) "faithful minister in the Lord"; although he quotes our present passage as an example of the meaning, "believing," "confiding," "trusting." The Revised Version, as will be seen, retains the translation 'faithful'; this, also, Alford prefers. The words 'in Christ Jesus' do not appear to make it necessary that we dismiss this latter meaning as inadmissible; the same form of expression, with the Greek preposition (*ἐν*, translated *in*), being frequently used in this Epistle, as in the place already noted (6 : 21), "faithful minister in the Lord," to indicate "the element, the life sphere," that relation, in other words, in which fidelity is exercised and shown. We own to a preference for this rendering of the word, and partly because of its more full expression of the apostle's meaning in characterizing those to whom he writes. The omission in Greek of the article before the word for 'faithful' brings the two clauses, 'saints which are at Ephesus' and 'faithful in Christ Jesus,' into close relation with each other. Perhaps, however, we may take the latter as comprehending along with those immediately addressed all those 'faithful in Christ Jesus' into whose hands the Epistle should come.

2. Grace be to you, and peace, from God our Father, and from the Lord Jesus Christ. Eadie calls attention to the *Christian* element in this "cordial and comprehensive" apostolical salutation, as "far more expressive than the ancient classic formula." Claudius Lysias (Acts 23 : 26) "unto the most excellent governor" sends greeting; Paul to the Ephesians, 'Grace be unto you, and peace, from God our Father, and the Lord Jesus Christ'; a salutation and a benediction in one. Ellicott, in his note, while saying that "the suggestion of Stier," that the "grace" may refer to "saints" and "peace" to "faithful," "does not seem tenable," still thinks these words should "not be diluted into mere equivalents of the ordinary forms of salutation." Attention should be given, also, to the association of 'the Lord Jesus Christ' with 'God our Father' as equally with him the source of grace and peace; benefits which, of the nature here intended, can be looked for, or expected, from no source less than divine.

3–8. THANKSGIVING FOR THE ELECTION OF GRACE, AND FOR REDEMPTION IN CHRIST JESUS THROUGH FAITH.

3. Blessed be the God and Father of our Lord Jesus Christ. A possible construction is: *Blessed be God and the Father of our Lord Jesus Christ*, and this would perhaps on doctrinal grounds be preferred by those who find a difficulty in the expression, "The God of our Lord Jesus Christ." Yet this latter form unmistakably occurs in ver. 17 of this chapter, and is quite in harmony with words of our Lord in John 20 : 17: "I ascend unto my Father and to your Father, and to my God and your God"; also in his cry from the cross: "My God, my God, why hast thou forsaken me?" In both these places our Lord speaks distinctively in his human nature, and the form used need in no way embarrass our conception of him as also divine. What seems the more natural construction may therefore be retained without doctrinal difficulty. Dr. Boise, in his note on the passage, seems to accept the usual rendering, though he quotes Meyer and Ellicott as preferring the other. Taking the words as they stand, they may be quoted as an example of that usage, alike by our Lord and by his apostles, which makes available to us all the preciousness of that fellowship with us in suffering and in service, into which our Lord is brought by his real participation with us in our human nature. **Who hath blessed us.** The juxtaposition of these two clauses, 'Blessed be God' and 'who hath blessed us,' brings to view a twofold usage of the emphatic word here that is somewhat difficult of clear discrimination. As applied to God, the word can only express the thanksgiving and the praise due to him from those who are made to know the perfections of his character, and are the recipients of his bounty. This is using

4 According as he hath chosen us in him before the foundation of the world, that we should be holy and without blame before him in love:

4 ual blessing in the heavenly *places* in Christ: even as he chose us in him before the foundation of the world, that we should be holy and without blemish

the word (εὐλογητός) "blessed" in its more exact meaning. It is a strong and fervent expression of praise (εὐλογία), whence our word "eulogy." The verb, however (εὐλογέω), has for one of its remoter meanings "to bestow blessings on," "to prosper," "to make happy." (Thayer's "Lexicon of the New Testament.") Thus the two clauses, 'Blessed be God,' 'who hath blessed us,' have a correspondence in meaning which justifies their significance in the present usage. They express that reciprocal interchange in which God's people bring to him their offerings of praise and thanksgiving, having received from him gifts of such a nature as that in the possession and enjoyment of these they, in their degree, come to share in that which makes *him* the object of their praise.

For these blessings so bestowed are **spiritual blessings in heavenly places in Christ.** The expression 'heavenly places' should first be explained. No word for 'places' appears in the Greek, and so it is printed as supplied, alike in the Common Version and the Revision. Whether it is the true word for completing the sense may be doubtful, although to find a better one is not easy. The Greek word here and elsewhere in this Epistle rendered 'heavenly *places*' (ἐπουρανίοις) is the same word which is found in John 3:12, where our Lord says to Nicodemus: "If I have told you earthly things and ye believe not, how shall ye believe if I tell you of heavenly things (τὰ ἐπουράνια)?" Again we find the word in Matt. 18:35, "my Leavenly Father"; again in 2 Tim. 4:18, "unto his heavenly kingdom." Again, almost singularly, the word occurs near the close of our present Epistle (6:12), "spiritual wickedness in high places," as given in the Common Version; "the spiritual hosts of wickedness in the heavenly *places*," as in the Revised Version. Other occurrences of the word in our Epistle are at 1:20, "at his right hand in the heavenly *places*"; 2:6, "made us sit with him in the heavenly *places*"; 3:10, "principalities and powers in the heavenly *places*." A local meaning seems clearly implied in all these instances. This local meaning, however, does not in all appear to govern the conception in the same degree. "Earthly things," those of which Jesus had been speaking to Nicodemus, concerning the new birth, etc., are by him put in contrast with "heavenly things," by which seems to be meant that higher range of revealed truth which concerns itself more with things more distinctively "heavenly." The "heavenly kingdom" of which Paul writes to Timothy is that kingdom which has heaven for its centre, and God as the Sovereign. Christ, at God's right hand in the "heavenly places," involves an idea more strictly local. But "spiritual hosts of wickedness in the heavenly places" must surely be understood in a way not to imply that there may be wickedness in heaven. Influenced by this variety of usage, apparently, Farrar and Maurice prefer the rather vague rendering, "the heavenlies," for all these instances in our present Epistle; while the writer in Schaff's "Commentary," Dr. M. B. Riddle, concludes that the word must have "a local sense, but a broad and comprehensive one"; and for the passage now immediately under consideration quotes Braune, as follows: "Every spiritual blessing which we have received springs from a higher world, is to be sought in a heavenly region, and thence to be obtained." This expansion of the local sense so as to comprehend the whole sphere of what is meant by 'spiritual blessings,' as found and realized 'in Christ,' may perhaps be accepted upon the whole as the best form in which to paraphrase a usage in the Greek for which we seem to have in English no entirely adequate expression.

4. According as he hath chosen us in him. The two first words the Revised Version renders *even as*. *Inasmuch as* is sometimes preferred. The connection of the thought is very close. The apostle, in speaking of the 'spiritual blessings' given and possessed 'in Christ,' looks back into the eternity past, **before the foundation of the world,** and finds the bestowment of these blessings as secured for us in that act of electing grace by which Christ is 'chosen' for his own high office, and his people 'in him' as their Representative and Head. The full force of the word for 'chosen,' is *chosen out*, making the act of choice more

5 Having predestinated us unto the adoption of children by Jesus Christ to himself, according to the good pleasure of his will,

5 ish before ¹ him in love: having foreordained us into adoption as sons through Jesus Christ unto himself, according to the good pleasure of his will,

2 Or, him; having in love foreordained us.

emphatic, and also individualizing it, as when our Lord chose his twelve apostles, one by one. **That we should be holy and without blame before him.** The word for 'holy' is to be taken here in a stronger sense than where it is used for a general designation of Christians as 'saints.' The accompanying clause, 'before him,' plainly implies that divine scrutiny which looks for perfection in character as alone pleasing to God. At the same time 'holy' and 'without blame' are not of identical meaning. They are, as Ellicott says, "positive and negative aspects of true Christian life." Of the word for 'holy,' Trench says ("New Testament Synonyms," p. 182) that, as we have already seen, "its fundamental idea is separation, and, so to speak, consecration and devotion to the service of Deity. . . . But the thought lies very near, that what is set apart from the world and to God, should separate itself from the world's defilements, and should share in God's purity." Holiness implies, therefore, more than that we should be without actual fault, and so is the "positive aspect" of perfect character. The "negative aspect," or freedom from fault, is implied in the phrase 'without blame.' What 'holy' and 'without blame' thus imply unfallen man would have been. That he may become this, redeemed man has been "chosen." It is, therefore, the ideal of our Christian profession. **In love.** Where to place these words, either in the pointing of the Greek text or in the translation, is among critics apparently undecided. Tischendorf so arranges the text as that 'in love' is connected with the words which begin the next verse: "Having in love predestinated us." The Revision, it will be seen, following the text of Westcott and Hort, connects them with the words immediately preceding, 'holy and without blame.' This Alford also prefers. Bengel, Meyer, Ellicott, Eadie, and others decide with Tischendorf. Others still, with much less reason than in either of these cases, place the two words in connection with 'hath chosen,' at the beginning of ver. 4, making the meaning to be, 'hath chosen us . . . in love.' This construction is made wholly unacceptable by the wide separation between the verb at the beginning of the verse and the qualifying words at the close. The objections to the arrangement in the Revised Version do not seem to be weighty. Adopting this, we find in the words 'in love' indication of that which is to be the distinguishing element in Christian character and in Christian life. If the other be preferred, then "in love predestinated us," etc., will direct attention to that originating motive in God which is so emphatically set forth in John 3 : 16. It will also be anticipatory of what is said below of the near relation to God into which believers are brought in the act of divine adoption.

5. Having predestinated us. *Foreordained* the Revisers prefer, alike here and in that place in Romans (8 : 29) of which this may remind us. "Predestinate" may be thought to imply a fatalistic idea which should not enter into our conception of God's electing grace. Thayer, however, in his "Lexicon," gives to the Greek word the strong meaning "to predetermine, decide beforehand." The foreordaining of ver. 5 is by the structure of the passage put in close relations with the choosing of ver. 4. As to which is the prior act, it is surely needless to inquire. **Unto the adoption of children.** *Of sons* is the true rendering. A further, or rather a co-ordinate purpose of the election. 'Chosen that we might be holy and without blame' expresses character; 'unto the adoption of sons' expresses relationship. **By Jesus Christ to himself**—that is, to God. Here the mediatorship of our Lord again enters in. It is necessary to distinctly recognize this mediatorship in the great transaction as described. No lower view of the office and mission of Jesus Christ, the Son of God, whether that lower view of him be as teacher, or as our pattern in righteousness, can satisfy the clear sense of the words here employed. In him the elect of God are 'chosen'; through him, by reason of their relation to him, they are brought into this new relation of sons by adoption. One fact it is also important to notice in this relation. It is a relation of sons by adoption; distinct from that which exists in the case of all men by virtue of their com-

6 To the praise of the glory of his grace, wherein he hath made us accepted in the beloved:
7 In whom we have redemption through his blood, the forgiveness of sins, according to the riches of his grace:

6 to the praise of the glory of his grace, ¹ which he 7 freely bestowed on us in the Beloved: in whom we have our redemption through his blood, the forgiveness of our trespasses, according to the riches

1 Or, *wherewith he endued us.*

mon origin in God's creative act. The force of the preposition 'to' or, 'unto' (εἰς), 'unto himself,' must also be remarked. The word, says Ellicott, "seems to bear its primary and most comprehensive sense of *to* and *into;* the idea of *approach* being also blended with, and heightened by, that of *inward union.*" He thus paraphrases: "God predestinated us to be adopted as his sons, and that adoption came to us through Christ, and was to lead us unto and unite us to God." **According to the good pleasure of his will.** The context clearly settles the question as to which of the two meanings of the word here rendered 'good pleasure' (εὐδοκίαν) shall be preferred; namely, whether (1) God's good-will toward us, or (2) his good pleasure in himself, that which it pleaseth him to will and to perform. There can be no real room for doubt that the apostle here means to say that in the acts of grace described God acts by his own free and sovereign will, doing that which for reasons infinitely good he wills to do.

6. **To the praise of the glory of his grace.** This must not be read as if it were, "To the praise of his glorious grace." The true sense of the passage is stronger and more emphatic than this would be. The marvelousness of the grace of God manifested, as here described, is the chief thing in the writer's mind. What he says to us is, therefore, that in the election of grace and redemption in and through Christ, God purposed an exhibition of his love to men "even while they were yet sinners," which should the more fully manifest the perfections of his character, especially his 'grace,' to all intelligences, and so command their 'praise.' **Wherein he hath made us accepted in the beloved.** This clause of the verse, so often quoted and a favorite with many, must now be given up as an imperfect rendering. The word in the Greek does not mean to "make accepted," but to graciously bestow gifts upon. The only other place in the New Testament where it occurs is at Luke 1: 28. "thou that art highly favored" (in the margin of the Revision, "en-

dued with grace"). The thought, then, is not acceptance in the Beloved, but the free bestowment of grace in him who is the Beloved One. The essentialness, however, of that relation in which the Mediator stands, alike to him who bestows and those who receive, is made as evident as is the freeness and graciousness of the redemption. It is 'in the Beloved' that the Giver and the recipient meet, and in him that grace and salvation are found.

7. **In whom we have redemption through his blood.** This presents to view another fact essential to a correct apprehension of that 'grace' of which the apostle speaks. The redemption so found 'in the Beloved' is 'through his blood.' Additional to all that in the Son which makes him the Beloved, and essential to any efficacy there can be for us in the faith that brings us to be 'in him,' there is this other element in the great transaction—the shedding of blood, sacrificial suffering on the part of the Beloved; upon this the bestowment of the grace being conditioned. The redemption of which we have the benefit is procured 'through his blood.' How vital among the doctrines of grace is this of the atonement becomes clearly evident. **The forgiveness of sins.** The original sense of the word translated 'forgiveness' seems to be "to send away." The forgiveness is not, therefore, a mere condoning of our transgressions, a passing of them over in that sort of imperfect forgiveness which is, perhaps, common with us, but is a sending away of our 'sins,' treating them as if they had never been—in the strong, figurative language of Scripture, "remembering them no more." This would seem to be necessary to that perfect reconciliation which takes place between God and the believing sinner, and made necessary also by the fact that this reconciliation takes place 'in the Beloved.' The favor that is his as the Beloved Son is given those who are thus made the subjects of this grace, and must involve such a sending away of their transgressions as shall make these as if they had never been. Two very important

8 Wherein he hath abounded toward us in all wisdom and prudence;
9 Having made known unto us the mystery of his will,

8 of his grace, ¹ which he made to abound toward us in all wisdom and prudence, having made known unto us the mystery of his will, according

¹ Or, wherewith he abounded.

words come thus into relation with each other: 'redemption' (ἀπολύτρωσιν), "deliverance effected by the payment of a ransom," and "the sending away" (ἄφεσιν) of transgression. The word 'redemption' here, in its strict meaning, may be studied in connection with the word translated "purchased possession," or "own possession," in ver. 14. No superficial conception of the great act of redemption will satisfy the meaning of such language; nothing less, indeed, than that which distinctly recognizes the vicariousness of that sacrificial suffering—'redemption through his blood'—by which we are saved. The distinction noticed by commentators between the word for "transgression," or "trespass," and the proper word for 'sins,' recognized also in the Revision, is not without its importance. Both are used in the first verse of the next chapter, and in a way to show that the distinction is a real one. The word for "sin" (ἁμαρτία) is a "generic one," meaning sin in general, and especially, perhaps, sin in the nature. The other (παράπτωμα) denotes positive and actual misdeed. This is the word used in our present passage, and has particular reference, perhaps, to the things of which we ourselves are most conscious as making 'forgiveness' necessary to us. **According to the riches of his grace.** Such extraordinary kindness to sinful men, when redeeming mercy meets them 'in the Beloved,' is not to be esteemed too great for God to bestow, nor this account too much to be true; for it is 'according to the riches of his grace.'

8. Wherein he hath abounded toward us. The verb means to "to make abundant" or "to furnish one richly, so that he shall have abundance." (Thayer's "Lexicon." Compare Matt. 13 : 12 ; 25 : 29.) This may be viewed as in some sense exegetical of the words 'riches of his grace.' **In all wisdom and prudence.** Two questions offer themselves: (1) What is the true connection? Does this clause belong with that which precedes, or that which follows? Shall we read, "hath abounded toward us in all wisdom and prudence"? or is this the true pointing, "hath abounded toward us; having in all wisdom and prudence made known to us," etc.? The latter is now generally conceded to be a forced construction. As will be seen, the Revisers decline to accept it. The words, 'in all wisdom and prudence' will then belong with 'hath abounded toward us.' (2) Are the words used of 'us,' or of God? Is it wisdom and prudence in which he himself abounds toward us? or are the gifts on his part, implied and contained in 'riches of his grace'? The latter is considered the preferable view. By Canon Barry in the commentary edited by Ellicott, "overflow" is preferred to "abound" in the immediate connection, so that the clause is made to read "caused to overflow to us in all wisdom and prudence"; "the word 'overflow,'" as the writer in question says, "having an emphasis which our word 'abound' has lost, and signifying here that the richness of God's grace not only fills the soul with the blessing of salvation, but overflows into the additional gifts of 'all wisdom and prudence' in us, which gifts are here dwelt upon in anticipation of the declaration of the next verse." 'Wisdom' (σοφία) is the more comprehensive word and has tho higher meaning. 'Prudence,' (φρόνησις) is less comprehensive.¹ The special significance of both words will perhaps be most clearly seen by noticing their relation to what follows in the succeeding verse.

9-24. ALL THINGS IN CHRIST.

9. Having made known unto us the mystery of his will. That knowledge of divine things which the believer has is not a gift of nature principally, but of grace. The connection of the thought is by some commentators made to suggest this; as Alford: "in that he made known"; Ellicott, "in making known to us." In this way God causes the riches of his grace to 'abound toward us in all wisdom and prudence.' The purposes and methods of divine grace, as re-

¹ Ellicott says: "σοφία denotes 'wisdom' in a general sense, φρόνησις is rather *intelligentia*, the application of the φρήν—in a word, an attribute and result of σοφία."

according to his good pleasure which he hath purposed in himself:
10 That in the dispensation of the fulness of times he might gather together in one all things in Christ, both which are in heaven, and which are on earth; even in him:

10 to his good pleasure which he purposed in him unto a dispensation of the fulness of the ¹ times, to sum up all things in Christ, the things ² in the

1 Gr. *seasons*........2 Gr. *upon*.

spects alike individual men and the race in its ultimate destiny, are not unfrequently in Scripture spoken of as 'mystery.' The word does not mean, of course, things unknowable, but the things which cannot be known otherwise than by revelation; as in Romans 11 : 25, in the Revelation (10 : 7), where we read of that which is there apocalyptically disclosed, as "the mystery of God," and in ch. 3 : 3, of this Epistle, where Paul speaks of a "mystery" made known to him "by revelation." In the phrase 'mystery of his will,' we seem to have all this abounding grace to men of which the apostle makes mention, referred for its ultimate source to the will and purpose of God, as is still further set forth in what follows: **According to his good pleasure which he hath purposed in himself.** It seems to be a main object of the writer in this part of his Epistle to make this thought clear; namely, that this whole method of salvation has its origin, wholly and alone, in God's own gracious purpose to redeem men "in Christ." The Revisers evidently prefer "in him"—that is, Christ. Alford, Ellicott, and Meyer, however, render "in himself," (reading αὑτῷ, in the text, instead of αὐτῷ). Dr. Riddell, in Schaff, also translates "in himself"—that is, God. The former may seem more in harmony with the general line of thought in the whole passage; yet the point is made doubtful by the fact, as Ellicott suggests, that the attention is here principally directed to the subject of the clause, which is God himself. It is partly a question of reading in the Greek text. Westcott and Hort, followed in the Revision, accept that of Tischendorf and Lachmann. Ellicott, Eadie, and Alford, that of Hahn. Our own judgment inclines to the rendering in the Revision.

10. That in the dispensation of the fulness of times. The change made in the Revision will be noticed, "unto" instead of 'that in,' and the indefinite substituted for the definite article. The Greek has no article. The meaning is *with a view to.* The mystery of God's will which he purposed in Christ was with a view to 'a dispensation of the fulness of times.' 'Dispensation' in this place is an obscure word. The Greek word, as found in the New Testament, has a somewhat variant meaning. In Luke 16 : 2–4, it is used for "stewardship." In 1 Cor. 9 : 17, Paul applies it to himself, as indicating that "stewardship" which had been entrusted to him as a minister of the gospel and an apostle. In Col. 1 : 25, he uses the word again, where he speaks of himself as "made a minister according to the dispensation of God." It is also the word (οἰκονομία) from which our "economy" comes. The root-idea of the word is that of setting in order, managing, directing. So that 'dispensation of the fulness of times' in this place comes to mean ordering or directing 'the fulness of times.' The thought is that of a divine purpose directing all times and events with reference to an end ultimately to be reached, and which, when the time for it should arrive, must surely be accomplished. **He might gather together in one.** The change made in the Revised Version should again be noticed. Fully expressed, we should read *to sum up for himself.* **All things in Christ.** The meaning of the 'all things' is made to appear in what follows. **Both which are in heaven and which are on earth; even in him.** There are other places in the New Testament in which what is here set forth is found under other forms of statement, as in Heb. 2 : 8, where the writer having quoted from the eighth Psalm, "Thou didst put all things in subjection under his feet," adds, "But now we see not yet all things put under him," the "yet" implying a time to come when this universal subjection shall be an accomplished fact. More express to a like point is that which is said in 1 Cor. 15 : 25-27; also in Col. 1 : 16–20. In our present passage, while the same general thought is implied, the form and application of it are different. Otherwise expressed, the word translated in the Revised Version 'to sum up,' means *to gather all under one head.* The apostle may be said to reach here the climax of his thought in this part of the Epistle. Christ's

11 In whom also we have obtained an inheritance, being predestinated according to the purpose of him who worketh all things after the counsel of his own will:

12 That we should be to the praise of his glory, who first trusted in Christ.

11 heavens, and the things upon the earth; in him, *I say*, in whom also we were made a heritage, having been foreordained according to the purpose of him who worketh all things after the counsel of

12 his will; to the end that we should be unto the praise of his glory, we who ¹ had before hoped in

---

¹ Or, *have*.

---

redeemed people, so he teaches us, are 'chosen in him' (ver. 4); in him and "through him" have the 'adoption as sons' (ver. 5); in him as 'the Beloved,' they obtain that 'grace' which is so 'freely bestowed' on them (ver. 7); in him they have 'redemption through his blood' (ver. 8). He now proceeds to show how, all these things being contained in that 'mystery' of the divine will which in the 'fulness of times' was to reach its complete accomplishment, their ultimate issue is to be to gather all things in the heavens and upon the earth under Christ as the Head; to sum up all in him. Two special thoughts seem to be presented: (1) the headship of Christ in the plan and purpose of redemption; (2) the comprehensiveness of this headship, being such as to "put all things under his feet." The words, 'to sum up all in Christ,' or, 'to gather all things under one head' in him, cannot rightly be understood as teaching that the results of his redemption shall be universal. As Meyer, quoted by Riddell, says, "The doctrine of *restoration*, according to which even those who have remained unbelieving, and finally devils, shall yet attain to blessedness, contrary as it is to the whole tenor of the New Testament, finds in this passage also no support." What we are to conclude from the passage is, "that physical nature and the world of mind, angels and men, will all stand in some new relation to each other and to Christ, their common centre, when this summing up in him is completed. . . . Evil spirits and unbelieving men shall then be recognized only as conquered and rejected." (Riddell.) The weight of the passage, however, is upon that which has been in the preceding verse the engrossing theme. Results of redemption as realized in the person of all the saved will be *summed up in him*, so that it shall at last completely appear how true it is that, as it is said in the closing words of this chapter, it is he that "filleth all in all."

11. In whom also we have obtained an inheritance. The words 'we have obtained an inheritance' are in the Greek represented by a single word; a word, also, which is a verb in the passive voice, and cannot be made to have the active signification given it in the Common Version. Neither does the word mean *to obtain* 'an inheritance,' but *to be made* 'an inheritance,' or, *heritage*. The Revision renders accordingly, and it should seem correctly, "in whom also we were made a heritage." It will be noticed that the Revision, instead of ending ver. 10 with the words 'even in him,' as in the Common Version, commences ver. 11 with "In him, *I say*," the two last words being supplied, and the repetition being with a view to re-establish the connection of the thought, which had become in a measure broken. We may recall in the use here of the word "heritage" or "inheritance," what is said (Deut. 32:9) of ancient Israel: "The Lord's portion is his people." In a higher and more spiritual sense, this is now said of his redeemed people. It is a strong way of expressing the value put upon the fruits of our Lord's redeeming work. **Being predestinated.** Foreordained is the better word. **According to the purpose of him who worketh all things after the counsel of his own will.** This re-affirms what has before been said of the origin of this whole redemptive scheme in God's own gracious purpose. The 'all things' must mean all things, whatever they may be, that can in any way affect the salvation and security of that saved people who have been made his "heritage." With what a sense of safety, as regards things present and things to come, the Lord's people may rest in the certainty of his promises, and his power and purpose to perform, may hence be inferred.

12. That we should be to the praise of his glory. The word 'we,' as shown by the clause immediately following—**who first trusted in Christ**—must be understood as referring to those Jewish Christians to whom the gospel was first preached, and who first received it in faith. *Who have before hoped*

13 In whom ye also *trusted*, after that ye heard the word of truth, the gospel of your salvation: in whom also, after that ye believed, ye were sealed with that Holy Spirit of promise,

13 Christ; in whom ye also, having heard the word of the truth, the gospel of your salvation,—in whom, having also believed, ye were sealed with

---

in Christ is the more correct rendering. The verb translated *have before hoped* is in Thayer explained as meaning "to repose hope in a person or thing before the event confirms it." Accordingly, commentators upon this passage think that the word in its proper force here looks back beyond that actual manifestation of Christ as the Saviour which took place in his ministry and death; or, as expressed by Canon Barry, the 'we' refers to those who, "taught by prophecy, entering into that vision of a great future which pervades the Older Covenant, looked forward to 'the hope of Israel,' and 'waited for the consolation of Israel'; and who accordingly in due time became, on the Day of Pentecost, the first fruits of his salvation." We can see no good reason for the limitation to the Day of Pentecost. The reference would seem to be to that assured expectation, based on divine promises of a Messiah who should come, and should "restore all things," which characterized the Jewish people and was especially marked in the more spiritual of those who were yet alive when Messiah actually came. Among these the gospel gathered its first fruits, and Paul himself, with others who received the gospel in faith much later than the time mentioned, would be included. That these should be here spoken of with a certain emphasis as being 'to the praise of his (God's) glory,' may be due to the fact of that confident hope with which, before Christ came, they looked for him, and the ready faith with which they received him when he came; testifying thus, in the first instance, to the certainty of the promise, and in the second instance, to the completeness of the fulfillment.

13. In whom ye also trusted. Here the Gentile Christians, as distinguished from those of the Jewish nation, are clearly meant. The word 'trusted' is supplied in the Common Version, though not, it will be observed, in the Revision. The Greek for 'in whom' is repeated before the close of the sentence, which remains incomplete till near the end of the verse. **After that ye heard the word of truth**—becomes, in the better rendering, "having heard the word of truth." So far as the Ephesians were concerned, this 'word of truth' they had 'heard' from Paul's own lips; and in reading what is here written to them, may have recalled that personal ministry with a sense of its value to them. **The gospel of your salvation.** This is the word of truth meant, this "good news" of a salvation which, through the faith they were enabled to exercise, had become theirs. **In whom also after that ye believed**—or, *ye had believed*. The changed form of the sentence in the Revised Version will be noticed. In the Common Version, an emphatic sense given by the writer to his own words by the form used, is wholly missed. The repetition of 'in whom' keeps the attention fixed upon the main thought in the verse, that all this benefit so received is 'in Christ.' It is to be observed how constantly the apostle keeps in view the faith which accompanies and conditions all these great benefits—"in whom having also believed"; the divine sealing next spoken of being granted to them as believers. **Ye were sealed.** The original meaning of the Greek word for "seal" is, "to set a mark upon," "to mark with a seal"; it means, also, to seal for purposes of security, as where in Rev. 20:3, it is said of the "dragon" shut up in the abyss, that a seal was put upon him. A passage in the Revelation more significant for our present purpose is that in chap. 7:3-8, where the servants of God are described as "sealed in their foreheads," that they might be safe amidst the judgments about to come on the world. Still more to the purpose are the words in 2 Cor. 1:22, "Who hath also sealed us, and given the earnest of the Spirit in our hearts." The purpose of the sealing is not simply that they may thus be set apart and and made known as "the children of God," but that it may serve as evidence to themselves, as in Rom. 8:16. In what the sealing consists becomes clear as we note the words which follow—**with that Holy Spirit of promise.** The 'Spirit of promise' is the more correct; and the word 'Holy,' in a literal translation, comes at the end of the clause, "the Spirit of promise, the Holy." The form in the Greek seems intended for

14 Which is the earnest of our inheritance until the redemption of the purchased possession, unto the praise of his glory.

14 the Holy Spirit of promise, which is an earnest of our inheritance, unto the redemption of God's own possession, unto the praise of his glory.

emphasis, not only as respects the Spirit himself, but as respects his mission and work in our behalf, that we also may be 'holy.' The Spirit was a 'Spirit of promise,' or a promised Spirit, even under the more ancient Dispensation, as in Joel 2: 28-33, quoted by Peter on the Day of Pentecost as fulfilled in the remarkable events then occurring; also in Zech. 12: 10 and in Jer. 31: 31-34. More especially is he the Spirit of promise in view of what is said of him by our Lord, as the Comforter who should come, as he himself departed. Perhaps, also, we may speak of him as 'the Spirit of promise,' though not perhaps strictly in the sense intended here, in view of that work which he performs within us, and in which such "exceeding great and precious promises" arrive at their fulfillment.

14. Which is the earnest of our inheritance. The nature and purpose of the sealing are best understood in connection with what appears in this verse. An 'earnest,' in the meaning of the Greek word (ἀρραβών), is money given in advance, as a pledge or security that the full amount promised shall be paid. In its spiritual use, as here and in 2 Cor. 1: 22, it must mean that assurance which the believer has in the work of the Spirit in the heart, and spiritual experiences of every kind, where real, and truly of the Spirit of God, that the ultimate blessing, of which he thus has now a foretaste, shall not fail. The reasoning of the apostle in Rom. 8: 16 is illustrative of the meaning here: "The Spirit itself beareth witness with our spirit, that we are the children of God, and if children, then heirs." It should be observed that 'the earnest of the Spirit' in our present passage and "the witness of the Spirit," in Romans, is not some vague, mystical experience of which no rational account can be given. It is, rather, the very work of the Spirit itself, in the meaning of those words in Phil. 1: 6, "Being confident of this very thing, that he which hath begun a good work in you will perform it until the day of Jesus Christ." The 'inheritance' thus acquires a significance which should be noticed. As "earnest money" is a part of that full amount which is ultimately to be made complete, so what a Christian experiences now is, while an 'earnest' of the 'inheritance' to be finally his in its fullness, a part of that very 'inheritance,' and in so far makes him know what the 'inheritance' as finally enjoyed shall be. So much of real spiritual blessing as he now enjoys is heaven already in his heart; what he has in the work and "fruits" of the Spirit is for him alike pledge and foretaste. **Until the redemption of the purchased possession.** The change in the Revised Version should be noticed: "Unto the redemption of God's own possession," the word in italics being supplied, because not in the Greek. The same rendering we find in Schaff (Riddell), where attention is called to the fact that the preposition (εἰς), translated 'until,' in the Common Version and "unto" in the Revision, is the same as that in the next clause, where we read "unto the praise of his glory." It is very properly held that "since the clauses are so similar, they should be regarded as parallel," and the preposition translated accordingly. The word "unto," indeed, makes the sense somewhat obscure, yet to use 'until' instead is to give the preposition a meaning that cannot be justified. The idea intended is not one of time, but of purpose, or end had in view, as in several other places in this chapter: ver. 10, 'unto [with a view to] a dispensation,' etc.; ver. 12, 'that [to the end that] we should be,' etc.; ibid, 'unto [for] the praise of his glory,' etc., in all which places the same preposition is used. The word for 'purchased possession' in this place is understood to mean what one has purchased, or laid by, for himself; 'the purchased possession,' therefore, does not express the whole idea. The thought is of the redeemed as ransomed or 'purchased' in the redemption, and thenceforth as the 'possession' of him by whom they are thus redeemed. And since the 'earnest' of a more full 'redemption' is given to them with a view to an ulterior and perfect result of the work in them and for them, we must understand 'redemption' of this 'purchased possession' as having in view that final, complete, and glorious work in which body and soul shall share. The thought is one which must always be precious to faith, since it involves alike the security of the true believer,

15 Wherefore I also, after I heard of your faith in the Lord Jesus, and love unto all the saints,
16 Cease¹ not to give thanks for you, making mention of you in my prayers;

15 For this cause I also, having heard of the faith in the Lord Jesus which is ¹among you, and ²the
16 love which *ye shew* toward all the saints, cease not to give thanks for you, making mention of *you* in

1 Or, in ......2 Many ancient authorities omit the love.

and the absolute completeness of that redemption to which he looks forward in hope. **Unto the praise of his glory.** This is the end or purpose of all as respects God; that which has just been considered the end or purpose as respects man. This intimate relation of the two clauses makes the more evident what is said above as to the preposition rendered in each, by the Revision, as "unto." If this be retained, the meaning in each case will be made more clear by viewing it as equivalent to that used in other places in this chapter mentioned above—"with a view to," or "for." What God does for his children here, in that earnest of the Spirit which they have in their regeneration, in the progressive work of their sanctification, and in all the various ministry of the Comforter, is with a view to their complete and perfect redemption ultimately, which shall also be for a manifestation to all intelligences of his glory in wonders of grace far exceeding even the wonders of creation and of providence.

15-23. Prayer for Increase of Knowledge and Spiritual Understanding.

15. Wherefore. Having dwelt thus far upon that truth which is so much the sum of the gospel message, the apostle now turns more directly to those addressed, in an expression of deep personal interest in their behalf, and in an assurance of his constant prayer for them, that they may more and more clearly apprehend alike the greatness of their own privilege and the exalted office now filled by him in whom they have believed and whom they serve. **I also, after I heard of your faith in the Lord Jesus.** So far as addressed to the Ephesians, these words can hardly mean their original acceptance of the Christian faith, for of this the apostle had been not only a personal witness, but a chief instrument. They would rather imply so much as he had been permitted to know since of their constancy and fidelity. Churches in the neighborhood of Ephesus, for whom as well as for the Ephesians it seems upon the whole safest to regard the Epistle as in a general way intended, had been planted by other hands, and

their 'faith in the Lord Jesus' had come to him as intelligence that had not only made him thankful and glad, but had prompted him to earnest prayer in their behalf. **And love unto all the saints.** In those ancient manuscripts, the Sinaitic, the Vatican, and the Alexandrian, which are regarded as the best authority in questions of the New Testament text, the word for 'love' is not found. As will be seen, the Revision omits this word. The American Company of the Revisers, however, prefer to retain the word, with the statement in the margin that "many ancient authorities omit" it. The sense of the passage is certainly somewhat obscure without the word 'love,' since we must then read, as in the Revision, 'faith toward all the saints' as well as 'faith in the Lord Jesus.' With a view, it should seem, to overcome, or at least lessen this difficulty, the text of the Revision supplies the words "*ye shew*." Westcott and Hort, whose Greek text the Revision follows, in accounting for this "difficult reading," refer in their note upon the passage to Philemon, ver. 5, "hearing of thy love, and of the faith which thou hast toward the Lord Jesus, and toward all saints" (although in the margin they give the alternative rendering, "thy love and faith"); to Titus 3 : 15, "them that love us in faith"; and to Rom. 1 : 12, "comforted in you, each of us by the other's faith." We cannot see that any real light is thus thrown upon the peculiarity of our present text, with 'love' omitted. There is manuscript authority for retaining the word, although not so good as for its omission; while, upon the other hand, there is force in the suggestion that "the omission," in the most ancient manuscripts, "can be readily accounted for." (Riddell.) Upon the whole, we incline to the judgment of the American Revisers, that it is better to retain the word, although with the understanding that manuscript authority for it is imperfect.

16. Cease not to give thanks for you. This thankfulness, in view of all he was enabled to know of the spiritual state of those to whom he writes, is quite as much evidence of

17 That the God of our Lord Jesus Christ, the Father of glory, may give unto you the spirit of wisdom and revelation in the knowledge of him:

17 my prayers; that the God of our Lord Jesus Christ, the Father of Glory, may give unto you a spirit of wisdom and revelation in the knowledge of him;

the genuineness of his interest in them as is that which follows. **Making mention of you in my prayers.** "Having remembrance of you" expresses the sense in a way less literal. "Making (to myself) a remembrance (of you)," Dr. Boise translates. The words do not imply actual mention in all cases, but, as used here, such a remembrance of them as that in all his prayers he might speak of himself as having them in mind. A like thing should be said of 'cease not to give thanks.' It is quite unnecessary to speak of either form of expression as "a popular hyperbole"; so Meyer. We may be said to pray for those who are not distinctively in our thoughts at the time of utterance, since they are, in our habitual mood of mind, always included, with the persons or things in whose behalf we are solicitous, and in whose behalf we constantly desire a blessing. So with thankfulness. The grateful feeling in behalf of specific objects may be latent, yet no less real, at any moment when gratitude is expressed.

17. That the God of our Lord Jesus Christ. We have here the same form as that commented upon in the note upon ver. 3. Alford considers it "as leading on to what is about to be said in ver. 20 of God's exaltation of Christ, to be 'head over all things to his church.'" Without attempting to explain a mystery so ineffable, we must recognize the fact of our Lord's real human nature, in union with the divine, and that in this real human nature he often acted and spoke. In such passages as that in John 5 : 30, "I seek not mine own will, but the will of him that sent me," we must, no doubt, as Dr. Hovey there explains, understand him as referring to that divine union of the Son with the Father, which makes it impossible that the Son should will aught else but that which the Father wills. In other places he establishes between himself and us that perfect fellowship in our relation to the Father, as in other respects, which results from the fact of his real humanity. His taking upon himself this humanity is also the first step toward, and the necessary condition of, that exaltation of which we read further on. **The Father of glory.** The phrase is peculiar, although others similar are found: "Father of mercies" (2 Cor. 1 : 3), "Father of lights" (James 1 : 17). The explanation in Ellicott seems forced, where the writer says: "I cannot help connecting it ('Father of glory') with the missing element in the preceding clause, and believing (with some old interpreters), in spite of the strangeness of expression, that God is here called 'the Father of the glory' of the incarnate Deity in Jesus Christ, called in 2 Cor. 4 : 6, 'the glory of God in the face (or person) of Jesus Christ.'" We can scarcely believe that the apostle can have intended a meaning so remote, and so little likely to be naturally suggested. It seems more probable that the phrase in question is employed with reference to that which follows, and in which Christ is soon to be spoken of as raised out of the humiliation into which he descended, to a place at the Father's "right hand in the heavenly places," with the "all power" given of which he himself spoke when soon to "ascend where he was before." As God is "the Father of mercies," while bestowing mercies upon the infinite object of his beneficence, so is the "Father of glory," in the sense that every manner of "might and dominion," and every form and measure of exaltation, are of his ordination, and most especially that which is so conspicuously seen in the person of Christ. **May give unto you the spirit of wisdom and revelation in the knowledge of him.** The Revision changes the article, rendering, "a spirit of wisdom," etc. It is quite consistent with New Testament usage to understand *the* Holy Spirit; the Greek word (πνεῦμα) being made definite by the following genitive. Taking into account what follows, this may be the better rendering; "wisdom and revelation," especially the latter, implying rather some divine illumination, than any action of the human 'spirit', however aided from on high. Meyer, Ellicott, and Braune prefer this view, and render accordingly. **In the knowledge of him.** This defines the nature and purport of the 'wisdom and revelation.' The word for 'knowledge' being a compound word,

18 The eyes of your understanding being enlightened; that ye may know what is the hope of his calling, and what the riches of the glory of his inheritance in the saints,
19 And what *is* the exceeding greatness of his power to us-ward who believe, according to the working of his mighty power,

18 having the eyes of your heart enlightened, that ye may know what is the hope of his calling, what the riches of the glory of his inheritance in the saints,
19 and what the exceeding greatness of his power to us-ward who believe, according to that working of

has an intensive force. The verb from which it comes means to "know thoroughly," and the meaning here is "precise, definite knowledge." For the possession of such 'knowledge' we are dependent upon a 'wisdom and revelation' which only the Spirit of Truth himself can impart. 'Of him' appears to mean of the Father, the connection of the thought making this, it would seem, necessary, as the verse immediately following shows.

18. **The eyes of your understanding** (or, *heart*) **being enlightened.** The peculiar expression, 'eyes of your heart,' is probably used to indicate that such 'knowledge' as is meant is more than may be comprehended in any act of the 'understanding,' the mere intelligence. The knowledge intended is spiritual, involves that which we mean by "experience," and engages the affections and the will in an especial manner. **That ye may know what is the hope of his calling.** In the call by which we are addressed in the gospel, a hope is presented as a motive and an end. The full appreciation of this hope requires much more than simply an ordinary act of the 'understanding.' The call, in fact, falls long, in most cases, upon unheeding ears, until in a way which, to the subject of it, may often seem mysterious, the familiar words of invitation acquire unwonted power, and prevail over the hardness and indifference which has held out so long. The 'hope of his calling' is then first known. But this is the beginning. The apostle is now addressing those who have passed this first stage. His prayer for them is that in the ministry of that 'wisdom and revelation' which the Spirit imparts they may come to have enlarged, definite, and more complete 'knowledge' of this 'hope.' But in order to this that 'knowledge of him,' of God, mentioned in the preceding verse, is necessary. In order rightly to comprehend, or even conceive, that which God promises or does, we must know himself; and he becomes thus known, really, through that wisdom and revelation in which he *makes* himself known.

And what the riches of the glory of his inheritance in the saints. The 'and' of the Common Version is rightly omitted in the Revision. This clause thus comes into closer connection with the preceding one, as if a continuation of the same thought—'what tho riches of the glory of his inheritance in the saints.' The phrase 'riches of the glory' is an example of that accumulation of descriptive words of which we find so many examples in this chapter. The writer seems to labor for terms in which adequately to express the sense he has of these wonders of divine grace, and seems almost willing to overload his style with descriptive epithets, heaped one upon the other. A question arises as to 'the inheritance' mentioned. Shall we take the passage (1) as parallel in some sense with ver. 11, where believers are spoken of as God's 'heritage,' and with ver. 14, where they are his 'own possession'? Or (2), as the commentators seem to prefer, is it the inheritance which the saints themselves are ultimately to receive? It is to be noticed that the inheritance is spoken of as 'his,' and that it is an inheritance '*in* the saints,' not *for* them. While the latter (2) of the two interpretations indicated may be in harmony with the immediate context, the language is so much like that found in ver. 11 and 14 that we strongly incline to the view which makes the meaning to be that 'inheritance,' that 'purchased possession' which God is spoken of as having in his redeemed people. This, however, involves glorious things for those who are thus made an inheritance; a 'glory,' the 'riches' of which is only apprehended, even by faith, as spiritual knowledge increases.

19. **And what is the exceeding greatness of his power.** "Surpassing greatness" is another form of expression of the same idea, perhaps also to be preferred. "Above measure," that which "excels," *supereminens*, in the Latin of the Vulgate. The thought is that, in this which now follows, God has given us an exhibition of transcendent power which

20 Which he wrought in Christ, when he raised him from the dead, and set *him* at his own right hand in the heavenly *places*,
21 Far above all principality, and power, and might, and dominion, and every name that is named, not only in this world, but also in that which is to come:

20 the strength of his might which he wrought in Christ, when he raised him from the dead, and made him sit at his right hand in the heavenly
21 *places*, far above all rule, and authority, and power, and dominion, and every name that is named, not only in this ¹ world, but also in that which is to

¹ Or, *age.*

could exist in himself alone. **To us-ward who believe.** The Revision retains the now antique form, 'to us-ward,' for "toward us"; in accordance with the judicious purpose to make as few changes as possible in the style of the older version. The manifestation of divine power is in that which is said of Christ in the verses following. But it is of Christ in his relation to his own redeemed people, and so is 'to us-ward.' **According to the working of his mighty power.** The Common Version fails to express adequately the force of the original, which, indeed, can only be done by making the rendering as literal as possible, "according to that working of the strength of his might"; an "extraordinary accumulation of words" as Dr. Boise says, "denoting power and activity."

20. Which he wrought in Christ, when he raised him from the dead. "I have power," said Christ, on one occasion, "to lay it [that is, *my life*] down, and I have power to take it again"; the word for "power" being that most usually employed to express "authority" or "right," yet, in that place, as Dr. Hovey justly says, in his note on the passage, combining "the two ideas of *right* and *might*." When, therefore, we read in the verse before us of the "working of the strength of God's might" in Christ when he raised him from the dead, we must keep in mind the divine oneness of the Son with the Father, so that the raising up is in full harmony with what is said of our Lord in chap. 4: 8-10 of this Epistle, that he himself "ascended on high, leading captivity captive, and giving gifts unto men." What we have before us, then, is the operation of the divine power in execution of divine purpose, rather than the attribution of such power exclusively to the Father alone. At the same time, we observe that the Son is spoken of in that character which he assumed in becoming man's Redeemer. He is here, not the Son, but the Christ; and what is said of him describes that fulfilment of divine plan, in the operation of transcendent divine power, which brings the whole work of redemption to its glorious consummation. **And set him at his own right hand.** We must not too much localize the idea here given us; but neither may we so treat the figurative sense as to weaken the true meaning of the words. The general idea is the exaltation of Christ, in his office as Redeemer, to complete and full participation in the universal sovereignty. God the Father is none the less God the Father; but the Son, having "ascended up where he was before," now in his mediatorial and redemptive office, is as if enthroned at his Father's right hand, "one" with him in exaltation and sovereignty, as in that "glory which he had with him before the world was." **In the heavenly places.** The local sense is here more distinctly applied than in the words at ver. 3 in this chapter. And still, we should not make our interpretation too exclusively local. Of heaven, we know but little, save as the home and rest of the redeemed, and the world in which the glory of the Infinite is manifested in ways unimaginable to us. Of its reality, however, we never doubt, while it is ever central in our conception of "those things which God hath prepared for them that love him." In the widest meaning of the phrase "heavenly places," as here used, it may include, with heaven itself, that sphere of spiritual things of which heaven is the centre, and over which Christ, as Head of the church, bears rule.

21. Far above all principality, and power, and might, and dominion. The words *rule* for 'principality,' *authority* for 'power,' and *power* for 'might,' are substitutions which make the meaning more clear. The amount of what is so said is, that the position and power held and exercised by Christ are absolutely divine, and, therefore, supreme. Writers are not altogether agreed whether 'all principality' here refers to those principalities against which, as in chap. 6: 12 of this Epistle, we are to "wrestle." Whether these be here

22 And hath put all *things* under his feet, and gave him *to be* the head over all *things* to the church, 23 Which is his body, the fulness of him that filleth all in all.

22 come: and he put all things in subjection under his feet, and gave him to be head over all things to the church, 23 which is his body, the fulness of him that filleth all in all.

expressly included or not, we know that they also are now under the sovereignty of our enthroned Redeemer. **And every name that is named.** "A name that can be uttered," says Meyer, "whatever it may be, Christ is above it, more exalted than that which the uttered name expresses." **Not only in this world, but also in that which is to come.** "This age" is the alternative reading here for the Greek word (αἰών). The meaning is not this *life* and the life to come, but the age, or Dispensation, now passing, and that which is to follow, when this shall end in the Second Coming of the Lord. We are thus assured that while the period of gospel propagation lasts, with its vicissitudes, its trials of faith, as well as its reassuring triumphs and satisfactions, Christ has, and exercises, a power which puts every manner of "rule, and authority, and power, and dominion" in absolute subjection to him, so that, in his own time and in his own way, every purpose of his mediatorial reign shall be fully accomplished. Also, that when this period comes to a close, and that "world which is to come," that consummating Dispensation has been reached, this same sovereignty will be in his hands; so that of all words of promise and prophecy spoken, not one shall fail.

22. And hath put all things under his feet. The word has a stronger meaning than simply to 'put under.' *Arrange under, subordinate,* implying absolute subjection. **And gave him to be head over all things to the church.** The purpose of the exaltation is here made known. It is in the interest of human redemption that all this is done. In this way it is provided that there shall be no possibility of opposition or hostility in any quarter with ability to mar in any way the perfection of the plan, or hinder or delay its execution. By 'the church,' here, is clearly meant that totality of all the redeemed, on earth or in heaven, and in all the ages, spoken of in the next verse as "his body." The more customary use of the word (ἐκκλησία), "the called out," the "chosen," is that of the local and organized company of believers. In a very natural figure, this local "assembly" is made to supply a name for the whole innumerable company of the saved.

23. Which is his body. This representation of the 'church' under the figure of a 'body' has occurred before in the writings of this apostle, as in Rom. 12 : 4, 5, where we read: "For as we have many members in one body, and all members have not the same office, so we, being many, are one body in Christ, and every one members, one of another"; also to a like effect in 1 Cor. 12 : 12-27. In the verse before us, however, Paul for the first time presents the conception of a *spiritual* unity of all the saved under a like figure. In the places just referred to he is occupied rather with "the members" of the body, and these in their relation to each other in the practical Christian life. Here he has in mind, not the body in any localizing view of the church, but the body as representing the redeemed in their spiritual totality and oneness. As such he sees in them 'his body.' **The fulness of him that filleth all in all.** The necessary sense of the clause as a whole would seem to make sufficiently clear the meaning of this word 'fulness,' concerning which commentators differ. Christ who "fills all in all," or, "in all things fills (for himself) all things," as Dr. Boise translates (see also Winer, p. 273), fills also that 'church' which is 'his body.' The 'fulness,' therefore, is simply the church as "that which has been filled" with the life of Christ himself. In the view of some there is here a reference by the apostle to the incipient Gnosticism believed to have thus early appeared in speculations which afterward became an element of exceeding mischief, especially in churches of the East, and in which this word (πλήρωμα) 'fulness' played a great part. One is at a loss to see how, in this place at all events, any such reference can be intended, though it is possible. The thought in the passage grows naturally out of what has gone before. The exaltation of Christ as 'head over all things to the church,' the spiritual unity of the church itself, the life of Christ filling the church, as 'his body,' the church, therefore, as so filled, and hence as his 'fulness'—these conceptions link in with each other in a perfectly natural way, and at least imply no necessity for going beyond the topic immediately in hand for even a remoter sense of the words employed.

SUMMARY OF THE EXPOSITION.

This first chapter of the Epistle may be viewed as in some sense an Introduction. It is a comprehensive survey of the great theme which subsequent chapters treat more in detail. In its three chief divisions it may be characterized as a Salutation (ver. 1, 2); as a Thanksgiving (ver. 3-14); and as a Prayer (ver. 15-23). In the first, Paul announces his own inspired and authoritative apostleship, derived from the "will" and appointment of God himself, and at the same time recognizes those to whom he writes in a truly Christian relation. In the second, he comprehends those features in the scheme of man's redemption which most claim the thankful recognition of all believers: (1) That divine foresight and foreordination in the eternity past, in which the condition of a fallen race was anticipated; (2) the gracious purpose and provision to which all subsequent acts of mercy are to be traced back, and in which the subjects of this grace are "chosen in Christ"; (3) that new relation into which believers are brought in their adoption as restored, forgiven, and redeemed; (4) and that gracious communication by God of his own redemptive plan, through which Christian knowledge becomes enriched. In the third is comprehended that which to Christian believers should be most a subject of aspiration and desire; the knowledge of God, and a true enlightenment in respect to all spiritual things, most of all the person and office, and divine sufficiency of Christ, their Redeemer and Lord.

Owing to the peculiar style of the writer, the several points of doctrine presented run into each other in such a way as to make any precise discrimination of them a matter of some difficulty. They deal directly with the fundamental facts and truths of our religion. Of special features in the general teaching of the chapter, we may notice those which follow: (1) The central place assigned in the redemptive scheme to our Lord Jesus Christ. Believers are "chosen" in him; their adoption as children is "by Jesus Christ"; they have "redemption through his blood"; in Christ, and under his leadership, when the consummation of the plan is reached, all results of redemption are to be gathered and summed, while under his sovereignty all things now are, in the interest of his redeeming work. This is, throughout the Epistle, a leading feature. (2) The clear and distinct manner in which human redemption is traced to "the good pleasure" of God in the counsels of a past eternity, "before the foundation of the world." (3) Distinct indication of the truth that redemption is not a contingency, even under the providential order of the world, but is in accordance with an election of grace, in which the saved of all ages are "chosen" as subjects of this great salvation. (4) The end had in view in such election; namely, the calling and preparation of a "holy" people, "without blame before him in love." (5) The new relation into which all such are brought, "adoption of children by Jesus Christ." (6) And lastly, that further truth so fundamental in the whole scheme, that "redemption" is "through the blood" of Christ, whereby we have "the forgiveness of sins according to the riches of" divine "grace." These features of the great redemptive plan come into view under special relations in subsequent portions of the Epistle, and supply the basis of that teaching in Christian morals in which, in closing portions of the Epistle, its doctrinal teaching is practically applied.

CHAPTER II.

AND you *hath he quickened*, who were dead in trespasses and sins:
2 Wherein in time past ye walked according to the course of this world, according to the prince of the

And you *did he quicken*, when ye were dead 2 through your trespasses and sins, wherein aforetime ye walked according to the ¹ course of this world,

¹ Gr. *age*.

Ch. 2. 1-10. THE SPIRITUAL DEATH AND THE NEW LIFE IN CHRIST.

1. And you hath he quickened. Many prefer, "You also," which is perhaps better, as making the close connection with the last verses of the previous chapter more evident. In language of great fervor, the methods of redemption, even to the crowning and consummating act of the enthronement of Christ in his mediatorial reign, have been set forth. The writer comes now to speak of the participation in this wonderful grace of those to whom he is writing. 'Also', besides what is thus seen in the general dispensation of this grace, 'you' yourselves have become participants. In what way, he describes. The words, 'hath he quickened' are not in the Greek, and so are supplied in the translation. The sentence, in fact, as originally written, reaching to the end of the third verse, is incomplete. There is no governing verb for the pronoun (ὑμᾶς), 'you.' Ver. 5 shows what the sense is. What the writer began to speak of is the quickening there and in subsequent verses described. The hurrying rush of thought bears him away, and the new conception crowds for utterance before that of the one already in mind is complete. **Who were dead in trespasses and sins.** A strong but true picture of the condition of unregenerate man. The Revision, it will be noticed, reads "through," not "in." There is no preposition in the Greek, so that the proper construction of the two nouns (παραπτώμασιν) 'trespasses' and (ἁμαρτίαις) 'sins' is taken to be as "the dative of manner or means." The condition described is one of spiritual death. How has this condition been occasioned? Through or by trespasses and sins. Each—the question and the answer—describes a condition: one being the cause of the other. The comment in Thayer's "Lexicon of the New Testament" describes the state here spoken of, as being "destitute of a life that recognizes and is devoted to God, because given up to trespasses and sins." Physical death is a condition in which the functions of physical life have ceased; spiritual death is that where the functions of spiritual life are no longer active, and indeed, apart from the intervention of divine grace are no longer possible;—those affections and that condition of the will, that whole attitude of mind and soul which involves right relations with God and communion with him. What is described is that "mind of the flesh" (Rom. 8: 7. Rev. Ver.) which is enmity against God; for it is not subject to the law of God, neither indeed can be. "The incapacity of the unregenerated mind for the exercise of spiritual affections, is what is meant by spiritual death." This condition the trespasses and sins cause. In these two words the apostle comprehends all that is true of man's sinful state; the word for 'sins' presenting that general view of this state which includes sin in the nature and sin as a general fact of man's condition; while 'trespasses' are the specific acts of sin, the "fallings-aside," as the word may import, of which men are more immediately conscious. Sin in the nature, in the habit of the soul, and repeated acts of transgression—to these is due that spiritual condition which the Scriptures characterize by the fearful word, "death."

2. Wherein in time past ye walked (or, *walked about*)—a picturesque expression for the life led by these Gentiles in that 'time past,' when as yet the grace of God in the gospel had not visited them. **According to the course of this world**—'the course,' literally, *the age* (αἰῶνα) *of this world*, the world in its present era, or age; in accordance with the world as it now is. The allusion seems to be to that moral state in which men in the world are everywhere found during this period of probation in which the purposes of God concerning our sinful race await their final accomplishment. Trench ("Synonyms of the New Testament," pp. 38, 39) says of the word translated 'course' in the Common Version and "age" in the Revision that, "signifying time, it comes presently to signify all which exists in the world under conditions of time; . . . and then, more ethically, the course and power of the air, the spirit that now worketh in the children of disobedience;

according to the prince of the [1] powers of the air, of the spirit that now worketh in the sons of disobe-

[1] Gr. power.

current of this world's affairs." Of the word translated 'world,' he says (p. 87): "Having originally the meaning of 'ornament' . . . from this it passed to that of 'order,' 'arrangement,' 'beauty,' as springing out of these. . . . Pythagoras is said to have been the first who transferred and applied the word to the sum total of the material universe, desiring thereby to express his sense of the beauty and order which everywhere reigned in it." Then, "from this signification of the word (κόσμος) as the material world, which is not uncommon in Scripture (Matt. 13:35; John 21:25; Rom. 1:20), followed that 'of the same word' as the sum total of the men living in the world (John 1:29; 4:42; 2 Cor. 5:19), and then upon this, and ethically, those not of the church (ἐκκλησία), the alienated from the life of God." The specific reference here may be to that Gentile world of which those immediately addressed still formed a part, and in whose moral condition they had 'in time past' fully shared. **According to the prince of the power of the air.** More literally rendered, we should read "ruler," while the 'power' meant is not power in the sense of force, but of control, authority. Thayer understands the word in connections like the present one as meaning "the leading and more powerful among created beings superior to man, spiritual potentates"; but here, specifically, "demons." The American Company of the Revisers prefer "powers" to 'power.' [There seems to be no ground for this preference in the Greek, which is a singular noun. 'Powers' may be right as interpretation, but scarcely as translation.—A. H.] The Greek for 'air' means the atmosphere in its lower regions, the upper being indicated by another word. The language used is difficult of explanation. That by the 'prince' or "ruler" Satan is meant, is sufficiently clear. What shall we understand by those 'powers of the air' over which he exercises sovereignty? Thayer, in his "Lexicon," appears to think the allusion to be to a Jewish notion that "the realm of air" is "filled by demons." Canon Barry, in the series of commentaries edited by Bishop Ellicott, prefers the view that as "the word [in the Greek] and its derivatives carry with them the ideas of cloudiness, mist, and even darkness, hence it is naturally used to suggest the conception of the evil power as allowed invisibly to encompass and move about the world, yet overruled by the power of the true heaven, which it vainly strives to overcloud and hide from earth." Ellicott himself appears to infer from the words in question that "all that supra-terrestrial but sub-celestial region [which the Greek word describes] seems to be, if not the abode, yet the haunt of evil spirits." That men, especially wicked men, are objects of the malignant activity of such spirits we are made to believe by many allusions to them in Scripture, and occasional express mention, which make the fact beyond doubt. Compare 6:12-16 of this Epistle. So much as this may be distinctly inferred from the words in our present passage. But if thus directly influencing the lives of men, we must suppose a presence and contact to which, in a meaning partly figurative, the expression 'powers of the air' may refer. It is not necessary to suppose that the apostle means to endorse any Rabbinic or Pythagorean fiction in this regard, as to what and where "the abode of demons" may be, but only that, invisible themselves, they are a part of our environment, and to be realized and dreaded as such. **The spirit that now worketh in the children of disobedience.** The word for 'spirit' is in the genitive, and accordingly must depend upon the word for 'ruler.' Satan is then described as ruler of the spirit working in 'the children of disobedience.' Little do wicked men realize what master they serve, or with what fearful reward in prospect for that obedience to him, which is disobedience to God. Winer speaks of such phrases as 'children of disobedience' as "called a Hebraistic circumlocution for certain concrete adjectives." Yet, referring to the passage here with others, he adds: "Every one must feel that these expressions are not mere circumlocutions, but phrases which bring out the meaning with greater *vivacity* and force." This phraseology, he adds, "is to be attributed to the vivid imagination of Orientals, which

3 Among whom also we all had our conversation in times past in the lusts of our flesh, fulfilling the desires of the flesh and of the mind ; and were by nature the children of wrath, even as others.
4 But God, who is rich in mercy, for his great love wherewith he loved us,
5 Even when we were dead in sins, hath quickened us together with Christ, (by grace ye are saved ;)

3 dience ; among whom we also all once lived in the lusts of our flesh, doing the desires of the flesh and of the ¹mind, and were by nature children of
4 wrath, even as the rest :—but God, being rich in mercy, for his great love wherewith he loved us,
5 even when we were dead through our trespasses, quickened us together ²with Christ (by grace have

1 Gr. *thoughts*........2 Some ancient authorities read *in Christ*.

presents mental and moral derivation or dependence under the image of son or child." It will be noticed that the Revised Version translates, "*sons* of disobedience."

3. Among whom also we all had our conversation in times past. Paul now speaks of himself and his Jewish brethren in distinction from those addressed, who were Gentiles. 'Had our conversation' is the very imperfect rendering in the Common Version for a word which means "to turn hither and thither," "to conduct one's self," "to live." "Were turned to and fro" is Dr. Boise's translation of the verb in the form it has here. The phrase 'times past' is a reference to that portion of their personal history which lay beyond the great fact of their conversion to faith in Christ and a new life. **In the lusts of our flesh.** Plainly implying that same spiritual condition which had just been described as that of the unconverted Gentile. **Fulfilling the desires of the flesh and of the mind.** "Doing the desires," etc., as in the Revision, seems harsh. In Thayer's "Lexicon," the meaning "to carry out," "to execute," is given for this Greek verb (ποιέω), in certain phrases where it occurs ; of which rendering the verse now before us is cited as an example. The rendering in the Common Version would thus seem to have good lexical authority. **And were by nature children of wrath.** The Greek word for 'children' here differs from that employed above, in 'children,' or *sons,* 'of disobedience.' It is the word used where an emphatic sense is intended, implying true, genuine children. Compare Thayer's "Lexicon." ' By nature' is not to be taken in an emphatic sense, the order of the words in the original forbidding this; yet their meaning is plain, as indicating that state, with reference to God. in which men are born by reason of inherited sin in the nature. "We were from birth," says Braune, "those who were forfeited to the divine wrath." The language asserts the condemned, because fallen, condition of the race, into which every individual of the race is born ; so that every instance of escape from this condemnation, and from its consequences, must be through the one Saviour, though it be that of the child not yet arrived at years of responsibility. **Even as others.** More is implied in this than simply a recognition of the fact that Jew and Gentile were, in the respect considered, in one common lot. The truth is also implied that, as the favored condition of the Jewish nation as to knowledge and opportunity had in no degree changed the fact of their participation in the common calamity and the common guilt, the condition described must be viewed as one belonging to the race as such.

4. But God, who is rich in mercy. The reading of the Revised Version, "being rich in mercy," while it is a more exact translation, expresses, also, the meaning much more fully. Meyer's—"since he is rich in mercy" makes the sense clearer still. The frequent recurrence of the word 'rich,' or "riches," in similar connections, may be noticed: "Riches of his grace" (1:7); "riches of the glory of his inheritance in the saints" (1:18); "riches of his grace" again (2:7); "riches of his glory" (3:16); and here, "rich in mercy." The word seems to be one of those which indicate strongly the writer's vivid sense of that which is throughout so much the theme of his meditation. the abounding grace of God in saving sinful men. **For his great love wherewith he loved us.** The Revision retains the 'for.' More of a causal sense should be given to the clause. *On account of, because of,* is, in this place, the proper force of the Greek preposition. It expresses "the ground or reason," says Thayer, "on account of which anything is, or is not, done." Since this is clearly the meaning here, there should be a more adequate expression of it in the translation.

5. Even when we were dead in sins.

We need to put this clause in its proper relation with the one just left, in order to get the writer's whole idea. It is not God's love in any general operation of that divine attribute, nor his love for those who, however they may have once been sinners, are now his redeemed children. It is God's love for men while they yet are sinners. He had just spoken of these same sinners, Jew and Gentile alike, as 'children of wrath.' Here it is God's 'great love' for the very same persons, 'even when dead in sin,' "dead through trespasses." (Revision.) It seems necessary to place the two momentous facts in association, in order to gain a proper conception of either. Upon the one hand, the 'wrath'—"displeasure," or "anger" were a better word, and more the exact meaning of the Greek—is not of that implacable kind which the word, as so often used in common speech, might denote; while, upon the other, the 'love' is by no means the love of more indulgence. The great fact is declared elsewhere (John 3:16) that "God so loved the world that he gave his only begotten Son, that whosoever believeth in him should not perish, but have everlasting life." This verse, no less striking because so familiar, "describes," to use the language of Dr. Hovey on the passage, "God's motive in the gift of his Son as love or good-will, not merely to the chosen or to the elect from every nation, but to all mankind; for," it is added, "this is the only tenable meaning of *the world* as here used." The passage now under consideration presents to view this love—this '*great love*'—as exercised toward those who were at the same time objects of severe and just displeasure. We approach any comprehension of all this only as we realize how men in the sight of God are at the same time objects of his creative power, "made a little lower than the angels," richly endowed by him, with purposes toward them of infinite kindness; and at the same time are "sinners." His love does not blind him to the sin; neither does the sin so alienate the love as that no further thought of kindness and no provision of grace can be hoped for. Into the deep mystery on the verge of which we thus stand, we cannot expect to enter. There abides, however, this great and precious truth —that God's love for us, even while yet "sinners," is a sure guarantee of access to him in the name of his Son, and of a far more abounding grace in redemption when sought and obtained through faith in the same prevailing mediation. **Hath quickened us together with Christ.** Here we return to the thought only partially expressed in ver. 1-3, with one other added, and in another of those phrases characteristic of this Epistle—'with Christ.' The meaning of the Greek is, 'made us alive together with Christ.' Alford, as quoted by Boise, says: "Our spiritual life is the primary subject of the apostle's thought; but this includes in itself our share in the resurrection and exaltation of Christ." In what has preceded there has been no reference to physical death, unless some such reference should remotely appear in the words 'dead in trespasses and in sins,' as implying the whole effect of sin in the fall of man. Nor is there anywhere in the direct connection a reference to the resurrection, unless it should be where, in the seventh verse below, mention is made of what God, "in the ages to come," is to make manifest of his "kindness toward us through Christ Jesus." What the apostle in the verse now in hand is speaking of, is a blessing already in possession by those who had believed in Christ—Jew and Gentile—and this, certainly, is a spiritual quickening. At the same time it is a quickening 'with Christ,' and so is a new life gained through his resurrection as the consummating act in his redeeming work. In all the effects of that redemptive work they share, in immediate and effective participation. This, no doubt, would remotely include quickening of the body in the final resurrection, as of the soul in present spiritual experience. Neither the one nor the other is to be thought of apart from Christ. We are now, and then shall be, "made alive *with* him." This the apostle emphasizes in the parenthetical clause which follows: (**By grace ye are saved.**) *Have been saved* is more exact, while also it brings to view more fully the fact that the salvation of a true believer is in a certain high sense not a pending work, with the result uncertain, but a completed fact. The whole great and wonderful proceeding is of grace, as is again forcibly set forth in verses which follow.

6. And hath raised us up together. In the Common Version these words carry the impression that believers are simply 'raised up' in unison—made to participate in a com-

6 And hath raised us up together, and made us sit together in heavenly places in Christ Jesus:
7 That in the ages to come he might shew the exceeding riches of his grace, in his kindness toward us, through Christ Jesus.

6 ye been saved), and raised us up with him, and made us to sit with him in the heavenly places, in
7 Christ Jesus: that in the ages to come he might shew the exceeding riches of his grace in kindness

mon benefit. In point of fact, the 'quickening together,' the 'raising up together,' and 'the sitting together' are all alike 'with Christ.' The Revision accordingly reads, "raised us up with him." We must be careful not to shift the main burden of the thought to that rising with Christ which is to come at the resurrection. The apostle is all along dwelling upon matters of present experience, while that which is yet a subject of hope and anticipation is collateral and implied. Out of that death in trespasses and sins we are, after being 'quickened,' also 'raised up,' the idea of a spiritual resurrection being made thus complete. And both are 'with Christ,' since *through* his resurrection and *in* his resurrection this 'grace' is made possible, not only, but actual. And made us sit together in heavenly places in Christ Jesus. It is 'sit together' *in him*. We notice that many commentators, by making too much, as it seems to us, of the local element in the phrase 'heavenly places,' appear to make the main force of the words now considered lie in a reference to the final glorification of the redeemed, as if the promise in Rev. 3 : 21 were here in some degree anticipated : "He that overcometh, I will give him to sit down with me in my throne, as I also overcame and sat down with my Father in his throne." The central thought in this phrase, 'heavenly places,' is no doubt that of heaven itself. But just as still in common speech, all that in thought, in hope, in experience, which centres in the 'heavenly' is itself characterized as heavenly, so it appears to be with the language of the apostle in this place. Whatever of reference there may be to that which until the final consummation must still be a hope, though an expectation also, what is specifically meant here is that present participation with Christ in the results of his redeeming work which is naturally consequent upon the being 'made alive with him' and 'raised up with him.' Let it be noticed also that these 'heavenly places' themselves are '*in*,' not 'with' Christ Jesus. The allusion seems to be, primarily, at least, to that present high spiritual privilege to which each believing soul is permitted to aspire. In raising them up with himself, he admits all such to a spiritual union and intimacy of intercourse, which while it anticipates what shall be when that glory which the Father gave to him he also will give to them, is at the same time a present holy and happy sitting together 'in heavenly places'; communing upon heavenly things, gladdened by heavenly anticipations, and foretasting the unspeakable bliss of heaven itself. It is a mistake to have the mind so occupied with what is future in the high meaning of this passage as to undervalue, however unconsciously, that which it assures us of concerning a great and wonderful privilege in the present.

7. That in the ages to come. There is much difference of opinion as to the proper meaning here of the phrase, 'ages to come.' Thayer understands by it, "the age after the return of Christ in majesty, the period of the consummate establishment of the divine kingdom and all its blessings." He refers to Luke 18 : 30, where a like phrase in the Greek occurs, and as rendered there it no doubt means, "the world to come"; also to Mark 10 : 30. The phrase as occurring in these two places (ὁ αἰὼν ὁ ἐρχόμενος) seems to mean "the world (or, *age*) to come," in strict contrast to 'the world' (or, *age*) that now is. In our present passage, however, the words used are in the plural, "in the coming ages" (ἐν τοῖς αἰῶσιν τοῖς ἐπερχομένοις). "Any special reference," says Ellicott, "to the then present and immediately coming age," which is the meaning given to the words by some commentators, "or to the still future kingdom of Christ," the view held by Harless, Olshausen, Thayer, and others, "seems precluded respectively by the use of the plural and the appended present participle (ἐπερχομένοις)." He takes the meaning to be "the successively arriving generations from that time to the Second Coming of Christ." This appears to be the more correct view of the phrase as here employed. He might show the exceeding riches of his grace. We must look to ver. 4 for the antecedent here. That 'God' might show 'the

8 For by grace are ye saved through faith; and that not of yourselves: *it is* the gift of God:
9 Not of works, lest any man should boast.

8 toward us in Christ Jesus: for by grace have ye been saved through faith; and that not of yourselves: **9** *it is* the gift of God; not of works, that no man

exceeding riches of his grace.' **In his kindness to us through Christ Jesus.** Trench ("Synonyms," p. 59) speaks of the word here translated 'kindness' as "a beautiful word." A little later on he distinguishes between it and the word for "goodness." A man, he says, "might display" what is meant by the latter "in his zeal for goodness and truth, in rebuking, correcting, chastising. Christ was working in the spirit of this grace when he drove the buyers and sellers out of the temple; when he uttered those terrible words against the Scribes and Pharisees." The spirit of the other word, 'kindness,' in our verse, "was displayed rather in the reception of the penitent woman (Luke 7 : 37; compare Ps. 24: 7, 8), in all his gracious dealings with the children of men." As used in our present passage, the word presents in a most engaging light the divine benignity of that attitude in which God 'in Christ Jesus' places himself before men while addressing them in the offers and invitations of the gospel—offers and invitations which were to be made during all those 'ages to come' which are embraced in the Gospel Dispensation.

8. For by grace are ye (*have ye been*) **saved through faith.** The use of the connecting particle 'for' seems to make it necessary for us to give the phrase 'the world,' or 'ages to come,' the meaning above indicated. Quite clearly the apostle now, in this verse, cites an example of the 'kindness' which it was God's purpose to thus show in the ages coming—the ages immediately following upon the consummation of his method of grace in the death, resurrection, and ascension of Christ. Such an example is afforded in those whom the apostle now addresses. "In the manifestation and exercise of this grace, ye yourselves have been saved." The change of 'ye are saved,' in the Common Version, to "have ye been saved," in the Revision, is made necessary by the tense of the verb in the Greek. It is the perfect passive, and denotes, as Ellicott says, "a present state, as well as a terminated action." The truth, as implied, is that the subjects of this 'grace' are 'saved' persons. One is at a loss to see how the fact could be otherwise. What takes place in the great transaction so described is this: A penitent sinner, truly penitent, comes to God in the name of Christ, exercising that faith to which the promise has been made. The 'grace' of God meets him, accepts him, and 'in Christ' he is made participant of the promised gifts of the Spirit, with all which results therefrom in a renewed heart, and spiritual life out of spiritual death. Is not such a one 'saved'? There remains, of course, the warfare for which he is equipped, as described in the sixth chapter of this Epistle; but it is quite impossible that, having once fully entered into the possession of this 'grace,' he shall ever so fall away as to be finally lost. **And that not of yourselves.** The Greek word for 'that' is neuter, so that the reference cannot be to 'faith,' since in that case it would be feminine. What is meant is the fact stated in the preceding clause. **It is the gift of God.** This clause has more of emphatic force in the literal translation—*not of yourselves; the gift of God.*

9. Not of works. In what sense 'works' are still expected of those whom grace has saved, is brought to view in the verse which next follows. What is said here is that this salvation is not in any sense merited by goodness in us, nor purchased by acts of obedience or acts of service. It is indeed restating, in another form of words, what has already been said, 'By grace ye are saved.' **Lest any man should boast.** The idea in this clause is one upon which the Apostle Paul often dwells with emphasis. Compare Rom. 3 : 27-4 : 25. There are these sufficient reasons why, in general, men should not claim as a merit in themselves what is due alone and wholly to the grace of God: (1) That such a claim is false in itself. (2) That the self-righteousness necessarily involved in such a claim tends to defeat the end sought in the bestowment of the gift; namely, the kind of character pleasing to God and commendable in man. (3) That it prevents all such exercise of gratitude to God as is due to him, and needful in man as an element of character worthy and ennobling. (4) That it robs God. There seems to be, how-

10 For we are his workmanship, created in Christ Jesus unto good works, which God hath before ordained that we should walk in them.

10 should glory. For we are his workmanship, created in Christ Jesus for good works, which God afore prepared that we should walk in them.

ever. in the clause considered, still a further thought. 'Not of works, *lest* any man should boast,' or *glory*. Even if it had been possible for man to achieve salvation as a reward of good deeds, it would have been undesirable. The pride natural to the heart of man, taking the form of self-righteousness, would have left his salvation incomplete in that which is most important, a thoroughly regenerate character. It is "he that humbleth himself" who shall be exalted. The giving of glory to God, as is his due, is not more the rendering to him of that which is his of right, than it is for the benefit of those who thus are emptied of themselves, that they may be filled with him.

10. For we are his workmanship. Ellicott and others prefer "handiwork," which is perhaps the better word. The Greek means simply "that which has been made." The verse, as a whole, brings to a climax what has occupied the thought of the writer in all this part of the chapter. Man's fallen, lost state; the grace of God in visiting him 'even when dead' through his 'trespasses'; the quickening divine energy which raises him out of that fallen condition, and makes him as regenerate, reconciled, and restored, to sit in 'heavenly places in Christ'—all as a 'gift of God' through faith, which is also his gift,—this is now summed up in the striking language of ver. 10. What a saved person thus becomes he is *made* to be. He owes all to the divine efficiency of the grace that has saved him, as really as the thing made (ποίημα) owes its existence to the hand that fashioned it. This is further made evident in what follows. **Created in Christ Jesus.** Two ideas, fundamental in the view which Paul gives of the saved man, are here expressed. (1) "It is a *creation*, a favorite conception of this apostle as representing that change in which a sinful human being becomes a child of God. It is more than a reformation, more than a change of the reigning purpose in life, more than change, however great a change, in the life itself. It is a work of renewal so radical as to be in its ultimate effect absolutely transforming. No word will adequately express the divine effectualness of this work of renewal short of that which declares how this same human being came to exist at all. (2) And it is 'in Christ Jesus.' The place which Christ Jesus fills in the new creation is in one way like that which he fills in the original one. We read of him that "all things were made by him, and without him was not anything made that was made." (John 1:3.) We even read that "in him was life." (John 1:4.) As incomplete as would be any idea of the original creation which did not include this all-efficient instrumentality of "the Word," would be any conception of the new creation which did not recognize 'Christ Jesus' as he "by whom are all things and we by him." (1 Cor. 8:6.) Every gift and every act of mercy coming to us in our salvation comes through him; so that when, as here, the whole is summed and expressed in the fact of a new creation, with a new nature and a new destiny, we trace all to his mediation in our behalf so entirely that we find it to be 'in' him. **Unto good works.** *For good works* expresses the sense better. The 'good works' here ought surely to have for us a very comprehensive meaning. So great a work, and at such a cost, can, in respect to this part of its design, have aimed at nothing less than that perfection of character toward which we are so often in the New Testament urged to aspire. **Which God hath before ordained.** *Before prepared* is the correct rendering. **That we should walk in them.** "There is, perhaps," says Canon Barry, "in all Scripture no stronger expression of the great mystery of God's predestination; for it is here declared, not only in reference to the original call and justification and regeneration of the soul, but also to the actual good works, in which the free-will and energy of man are most plainly exercised; and in which even here we are said not to be moved, but to 'walk' by our own act." This writer seems to find in the passage one element of meaning which may not strictly belong to it; perhaps as influenced by the word 'ordained' in the Common Version, which as we have seen is an incorrect translation. What Dr. Boise quotes of Beveridge, as found in a note by Ellicott, is better: "God, *before* we were created in Christ, *made ready* for us; prearranged, prepared a sphere of

11 Wherefore remember, that ye *being* in time past Gentiles in the flesh, who are called Uncircumcision by that which is called the Circumcision in the flesh made by hands;
12 That at that time ye were without Christ, being aliens from the commonwealth of Israel, and strangers

11 Wherefore remember, that aforetime ye, the Gentiles in the flesh, who are called Uncircumcision by that which is called Circumcision, in the flesh, made by hands; that ye were at that time separate from Christ, alienated from the commonwealth of Israel,

moral action, or (to use a simile of Chrysostom) a road, with the intent *that we should walk in it* and not leave it." Not, however, surely, as a mere outward conformity to rule or to precept, but as a yielding up of the whole life, inward and outward, to a principle of obedience which shall in all ways express that transformation "by the renewing of our mind," in which we shall fully "prove what is that good, and acceptable, and perfect will of God." (Rom. 12:2.) It is to be noticed that Paul in ver. 9 and 10 speaks of 'good works' in those two contrasted aspects of them which it is so important to keep in mind. 'Works,' however 'good,' as is shown in ver. 9, make no part of that ground of justification in which the saved person stands accepted with God. "By grace ye have been saved, through *faith*." Yet, as appears by ver. 10, there are still to be 'good works' as fulfilling that divine idea in our salvation which aims at nothing less than renewal of the moral nature, and perfection in character and in life.

11-22. GENTILE AND JEW MADE ONE SPIRITUAL BODY IN CHRIST.

11. Wherefore remember. The apostle is now to speak of a result of that which in previous verses has been set forth which must place this grace of God in a new light. Thus far he has spoken of this grace as it affects the individual saved soul. Now he comes to show how, what operates thus in the individual, reaches in its effect beyond him so as to be an element of union, not only of man to God, but of men with one another. To begin, he points these Gentile Christians once more to that which had been their sad condition. It is this he would have them 'remember.' **That ye being in the time past Gentiles in the flesh.** He does not mean, just here, 'in the flesh' in the sense of being as yet unregenerate, but Gentiles by nature and by birth, as distinguished from Jews. **Who are called Uncircumcision by that which is called Circumcision.** As preparatory to what next follows in development of the whole thought of the writer, attention is once more called to that distinction, not only of race, but of condition, in which, during so many centuries, the Gentile had stood apart from the Jew. He is to show, directly, how these are made one. He begins by reminding the Gentile Christians how entirely they had once been "alien from the commonwealth of Israel." **In the flesh made by hands.** This distinction had been, after all, very much an outward one. So far as concerned Jewish pride itself, the distinction was wholly an outward one, and rested in the fact of the presence or absence of an outward sign, of whose real significance the Jew himself was all too little aware.

12. That at that time ye were without Christ. Here was a fact in their condition of far greater importance than that of which the Jew was accustomed to make so much. In respect to this other fact, the Jew, if unconverted, was in no better state than the unconverted Gentile, save that, as one of that nation of whom Christ was to come and who had inherited the "covenants of promise," the Jew was, so far, not 'without Christ' in the same sense as the Gentile. "Separate from Christ" is the rendering of the Revision. More seems to be meant than that which is true of every unconverted person. The expression implies, also, what is comprehended in the clauses which follow. Until Christ actually came, and the world-wide purpose of his mission had been disclosed in the preaching of the gospel to "the Gentiles also," these latter had, only in exceptional cases, and in these only in very imperfect measure, any knowledge, even, of that wealth of Messianic promise which had been from age to age the heritage of Israel. Wandering thus amidst the deep darkness of Pagan ignorance and Pagan idolatries, they were in a most melancholy sense 'separate from Christ.' **Being alienus** (or, *alienated*) **from the commonwealth of Israel.** Thayer explains the word for 'alienated,' "shut out from one's fellowship and intimacy." The adjective from which the verb comes means, primarily, "belonging to another." We are apt to give the word 'alienate,' or 'alienated,' more of a subjective meaning—a state of mind in ourselves

from the covenants of promise, having no hope, and without God in the world:
13 But now, in Christ Jesus, ye who sometime were far off are made nigh by the blood of Christ.

through which, in feeling and in respect of sympathy and fellowship, we are made to hold ourselves aloof. This is not the meaning here. The Gentiles were '*shut out* from the commonwealth of Israel.' This was partly as a necessary effect of that divine appointment in which, with a view to certain most important purposes, Israel was made the chosen people; and partly an estrangement due to Jewish pride, upon the one hand, and Gentile disdain upon the other. **And strangers from the covenants of promise.** The expression is peculiar, though the Revision retains it. We could not change it to read, more in accordance with English idiom, 'strangers *to* the covenants of promise.' The Greek will not allow this; besides which, that is not what the writer means to say. The word for 'covenants' is in the genitive—the "genitive of the point of view." So Ellicott, as quoted by Boise. Strangers *in respect to* the covenants of promise, appears to be the meaning. 'The covenants' must be those which had been made especially with Israel as the chosen people; that with Abraham, in behalf of his posterity; and that with Moses, as representing the Israelitish nation. The Gentiles were not strangers in respect of these, in the sense that they were never to have part in what the promise contained, since in Abraham and his descendants "all nations" were to be "blessed." They were strangers in the sense that until Christ, the Promised One, had actually come, they had not only had no part in what the covenant had provided, but had not even been aware that any such privilege was possible for them; and in the sense that after Christ had come they still remained aloof until the gospel of God's grace had reached them. **Having no hope.** Scarcely any form of words could better express the condition of a Pagan people. In the previous descriptive clauses of the verse, the allusions have been more to what expressed outward relations. Between Jew and Gentile there had been that "middle wall of partition" mentioned in ver. 14, as a consequence of which the Gentiles had been both aliens and strangers, as to the commonwealth of Israel and as to those 'cove-

and strangers from the covenants of the promise,
13 having no hope and without God in the world But now in Christ Jesus ye that once were far off are

nants' which from the time of the patriarchs had singled out the descendants of the patriarchs as "a peculiar people." Now the apostle comes to another and a deeper fact in their condition. 'Having no hope.' Their religions and their philosophies had alike failed to answer those questions which the soul of man is compelled by the very constitution of its nature to ask. **And without God in the world.** Thayer quotes Ælian as saying that there is no one, even of the barbarians, without God, using the same Greek word as Paul uses here (ἄθεος), and meaning to say that even barbarians have a kind of religion and gods whom they worship. Upon the other hand, Paul declares, of all the Gentile races and nations, that they were (ἄθεοι) ' without God.' Countless deities, but no God! Men of superior intelligence, even among the cultivated Pagan nations, were wont to say substantially the same thing, while showing in many ways how little value they found in the inventions of mythology; and while indicating, in the speculations of their philosophy, how confused and uncertain were all their own ideas of God. 'In the world' appears to mean simply the life of men as led amidst present surroundings and conditions. There may be an intimation in the words how much men need 'God in the world,' and how truly calamitous it is to be without him. Indeed, it might not be going far astray to see something characteristic in the successive clauses of the verse, suggesting that of all that had been calamitous and lamentable in the condition of the Gentile nations, this was greatest and worst, that they were 'without God in the world.'

13. **But now.** From this view of the sad condition of the Gentile nations, with particular reference to those addressed, the apostle now turns, as if gladly and gratefully, to speak of that which, as "the apostle to the Gentiles" must have been to him a matter of great satisfaction. **In Christ Jesus ye who sometimes** (or, *once*) **were far off are made nigh by the blood of Christ.** It is to be noticed how the thought which in all this part of the Epistle seems uppermost in the writer's mind, finds expression twice in this short verse.

14 For he is our peace, who hath made both one, and hath broken down the middle wall of partition *between us;*
15 Having abolished in his flesh the enmity, even the

14 made nigh in the blood of Christ. For he is our peace, who made both one, and brake down the 15 middle wall of partition, having abolished in his flesh the enmity, *even* the law of commandments

'In Christ Jesus' . . . 'by the blood of Christ.' The second of these in some sense explains the first. 'In Christ Jesus' may have seemed to the writer not sufficiently explicit. He adds, 'by the blood of Christ,' that there may be no misapprehension as to the relation Christ bears to this of which he is now to speak. In ch. 1 : 7 of this Epistle we have the same thought: 'In whom we have redemption through his blood.' That result of this redemption held in view in our present passage is implied very clearly in our Lord's own words (John 12: 32): "And I, if I be lifted up, will draw all men unto me." In drawing all men unto himself he draws them into a unity and fellowship which annihilates those distinctions by which they have been sundered, and set in positions, often, even of antagonism. It is thus that these believing Gentiles to whom Paul writes have been 'made nigh.'

14. For he is our peace who hath made both one. The position of the words (αὐτὸς γάρ, 'for he') makes them emphatic: "he and no other." Orelli ("Old Testament Prophecy," p. 310) views the word 'peace,' in this place, as "borrowed" from Micah 5 : 5, "He shall be peace." Speaking of the Hebrew word for 'peace,' he says: "Such a word is capable of unlimited intensification, and has found it in the Bible. Only the completed revelation has disclosed all its depths of meaning. In the Hebrew language the word (שָׁלוֹם, peace) was an every-day word, a common greeting, a trivial wish. It denoted what every one desired for himself and wished for any one with whom he was on good terms; freedom from harm and disturbance, peace, rest, well-being. Among the peace-loving Orientals peace was, and is, in the profane sphere of thought, the highest good. And in the religious life the sum of salvation may be comprised in it. When prophecy promises peace in the time of consummation, and calls the Messiah Peace absolutely, it means peace in inner and outer perfection, man being completely at one with God, and men having become through his revelation one with each other. This will be Messiah's gift. Such peace, in fact, the Prince of Peace from Bethlehem brought to the world, only far more gloriously than human heart could conceive under the Old Covenant. And in the sense in which he established peace, it is the highest good to the Christian. Hence everything we have in Christ may be summed up in the word borrowed by the apostle from our prophet." Other such intimations may be seen in Isaiah 9 : 5, 6, where Messiah is named "Prince of Peace," in the song of the angels, where his coming brings "peace on earth," and his own words to his disciples in taking leave of them: "My peace I give unto you." In our present passage he is that 'peace' itself in bringing to pass the twofold reconciliation—man with God, and, in that very fact itself, of men with each other. For 'he hath made both one'—both Jew and Gentile. **And hath broken down the middle wall of partition between us.** The words 'between us' being supplied in the Common Version, although not necessary to the sense. The force of the metaphor is quite sufficiently plain. The expression 'middle wall of partition' might seem tautological in English, though it is not so in the Greek. The words for 'middle wall' and 'partition' are an example, as Winer explains (§ 59, 8, a), of "the genitive of apposition." We should say "partition wall."

15. Having abolished in his flesh the enmity. There is a question here as to the pointing of the Greek. Tischendorf makes the passage read, "the middle wall of partition, the enmity"; 'enmity' being in apposition with the clause which precedes, and epexegetical of it. In this pointing, 'having abolished in his flesh' is connected, not with 'enmity,' but with "the law of commandments" immediately following. We should then read, "hath made both one, and hath broken down the middle wall of partition, the enmity, having abolished in his flesh the law of commandments," etc. It is a question of construction rather than of meaning, save that in the arrangement of Tischendorf the word 'enmity' comes to explain so clearly the force of the imagery in 'middle wall of partition.' The Revision follows the pointing of Westcott and Hort. By 'the enmity' is no doubt in-law of commandments *contained* in ordinances; for to make in himself of twain one new man, *so* making peace;

16 And that he might reconcile both unto God in one body by the cross, having slain the enmity thereby:

contained in ordinances; that he might create in himself of the twain one new man, so making

16 peace; and might reconcile them both in one body unto God through the cross, having slain the enmity

17 thereby: and he came and ¹ preached peace to you

¹ Gr. *preached good tidings of peace.*

---

tended the feeling of mutual hostility long existing between Jews and Gentiles, with remoter allusion, probably, to that "enmity with God" which is characteristic of the "mind of the flesh" always. The arrangement of Tischendorf, which Ellicott also adopts, seems on this account preferable. **Even the law of commandments contained in ordinances.** Following the pointing of Westcott and Hort, and translating as in the Common Version and the Revision, this 'law of the commandments contained in ordinances' comes to be explanatory of 'the enmity.' It may be doubted if this is what the apostle intends. In what *sufficing* sense, can 'the law of commandments in ordinances' represent or explain 'the enmity'? The alienation, amounting to hostility, between Jew and Gentile, was due to many causes, and not simply, we must suppose, to the character and effect of Jewish institutions. Indeed, when Paul speaks here of the abolition of that which distinctively characterized Judaism, he seems to allude to the removal rather of that which was a hindrance to union than that which was a cause of enmity. The 'commandments in ordinances' must mean the ceremonial law, or rather that system in general of special Mosaic legislation which was done away in the gospel. **For to make** (*that he might create*) **in himself of twain one new man; so making peace.** '*Might create in himself*,' a stronger word than simply 'make.' Jew and Gentile, though retaining their individuality otherwise, became "one in Christ Jesus." In bringing this to pass that work of spiritual renewal is effected in each of which the apostle so often speaks as 'a new creation.' They are thus brought into that spiritual fellowship and unity, by reason of their common faith in Christ, which warrants the characterization, 'one new man.' It is doubtful if the rendering '*so* making peace,' the italicized word being supplied, is the preferable one. Dr. Boise views the participle in the Greek for 'making,' "as denoting means as well as time; *while* making, and *by* making peace." The peace is made before the unity, and becomes a *means* of unity.

16. And that he might reconcile both unto God in one body by the cross. The pivotal word here is the word translated 'reconcile.'¹ Thayer appears to regard our present passage as an example of the meaning, "to draw to himself by reconciliation, or so to reconcile that they should be devoted to himself." The second of these meanings which Trench finds in the word must surely imply the first, for reconciliation in the sense of restored favor with God must be the invariable condition of all which most characterizes the Christian state, whether with reference to God or with reference to men. This becomes evident as we consider what follows in the verse. **Having slain the enmity thereby**—that is, by "the cross." The condition as described is clearly one in which all that was wrong in the relation of these Jewish and Gentile Christians with God, or with each other, had been fully made right. The 'enmity' is 'shin'— alike that alienation of heart which had characterized their unregenerate condition, and that mutual alienation which had made any fraternal tie between them wholly impossible. This had been slain by 'the cross.' It is that result which so often in Christian history has followed upon a true and a truly transforming reception of the gospel of Jesus Christ. 'Peace with God' prepares the way for peace with all

---

¹ Of this word, Trench says ("Synonyms," pp. 137, 138): "The Christian καταλλαγή has two sides. It is first a reconciliation, '*qua Deus nos sibi reconciliavit*,' laid aside his holy anger against our sins, and received us into favor, a reconciliation effected once for all for us by Christ upon his cross.... But καταλλαγή is secondly and subordinately the reconciliation, '*qua nos Deo reconciliamur*,' the daily deposition, under the operation of the Holy Spirit, of the enmity of the old man toward God." Of this latter he quotes 2 Cor. 5:20 as an example.

17 And came and preached peace to you which were afar off, and to them that were nigh.
18 For through him we both have access by one Spirit unto the Father.
19 Now therefore ye are no more strangers and foreigners, but fellow citizens with the saints, and of the household of God;

that were far off, and peace to them that were nigh: for through him we both have our access in one Spirit unto the Father. So then ye are no more strangers and sojourners, but ye are fellow-citizens with the saints, and of the household of

---

men. It is that new nature whose living principle is love—love to God and love for the neighbor.

17. And came and preached peace. It is Christ Jesus, named in ver. 13. The immediate connection of our present verse is with ver. 14: 'For he is our peace, who,' etc. . . . 'and came and preached peace,' etc. This cannot refer to the personal ministry of our Lord; partly because what is specifically mentioned here did not characterize that ministry —the mission of his gospel to the Gentile world being left for his apostles to make known, and partly, also, because what is here mentioned in ver. 17 clearly follows in the order of thought what is mentioned in ver. 15, 16. It was after 'by the cross' he had prepared the way for the work of reconciliation described, and in some sense effected it, that he 'came and preached peace.' The allusion must be to that which was foreshadowed in the promised ministry of the Holy Spirit, who should "not speak of himself"; he should "receive of mine and show it unto you." In a word, in the gospel as preached to Jew and Gentile alike, Jesus himself, in the attendant ministry and effectual calling of that Spirit of Truth whom he both promised and sent, 'preached peace.' **To you which were afar off, and (peace) to them that were nigh.** The allusion is supposed to be to Isa. 57: 19: "I create the fruit of the lips. Peace, peace to him that is afar off, and to him that is near, saith the Lord, and I will heal him." Such an allusion is possible, though if existing at all, it must be indirect and general. In the Greek the word for 'peace' is repeated, for the sake of emphasis, evidently; as in the Revision, "peace to you that were far off, and peace to them that were nigh."

18. For through him we both have access by one Spirit unto the Father. Dr. Boise calls attention to the fact that we have here presented the three persons of the Godhead: "Through him," Jesus Christ, the Son, "we have our access in one Spirit [Revision] unto the Father." There is a suggestion, also, in this mention of the Spirit's ministry as to the sense which the words 'came and preached peace' should bear. Thayer's first meaning for the word translated 'access' is "the act of bringing to, moving to"; and his second, "access, approach." He quotes Ellicott as insisting upon the transitive sense, "introduction." The word 'access' does not, indeed, seem to express all which is intended. Privilege, opportunity of approach, is secured in that work of 'reconciliation,' which is effected in the 'cross' of Christ; but the ministry of the Spirit has a purpose and effect of its own, being nothing less than that "preparation of heart and answer of the tongue" which are also and both "from the Lord." (Prov. 16:1.)

19. Now therefore ye are no more strangers and foreigners. "So then" and "strangers and sojourners" are changes made in the Revision. The apostle now shows what is the inference from that which has gone before. Gentile Christians, in view of their full participation in the benefits of the gospel, are in wholly changed relations as respects that which was the highest privilege of the Jew. Two results follow from this new order which the Dispensation of God's grace in the gospel has introduced: (1) The Jew is no longer, in any sense, in an exclusively favored position. The object of his calling and separation among the nations of the world has been accomplished. (2) In the New Order so introduced all men are alike included, without distinction of race, nation, or condition. In this New Commonwealth, citizenship is free to all who will accept it upon the terms offered. These to whom the apostle writes have so accepted. They are therefore no longer 'strangers,' citizens of another commonwealth or country, nor "sojourners," merely resident foreigners. **But fellow citizens with the saints.** All the rights of citizenship are theirs; they are at home, and every privilege open to the citizen is open to them. **And of the household of God.** "To the right of the citizen," says Braune, quoted by Riddell, "is added that of the house, of the child, of the heir." A great

20 And are built upon the foundations of the apostles and prophets, Jesus Christ himself being the chief corner stone;

20 God, being built upon the foundation of the apostles and prophets, Christ Jesus himself being the chief

and wonderful change from the "alien" condition once true of the whole Gentile world.
20. And are built. The figure used now once more changes. In ver. 15, 16, the reconciliation effected 'by the cross' is represented under the idea of a blending in one personality of these 'twain' between whom such long continued and inveterate enmity had existed, so making one new (*renewed*) man, while 'both' are reconciled unto God 'in one body.' Next the unconverted Gentiles were viewed as before aliens and foreigners; but now, as converted, brought into all the privileges of citizenship. The result of the same gracious work is next represented as a building in which material, diverse and apparently incapable of harmonious union in one structure, is brought together and wrought into unity of plan and result with divine skill. **Upon the foundation of the apostles and prophets.** The commonly accepted view we suppose to be that by 'prophets' are meant the prophets of the Old Testament. A careful study of the passage suggests objections to this. 1. It is not clear that in writing to Gentile Christians, Paul would name in such a connection what would be in any good measure appreciated only by those familiar with the more ancient Scripture. 2. Some weight, perhaps, should be allowed to the objection founded on the order of the words used. It would be natural to expect that if Paul were speaking of those ancient men held in such reverence by every Jew, he would have named them first. 3. It is further urged that throughout the entire connection of the passage Paul occupies the attention of his readers with things present, and is therefore less likely to introduce what is, in this respect, so remote from the general order of his thought. 4. In 3:5, of this Epistle, and in 4:11, especially in the former place, Paul names in a like connection with each other "apostles and prophets." The thought in 3:5, in particular, is so much like what we have here, that one seems in a measure forced to the conclusion that here, as there, he is speaking along with the 'apostles,' of those in the church at that time who were endowed with the prophetic gift, and who might therefore with propriety be associated, as here, with those who as apostles held the leading place. But in what sense were apostles and prophets a 'foundation'? Perhaps in a twofold sense: 1. As inspired teachers, making known that truth upon which all that bears the name of Christian must rest. 2. With particular reference to the apostles, as exercising apostolical authority, and entitled to be received in that representative character with which their Lord in sending had endowed them. The words of Christ to Peter (Matt. 16:18), however interpreted in their more precise meaning, certainly seem to imply an apostolical office and function, for which large occasion appeared in the years immediately following his own ascension, and preparation for which was quite as certainly promised in the assurance that the Spirit of truth, in his own ministry for them, should "guide" them "into all truth." It is, therefore, but the recognition of what had been thus appointed when for the 'apostles' as a body, and for the 'prophets' whose service bore such an intimate relation with their own, a place and function so fundamental is indicated. **Jesus Christ himself being the chief corner stone.** "As the corner stone," says Thayer, "joins together two walls, so Christ joins together as Christians, into one body dedicated to God, those who were formerly Jews and Gentiles." The general reference will be to that fundamental place which Christ fills in all that which is to a Christian matter of faith or a rule of life.

21. In whom all the building. The Revision reads, "each several building," and in the margin "every building." Winer (18. 4) does not recognize a necessity for this change "As Paul," he says, "is speaking of the Christian Church as a whole, 'the whole building,' is the proper translation." Alford, Ellicott, and Braune, among commentators, also prefer this rendering, though the Revision agrees with Meyer. Dr. Boise also agrees with him. "In one vast temple," he says, "are many 'buildings' (οἰκοδομαί)," and refers to Matt. 24:1. "the buildings of the temple." Riddell seems to understand by "buildings," "the separate Christian congregations" and speaks of these as "each of them growing in the same way, in the personal Christ." The

21 In whom all the building fitly framed together groweth unto a holy temple in the Lord: 22 In whom ye also are builded together for a habitation of God through the Spirit.

21 corner stone; in whom ¹ each several building, fitly framed together, groweth into a holy ² temple in 22 the Lord; in whom ye also are builded together ³ for a habitation of God in the Spirit.

1 Gr. *every building*.... .2 Or, *sanctuary*.......3 Gr. *into*.

allusion does not seem to be to congregations, or to churches, but to individual Christians, such as these to whom Paul writes. One finds in the passage a general sense much like what appears in 4 : 16, below, where mention is made of "the whole body." The omission of the article in the Greek makes the usage in the verse under consideration exceptional, yet one which occurs in other places, cited by Winer, as in this Epistle (1 : 8), and in James 1 : 2. It seems most in consistence with that emphasis which the apostle is placing upon the idea of unity, and with the figurative method of illustration employed throughout this part of the chapter, to understand him as representing all Christians, however diverse in other things, yet by their common faith and their common union with Christ, themselves so brought into unity as to constitute this spiritual "temple in the Lord." **Fitly framed together.** The language is much like that in 4 : 16, "the whole body fitly joined and compacted," etc. **Groweth unto a holy temple in the Lord.** The conception seems to be that of the church of Jesus Christ in its spiritual sense. Made up of those who are true believers, it is 'fitly framed together,' and as the number of these increases from age to age it becomes more and more worthy a fulfillment of that typical "holy temple of the Lord" in whose holiest place the Shekinah dwells.

22. In whom ye also are builded together. Ye Gentiles, not as churches, but as individual believers, have each and personally a place. The words 'in whom' should be noted as a reiteration of what has so frequently appeared in these first two chapters of the Epistle. Each privilege of the believer, all the grace manifested and experienced, is always 'in Christ.' **For an habitation of God through the Spirit.** The three divine Persons again grouped in a single verse. 'In' the Son believers are brought into the unity of this 'temple of the Lord' in which the Father, 'through the Spirit,' or 'in the Spirit,' as the special form of divine manifestation, dwells. The figurative allusion to the ancient sanctuary is made more evident by the fact that the word used for 'temple' is not that which denotes the temple in general, but that which indicates the "sanctuary," where stood the altar of incense, and in the holiest place of all, the mercy seat—"shadows of good things to come"—with the Divine Presence itself manifested in impressive symbols.

SUMMARY OF THE EXPOSITION.

In this chapter the apostle enters more directly upon the specific theme of the Epistle. He is addressing a church made up mainly or wholly of converted Gentiles. Two things are true of them in their present condition: 1. They are renewed persons, changed by the grace of God from their former heathen state into a spiritual condition which is for them as life from the dead. (1-10.) 2. They have been brought into full enjoyment of those privileges which were once thought to be the exclusive possession of the chosen people; so that now, in this respect, the distinction of Jew and Gentile exists no longer. (11-13.)

As regards the former of these particulars, however, Jew and Gentile had been recipients of a like mercy. Paul recognizes the fact that those like himself who had been wont to claim a peculiar interest in God's favor had been 'sons of disobedience' not less than the Gentiles. They also had been 'dead in sins,' and had been also 'raised up' through the same renewing grace of 'God, who is rich in mercy.' Thus, apart from that act of divine beneficence in which the door to all spiritual privilege had been thrown open to the Gentiles, a perfect union of Jew and Gentile had been prepared in the fact that out of a common condition of deadness in sin they had been raised in the same act of renewing grace into possession of one and the same new life in Christ.

Upon this thought, from ver. 14 to the close of the chapter, the writer mainly dwells. Jew and Gentile are henceforth one. Their common regeneration, supplanting 'enmity' with love; their common access to God by virtue of their admission to the same new relation with

CHAPTER III.

FOR this cause I Paul, the prisoner of Jesus Christ for you Gentiles,

1 For this cause I Paul, the prisoner of Christ Jesus

the Father through the Son,—these are recognized in a setting aside of all that in 'the law of commandments contained in ordinances' which had heretofore been 'a middle-wall of partition' between them. They are now one spiritual building, growing 'unto an holy temple in the Lord,' with the foundation in that revealed truth of which 'apostles and prophets' were the ministers, Jesus Christ being the corner stone.

It is worthy of particular remark that to him who in his earlier life had been peculiarly characterized by Jewish prejudice—" a Pharisee and the son of a Pharisee" (Acts 23 : 6) —not only had an especial mission to the Gentiles been committed, but to him also it fell, as in this Epistle, to set forth in express terms the truth that in this kingdom of God which he and others had been sent to proclaim there was thenceforth, forever, to be 'neither Jew nor Greek.' Of this truth he was himself, in his complete conversion from a prejudiced and persecuting Jew to a large-minded Christian with the whole world embraced in the circle of his sympathy and self-sacrifice, a preeminent example and witness.

Ch. 3 : 1-13. PAUL A PRISONER OF CHRIST JESUS FOR THE GENTILES.

1. For this cause. "Because ye are so called and so built together in Christ." (Ellicott.) On account, therefore, of what he had just been saying, and most especially in ver. 19-22 of the foregoing chapter. In these four verses he sums up what had before been said of the grace of God to the Gentiles, in opening for them, in free access and enjoyment, the whole great treasure of gospel promise and privilege. 'For this cause,' he proceeds to say—but breaks suddenly off from the thought in his mind, being diverted from it by the more personal one suggested in the words which follow. The thread of connection, thus dropped, is taken up again at ver. 14. What he began to say is that because of the great gift of grace to these Gentile believers, he prayed for them, that they might attain to all that measure of spiritual experience described in the closing verses of the chapter. The connection, then, is: "For this cause . . . I bow my knees unto the Father of our Lord Jesus Christ," etc. **I Paul, the prisoner of Jesus Christ.** "Of Christ Jesus" in the Revision. The break in the connection just described the old commentators sought to avoid by supplying, in the Greek text, the Greek verb for 'I am' (εἰμί), making the verse read: "For this cause, I, Paul, *am* the prisoner of Jesus Christ." For such a change in the text there seems to be no manuscript authority, although one ancient version—the Syriac—and two more modern ones—the Genevan, and that of Tyndale—have it. Such authorities as Chrysostom, Theophylact, Anselm, Erasmus, and Beza, also approve it. Meyer, too, prefers this emendation.[1] Since we have had already, in 2 : 1-5, an example of this peculiarity of style, it certainly seems unnecessary to resort to an expedient so doubtful as a change in the Greek unwarranted by the manuscripts. The expression 'prisoner of Christ Jesus' does not mean for the sake of Christ Jesus. We have the same idea again in 4 : 1, "Prisoner in the Lord." With that vivid conception of the meaning of such incidents in his ministry so often noticed in him, he sees himself to be a prisoner, not because his enemies have prevailed, nor because of any unjust sentence of his Roman judges, but as what is, in truth, not even so much a permitted incident of his ministry, as indeed *a part of it*. And so, with a turn of thought and phrase not unusual with him, he calls himself Christ's prisoner, as he is Christ's minister; doubtless also finding unspeakable comfort in so interpreting these events, which, as is shown elsewhere (Phil. 1 : 12), he feels so sure self ὁ δέσμιος ("the prisoner"), when he so well knew others were suffering like himself, the other explanation is to be preferred."

---

[1] Ellicott, however, says of this view: "On account of the tautology in τούτου χάριν ("for this cause"), and ὑπὲρ ὑμῶν ("for you"), the analogy of 4 : 1, and, still more, the improbability that St. Paul would style him-

2 If ye have heard of the dispensation of the grace of God which is given me to you-ward:
3 How that by revelation he made known unto me the mystery; (as I wrote afore in few words;

2 in behalf of you Gentiles,—if so be that ye have heard of the ¹ dispensation of that grace of God
3 which was given me to you-ward; how that by revelation was made known unto me the mystery,

1 Or, *stewardship.*

---

have "fallen out rather to the furtherance of the gospel." The word for 'prisoner' means one who is bound, as was the case with Paul at this time—bound with a chain to the soldier who kept guard over him. **For you Gentiles.** We may remind ourselves here of the incidents accompanying Paul's arrest at Jerusalem (Acts 21:27-40): in the first place, great offense taken, on the part of the Jews, at what seems to have been known of his ministry among the Gentiles; and then, secondly (Acts 21:29), because "they had seen before with him in the city, Trophimus, an Ephesian, whom they supposed that Paul had brought into the temple." The words we are considering, however, should not be regarded as fully explained by these incidents. Doubtless he means to say that his imprisonment was a consequence, in general, of his ministry to the Gentiles, in accordance with that which had been signified to him as his especial mission (Acts 22:21), and so was in their behalf.

2. If ye have heard. The mention of this ministry to the Gentiles suggests to him another train of thought, which he abruptly takes up and follows as far as to ver. 14. That the Ephesian Christians themselves had 'heard' of that of which he was now to speak, there could be no doubt at all. They had heard of it many times, and from his own lips. The peculiar form of expression might be understood as intended to remind them the more impressively that they *had* so 'heard.' There is reason, at the same time, for the view noted in the "Introduction," that the language used rather goes to confirm the theory that this Epistle was really intended for others besides the Ephesians, churches in places near Ephesus, which Paul himself had not personally visited. In each case, however, there is undoubtedly what Ellicott speaks of as "a gentle appeal, expressed in a hypothetical form, and conveying the hope that his words had not been quite forgotten." The Greek (εἴγε), fully translated, will read, "if indeed," giving a degree of emphasis to the words which follow. **The dispensation of the grace of God.** The Revision, it will be seen, has "steward-

ship" in the margin for 'dispensation.' Thayer understands by the Greek in this place, "that dispensation (or arrangement) by which the grace of God was granted to him." The commentators appear to agree that the words should be so taken. The connection, however, seems to show that the 'grace' spoken of is not the grace shown to Paul himself as a forgiven sinner, but that implied in the "revelation" spoken of in the following verse. **Which is given me to you-ward.** The meaning is not exactly "in your behalf." The Greek preposition (εἰς) is to be taken, says Ellicott, "with its proper force (ethical direction), 'toward you,' 'to work in you,' or, perhaps, 'among you.'" It was a ministry, with this "mystery" of which he proceeds to speak as the subject of it, to be fulfilled among the Gentiles, and *in* them.

3. How that by revelation. It is well remembered how, on various occasions, in his address to the Jews (Acts 22:1-21), before Festus and Agrippa (26:1-26) and in his Epistle to the Galatians (1:11-21), Paul relates the circumstances of his conversion with evident purpose: (1) To show what a truly supernatural event that was; and (2) To make it evident that both a revelation and a mission had at that time been given to him. His conversion had not occurred under the preaching of any of those who were afterward his fellow-apostles; neither had he received his knowledge of these things at the hands of any human teacher. He "neither received it of man, neither was he taught it, but by the revelation of Jesus Christ." He could not more strongly affirm his consciousness of acting and speaking by divine inspiration. So here it is 'by revelation.' **He made known unto me the mystery.** Tholuck, as quoted by Riddell, explains the word 'mystery' in its New Testament use as meaning "(1) such matters of fact as are inaccessible to reason, and can only be known through revelation. (2) Such matters as are patent facts, but the process of which cannot be entirely taken in by the reason." Paul seems himself to explain in a measure his own use of the word in his paren-

4 Whereby, when ye read, ye may understand my knowledge in the mystery of Christ,)
5 Which in other ages was not made known unto the sons of men, as it is now revealed unto his holy apostles and prophets by the Spirit;

4 as I wrote afore in few words, whereby, when ye read, ye can perceive my understanding in the 5 mystery of Christ; which in other generations was not made known unto the sons of men, as it hath now been revealed unto his holy apostles and pro-

thetic reference, here immediately following, to what had before been said of this 'mystery.' **As I wrote afore in a few words.** The reference is not to be understood, as some have thought, as being to some former epistle to the Ephesian Church, but to previous words in this same Epistle; as Ellicott and Eadie think, to 1 : 9 of this Epistle, where we read of "the mystery of his (God's) will, according to the good pleasure which he hath purposed in himself," etc.; and to 2 : 13 and following verses, where mention is made of the gathering in of the Gentiles.

4. Whereby, when ye read, ye may understand my knowledge in the mystery of Christ. The word 'understand' does not represent the meaning properly. "*Perceive my understanding,*" as in the Revision, expresses the thought more exactly. He does not mean, however, *full* 'understanding.' Eadie translates: "You can while reading perceive my insight in the mystery of Christ." They may perceive that measure of 'understanding,' that apprehension of the great mystery of Christ which had been given to him 'by revelation.' But in what sense is this mystery of which he speaks 'the mystery of Christ'? It seems unnecessary to search, as Ellicott appears to do, for some recondite meaning here. The verses immediately following, especially ver. 6, explain the phrase in so far, at least, as its general sense is concerned. Tholuck's first definition of the word 'mystery' is covered in what is said in that verse of the purpose of God to receive the Gentiles fully into the privileges and fellowship of the gospel: a purpose which was "a matter of fact inaccessible to reason, and only to be known through revelation." But the fulfillment of this purpose was so in Christ, and through him, as that he himself may stand for and represent the whole.

5. Which in other ages was not made known unto the sons of men. *In other generations* is the correct rendering. The only other place in the New Testament where the phrase "sons of men" occurs is at Mark 3 : 28: "All sins shall be forgiven unto the sons of men," etc. It corresponds to the simple word "men" in the parallel passage in Matthew. When it is said here, therefore, that this mystery of a world-wide redemptive scheme had not in other generations been made known to the sons of men, there is no want of consistency with the fact that in prophecies of the Older Dispensation foretokenings of it had appeared. Not only had not that 'revelation' of the 'mystery' been made to all men as is now done in the preaching of the gospel given to us by inspiration, but even to those favored persons, like Abraham and others, who were made depositaries of that earlier revelation, only far-away glimpses of the great truth had been granted. "Prophets and kings *desired* to see the things which we see," but "died without the sight." **As it is now revealed unto his holy apostles and prophets.** That the 'prophets' meant are the New Testament prophets, see under 2 : 20. This also is clearly implied in the language here. There is thus a manifest claim on behalf of those by whom the foundations of Christian doctrine were laid, to exceptional knowledge of the mind and purpose of God as respects the things made known by them. This exceptional knowledge on their part was even beyond what had been allowed to inspired men of the 'other generations.' And this exceptional knowledge was, as of necessity it must be, 'revealed' knowledge. We have thus a clear expression of that consciousness of a divine inspiration by which the founders of our religion acted and spoke. That Paul here speaks of the 'apostles and prophets' as 'holy' is not to be thought inconsistent with a due sense of personal imperfection on his own part, neither can it furnish ground for questioning the Pauline authorship of this Epistle. (De Wette.) Not only is he speaking of the apostles and prophets in a general way, without particular reference to himself, but the word for 'holy' is the word which we have already found used as a designation for all Christians, and translated 'saints.' Besides which, as Ellicott suggests, it may be meant as in some degree antithetical to 'sons of men' above. It has no especially designed reference to personal character, but to that per-

D

6 That the Gentiles should be fellow heirs, and of the same body, and partakers of his promise in Christ by the gospel:
7 Whereof I was made a minister, according to the gift of the grace of God given unto me by the effectual working of his power.

6 phets in the Spirit; to *wit*, that the Gentiles are fellow-heirs, and fellow-members of the body, and fellow-partakers of the promise in Christ Jesus
7 through the gospel, whereof I was made a minister, according to the gift of that grace of God which was given me according to the working of his

sonal consecration in which they were given to the Lord in service and sacrifice. In what light as compared with other such 'saints' Paul viewed himself, is made clear by what we read in ver. 8, below. **By the Spirit.** The source of the revelation is here indicated. It was promised by our Lord that "the Spirit of truth" should "guide" these to whom such a weighty charge had been given "into all truth." The things of Christ, pre-eminently such things as are here in question, he should "declare unto" them. It is precisely of this that Paul is now speaking.

6. That the Gentiles. One observes a peculiar persistency in dwelling upon this truth of the opening of gospel privilege to the Gentiles. In this sense, as in the general sense of his apostleship, Paul magnifies his office. (Rom. 11:13.) It seems clear, also, that he earnestly desired to impress his Gentile brethren themselves with a strong sense of the mercy of God toward them in this regard. **Should be** (better, *are*) **fellow heirs, and of the same body, and partakers of his promise in Christ.** 'That the Gentiles are.' The sense of privilege is made more vivid by this translation, since the privilege is thus viewed as a present possession, not simply as a provision. The rendering, in the Revision, of what follows, is also preferable, especially "fellow-members of the body," although the expression seems a little heavy, and although in the Greek this whole phrase is represented by a single word (σύνσωμα). The literal meaning is, as in the Common Version, 'of the same body.' There is an advantage, however, in giving to the three descriptive phrases used the form which in each case makes the idea of *participation* so emphatic. Nor are these phrases in the least degree tautological. 'Fellow heirs' points to that general provision of grace by which Gentiles are admitted to all that privilege of an inheritance in Christ once supposed to be the possession of Israel alone. Fellow members 'of the same body' describes those Gentiles who, having become subjects of this redemption, are now of the mystical body of Christ.' Fellow 'partakers of his promise'

describes them as being 'justified by faith,' having 'peace with God,' and now 'rejoicing in hope of the glory of God.' The thought as so presented is progressive, and implies that whole process by which privilege becomes possession; and promise, realization. **By the gospel.** Referring to the somewhat peculiar expression, 'the promise in Christ Jesus through the gospel'—not 'by the gospel,' as in the Common Version. Ellicott, following Meyer, says: "The former ['the promise in Christ'] points to the objective ground of the salvation, him in whom it is centred, the latter ['through the gospel'] the *medium* by which it was to be subjectively applied."

7. Whereof I was made a minister. The word translated 'minister' here (διάκονος) has been supposed to be derived from two Greek words, meaning literally "one covered with dust." But the more correct view now finds its origin in an obsolete word for "I hasten." The root signification would point to eagerness and activity in service. It is the word ordinarily used in the Epistles to denote what we commonly mean by a "minister," as in Col. 1:25; 1 Cor. 3:5; 2 Cor. 6:4; 1 Thess. 3:2, and many other places. It is also used, as in Phil. 1:1 and in 1 Tim. 3:8, to denote specifically the office of deacon. This last is simply the case of a general term employed for a specific purpose. Where the word denotes the ministry in general, connecting words commonly explain its use to that effect, as "minister of the word," "ministers of God," or "of the church." The connection here, also makes it sufficiently plain in what sense Paul applies the word to himself. Eadie, Ellicott, and others prefer "became a minister" to "was made a minister," which latter form, Eadie thinks, "might show that he had no concurrence in the act." The Revision, however, as will be seen, retains "was made," and this seems quite in harmony with the general thought in the passage, as what immediately follows will show. **According to the gift of the grace of God.** The apostle is showing, it must be observed, not how he became a Christian, but how he became a

8 Unto me, who am less than the least of all saints, is this grace given, that I should preach among the Gentiles the unsearchable riches of Christ;
9 And to make all *men* see what *is* the fellowship of the mystery, which from the beginning of the world

8 power. Unto me, who am less than the least of all saints, was this grace given, to preach unto the 9 Gentiles the unsearchable riches of Christ; and to ¹ make all men see what is the ² dispensation of the mystery which from all ages hath been hid in God

1 Some ancient authorities read *bring to light what is*... .2 Or, *stewardship*.

'minister,' although the former is, of course, implied in the latter. It was a 'gift of the grace of God' that he should be called to this service. **Given¹ unto me by the effectual working of his power.** The words 'by the effectual working of his power' express once more that strong sense which the apostle manifests, in repeated instances, of the supernatural character of that change by which he who was at one time "a blasphemer and a persecutor," was made, not only a Christian, but "a preacher of that faith which once he destroyed." (Gal. 1 : 23.) What adds to the surprising nature of this change is the fact that one whose devotion to his own national faith, as a Jew, amounted almost to fanaticism, should be a preacher of this new faith to the Gentiles. Paul himself could account for all in no other way than as due to 'the effectual working' of God's own mighty power, seeing, says Olshausen, in all this "an act of omnipotence."

8. Unto me, who am less than the least of all saints. The phrase 'less than the least of all saints' is, in the Greek, a single word (ἐλαχιστοτέρῳ), of which Winer says (xi, 2, 6), that it is a form belonging "specially to the diction of poetry, or to later Greek, which sought to strengthen the comparative, become weak in popular usage." It is a comparative, formed from the superlative, meaning "least." Ellicott terms the translation, retained also in the Revision, a "most felicitous" one. He also says, what is most just as regards the general sense of the passage, that "it is perfectly incredible how, in such passages as these, which reveal the truest depths of Christian experience, Baur (*Paulus*, p. 447) can only see contradictions and arguments against the apostolic origin of the Epistle." **Is this grace given.** The word for 'grace,' in this place and in the connection, is taken here as in the sense of the Latin word for "office." That service which had, during many years, involved so much of hardship and danger, and now imprisonment, he views as an especial and peculiar 'grace,' or unmerited favor. **That I should preach among the Gentiles.** "Unto the Gentiles," in the Revision. This is in accordance with the text, which omits the preposition for "in" (ἐν) upon the authority of four very ancient manuscripts (א A B C). This text also Alford prefers. Eadie and Ellicott retain the preposition, and translate "among the Gentiles," citing authorities which, according to the latter, "fairly preponderate." The preponderance of authorities is, it would seem, in number only. In other respects it certainly favors the omission of the preposition (ἐν), in which case we translate 'to the Gentiles.' **The unsearchable riches of Christ.** We have here, again, the word 'riches,' by which the writer of this Epistle so often seeks to represent the fullness and abundance of the mercies of God in Christ the Saviour. The meaning must be 'of Christ' as representing "the exhaustless blessings of salvation" (Ellicott): exhaustless, no doubt, in ways of which in this world and in this life it is possible to have only the most inadequate conception.

9. And to make all men see. More is meant than simply to convince the reason or enlighten the understanding. Thayer explains the verb as denoting, in "a use only biblical and ecclesiastical, to enlighten spiritually, imbue with saving knowledge." The same word occurs in the Greek at John 1 : 9, where the Word, Christ, is spoken of as "the true light which lighteth every man that cometh into the world." Paul seems here to have in view that apostolical sufficiency, realized in gifts of the Spirit, by which in this ministry the minds of men were acted upon with pecu-

¹ Meyer, Ellicott, Eadie, and Tischendorf, following the Sinaitic manuscript, with the Syriac Version and the Greek Fathers, adopt in the case of one word a different reading from that of Westcott and Hort in the Revision; namely, τὴν δοθεῖσάν, 'given,' in the accusative, agreeing with τὴν δωρεάν, 'the gift,' instead of τῆς δοθείσης agreeing with τῆς χάριτος, 'the grace,' in the genitive. The point is not material, save that in the latter case the 'grace' manifested in 'the gift' is perhaps more emphasized.

hath been hid in God, who created all things by Jesus Christ:
10 To the intent that now unto the principalities and powers in heavenly *places* might be known by the church the manifold wisdom of God,

10 who created all things; to the intent that now unto the principalities and the powers in the heavenly *places* might be made known through the church

liar power and effect. **What is the fellowship of the mystery.** The word, in the Greek, is the same which has several times before been translated 'dispensation,' and there can be no good reason for representing it here by 'fellowship.' The Common Version, however, follows the Elzevir text in the word 'fellowship' (κοινωνία), instead of 'dispensation' (οἰκονομία), which the best authorities require. 'Dispensation of the mystery' means that order or arrangement under divine purpose by which the Gentiles also were made partakers in the gospel blessing; a mystery in the sense that it remained hidden in the secret purposes of God, save so far as intimations were given in the Older Dispensation, till it pleased him to make it known by his apostles and prophets. **Which from the beginning of the world hath been hid in God.** Literally, *which from the ages*, a New Testament phrase, meaning from the beginning of time. 'Hid in God' will mean, in the mind, the as yet unrevealed purpose of God. **Who created all things by Jesus Christ.** The Revision omits the last three words. They are not found in either of the three oldest manuscripts—Sinaitic, Vatican, Alexandrian—and are consequently omitted by Westcott and Hort, by Ellicott, and "most recent editors." A question is raised by some commentators as to the precise force, in such a connection, of the words 'who created all things.' It may be sufficient to see in them a recognition of that sovereignty in God, based upon the fact that 'all things' owe their origin to him, by virtue of which he not only of right appoints events "according to the good pleasure of his will" (ch. 1:5), but times their fulfillment as his infinite wisdom sees to be in all respects fitting and right.

10. To the intent that now unto (*the*) principalities and powers in (*the*) heavenly places. A third example of use of the phrase 'heavenly places.' By 'principalities and powers' are, on all hands, understood angelic beings in their several orders. Some writers, such as Bengel, Hofmann, Olshausen, mentioned by Eadie, understand evil angels as well as good. "The general tenor of the passage," as Ellicott says, "makes this view inadmissible," while also "evil angels more naturally recognize the *power*, good angels the *wisdom* of God." The '*now*' of the passage should be noticed as suggesting the fact that what once had been 'hid in God' has now, the time for it having arrived, been revealed. **Might be known by the church.** Two things are implied: (1) that angelic beings are not only interested in, but are occupied in observing and studying, that which appears in 'the church,' more especially as it is a scene of divine manifestation, perhaps unexampled in the universe of intelligence; (2) a meaning in the word 'church,' founded upon its literal one, yet far more comprehensive and exhaustive. What is here the particular object of interest and study to angelic beings is that work of redemption of which the church is alike the subject and the scene, while on its own part 'the church,' in that meaning of the phrase contemplated here, is the whole company of the redeemed in all ages, on earth and in heaven. The conception of the church as a local assembly (ἐκκλησία) of saved persons is expanded so as to comprehend *all* the saved. **The manifold wisdom of God.** The Greek word for 'manifold' occurs only in this place in the New Testament. It is used in classic Greek to denote that which appears "much variegated, in a great variety of colors." (Thayer.) Farrar translates, "richly variegated." This does not seem, however, to express the thought here. Another meaning for the word is "much varied," having many forms. And this would certainly appear to be what the apostle intends in this place. The wisdom of God, in the history and in all the varied fortunes of his church, is manifested in multiform ways; in ways peculiar to this peculiar scene of divine procedure, and, as observed and studied by the higher intelligences, opening to them discoveries of divine perfection unseen elsewhere. As to the connection of the thought, commentators differ. To what do the words in the beginning of the verse, 'to the intent that,' refer? Meyer under-

11 According to the eternal purpose which he purposed in Christ Jesus our Lord:
12 In whom we have boldness and access with confidence by the faith of him.
13 Wherefore I desire that ye faint not at my tribulations for you, which is your glory.

11 the manifold wisdom of God, according to the ¹eternal purpose which he purposed in Christ
12 Jesus our Lord: in whom we have boldness and access in confidence through ²our faith in him.
13 Wherefore I ask that ³ I may not faint at my tribulations for you, which ⁴ are your glory.

1 Gr. *purpose of the ages*......2 Or. *the faith of him*......3 Or, *ye*.........4 Or, *is*.

stands, "the concealment of the mystery." (Ellicott.) Harless, "the past act of creation." (Ibid.) Ellicott himself understands, "the general Dispensation described in the two foregoing verses"; Eadie, the entire preceding paragraph. This last would seem to be correct, emphasis being placed upon that which the apostle himself makes prominent—the 'mystery,' now revealed in the announced world-wide comprehensiveness of the scheme of redemption. It is not simply that redemption is provided, nor simply that to "the Jew first" the announcement was made, nor even alone that it is "now also to the Gentile," but in addition that dispensation of the mystery, that order, adjustment, and final accomplishment of a great and wonderful divine plan; all this, made 'known by the church,' commands the adoring attention of 'principalities and powers in the heavenly places.'

11. According to the eternal purpose—literally, "purpose of the ages." New Testament usage, however, requires that we shall understand eternity as implied. The apostle is as if answering the question *when* this purpose was formed. This answer is, in eternity; before the foundation of the world, as in ch. 1:4. **Which he purposed in Christ Jesus our Lord.** The Revision retains 'purposed' as a translation of the Greek verb (ἐποίησεν). Thayer quotes this verse as an example of the meaning " to carry out, execute." Alford would agree with the Revision, influenced by the fact that the purpose is spoken of as 'eternal,' and not seeming to involve the idea of execution or fulfillment. Ellicott translates, "wrought in Christ"; in his view the words 'in Christ Jesus our Lord,' seeming "so clearly to point to the realization, the carrying out of the purpose in *Jesus* Christ—the Word made flesh." Dr. Boise appears to prefer this, yet adds: "Is it not just possible that the writer had both in mind—the forming of the eternal purpose, and the execution?"

12. In whom we have boldness and necess. The first meaning given by Thayer for the word here translated 'boldness' is "freedom in speaking, unreservedness of communication." His second meaning is "free and fearless confidence," "cheerful courage." Under this he quotes our present passage. The former would seem more appropriate for that place where the word occurs in a like connection (Heb. 4:16), "Let us therefore come with boldness to the throne of grace." It is needless to say that nothing savoring of presumption can be intended; yet doubtless it is meant that we shall realize how great a privilege, alike of access and of utterance, must be afforded us, since the **confidence** with which we are to approach is **by the faith of him.** Christ is the *medium* of approach; 'confidence' recognizing his worthiness, not our own, the state of mind in which we come.

13. Wherefore I desire. Some would here resume the connection that was broken at ver. 2. This, however, is more properly at ver. 14, next following. The reference here is to all he has been saying from ver. 2 to ver. 12, inclusive, and is an appeal to those whom he addresses, that, in view of all, they share with him the courage and faith by which he is himself sustained in his imprisonment. **That ye faint not at my tribulations for you.** "I entreat you not to lose heart" is another translation. Still another is that preferred by the American Company of the Revisers, who would read, "I ask that *I* may not faint." The Greek will admit of either construction, the verb for "faint" being in the infinitive, while the pronoun "I" or "ye" is to be supplied in translating. It would be necessary, so Eadie thinks, to supply also another word, so that the clause shall read, "I desire *God* that I faint not." His objection to this rendering is "that there is in the clause no formal or implied reference to God; that it is awkward to interpose a new subject, or make the object of the verb and the subject of the infinitive different; and," especially, it would seem, "that the apostle possessed little indeed of that faintheartedness against which he is supposed to guard himself by prayer." As Ellicott says: "Such a prayer would here

14 For this cause I bow my knees unto the Father of
our Lord Jesus Christ,
15 Of whom the whole family in heaven and earth is
named,

14 For this cause I bow my knees unto the Father,
15 from whom every ¹ family in heaven and on earth

¹ Gr. *fatherhood.*

---

fall strangely indeed from the lips of the apostle, who had learned in his sufferings to rejoice (Col. 1:24) and in his very weakness to find ground of boasting (2 Cor. 11:30; 12:5)." Recent commentators seem generally in accord that the '1 faint not' is inadmissible, the clause being simply an expression of desire that his brethren to whom he writes shall not "lose heart" on his account. **Which is your glory,** or, "are your glory"; namely, the 'tribulations.' "The thought is," says Riddell, "not that it would be a disgrace to them to have a founder who fainted in tribulations, but that the reason they should not faint is the character of his tribulations as the apostle to the Gentiles." To suffer in a good cause is an honor to him who suffers. We are accustomed to speak of "*the crown* of martyrdom." And they in whose behalf the suffering is borne, while in sympathy and fellowship they suffer with him, may feel that to be so represented in some great trial of faith and constancy, not only encourages a like virtue in themselves, but also admits them to a share in the merited praise he has won. Above all, should his constancy be an example for them.

14-19. A Prayer.

14. For this cause I bow my knees unto the Father of our Lord Jesus Christ. The connection that was broken at ver. 2 is here resumed. The words 'for this cause' look back in their meaning, as already shown, to the closing verses of the previous chapter—perhaps, however, not exclusively. What has been said parenthetically (ver. 2-13) is an expression of personal interest in behalf of these Ephesian brethren, instanced alike in his 'ministry' for them and his 'tribulations' on their account, which prepares them for the fervent supplication to which he now gives utterance. The burden of the prayer, however, must be regarded as having respect to them as the object of such beneficent favor as the second chapter, and especially the closing verses of it, describes. His prayer for them is that the full measure of spiritual blessing so provided, they may enjoy. The omission of the words 'of our Lord Jesus Christ,' now conceded as necessary, is important to the sense. "The whole family"—"every family," as in the Revision—is then named, not of our Lord Jesus Christ, but the Father. We thus retain, also, the evidently designed paranomasia, or correspondence of sound, in the Greek words for "Father" (πατήρ), and "family" (πατριά). The omission is demanded by the fact that the words do not appear in the four oldest manuscripts, אֵ A B C, and are now rejected by such critics as Meyer, Olshausen, Stier, Alford, and Ellicott, with whom Eadie, after some hesitation, agrees.

15. Of whom the whole family in heaven and earth is named. The Revision gives, in the margin, "fatherhood" as an alternative rendering instead of 'family,' as in the text. 'Of whom the whole fatherhood'—or, *every fatherhood*, as the translation should be—'in heaven and earth is named,' yields a sense which we might be glad to adopt, as it is a truly noble one. We observe, also, that Farrar does adopt it in his translation of the passage. The lexical meaning of the word for 'family' (πατριά) "race," "lineage," "family," does not admit of this, neither does its New Testament use in such passages as "all the families (πατριαί) of the earth" (Acts 3:25), and "of the house and lineage (πατριᾶς)—or family—of David," authorize the suggested rendering. It might seem that 'family'—at least, as that word is commonly understood, yields a sense too limited. Ellicott appears to prefer "race." This may be too broad, while "lineage" is perhaps too vague. Upon the whole, it may be best to retain 'family,' though in that wide sense which simply implies a common ancestry. "Every family," says Davies, "every clan (πατριά), has its bond in a common father; and an earthly father is an image and representative of the heavenly. All family unions, all fellowships which acknowledge a father (πατήρ) are based in the name of the one Father. It is not obvious," he adds, "why St. Paul introduced *here* this unfolding of what is contained in the Name of the Father.

16 That he would grant you, according to the riches of his glory, to be strengthened with might by his Spirit in the inner man;
17 That Christ may dwell in your hearts by faith; that ye, being rooted and grounded in love,

16 is named, that he would grant you, according to the riches of his glory, that ye may be strengthened with power through his Spirit in the inward man;
17 that Christ may dwell in your hearts through faith; to the end that ye, being rooted and grounded in

It is enough to say that it helps to make the whole grand image of the filial fellowship of men with God in the Son a more living one." It seems clear, then, that we must dismiss the interpretation so common of 'the whole family in heaven and earth,' as meaning simply *the redeemed church of all ages.* For the 'whole family' we must read 'every family,' and view the passage as teaching that whatever, in heaven or in earth, among angels or among men, grounds itself in a fatherhood, has its ultimate origin and ground in the fatherhood of God. To him, accordingly, as the universal Father, the apostle, 'the prisoner in Jesus Christ for these Gentiles,' to whom he writes, bows the knee in fervent prayer on their behalf.

16. **That he would grant you according to the riches of his glory.** We have in 1:7 of this Epistle "according to the riches of his grace," and ver. 18 of the same chapter 'riches of the glory of his inheritance in the saints'; here it is 'riches of his glory.' The apostle has in mind the infinite perfections of God, and asks for his brethren that out of the fullness of this divine sufficiency they may receive the blessing sought in their behalf. **To be strengthened with might.** This does not mean that they may be mightily strengthened. What is asked is that actual '**might,**' *power*, may be communicated to them. There is some questioning among commentators as to the kind of power sought, and as to the special need to be supplied by means of it. Meyer assumes a reference to the exhortation in ver. 13 that they 'faint not,' and supposes the request in their behalf to be that in this respect they might be 'strengthened.' The earnestness and emphasis of the words used seem, however, to imply more than this. Eadie conceives "the form of expression to be in unison with the figure which the apostle had introduced into the conclusion of the second chapter. He had likened the Ephesian Christians to a temple, and in harmony with such a thought he prays, that the living stones in that fabric may be strengthened, so that the building may be compact and solid." It seems to us that the explanation is to be sought in what follows, rather than in what goes before. How this appears will be seen directly. **By his Spirit in the inner man.** The 'power' sought in their behalf is spiritual power, to be communicated "through his Spirit" (Revision) and realized as an inward endowment—with a view to what end he proceeds immediately to show.

17. **That Christ may dwell in your hearts by faith.** It is not here a different gift from the former one which he seeks. The indwelling of Christ through faith is precisely what he asks that the Spirit may secure to them, and in this the 'might,' the 'power' will consist. This, too, is the special office of the Spirit's ministry. Not only so, it is in this way, above all, that spiritual power is to be gained. "Issue and result," says Ellicott, "not purpose, of the spiritual strengthening." The expression 'dwell in your hearts' should be noted. As the writer just quoted says: "The indwelling of Christ, the taking up of his *abode*, is the result of the working of the Holy Spirit on the one side, and the subjective reception of man on the other." He quotes from Calvin: "*Non procul intuendum esse Christum fide, sed recipiendum esse animæ nostræ complexu.*" *Christ is not to be looked upon from afar off in our faith, but to be received in our very soul's embrace.* **That ye being rooted and grounded in love.** The two metaphors here employed are in substance one and the same. As Thayer shows, while the literal sense of the word 'rooted' is "strengthened with roots," still tropically it means "to render firm, fixed, established," which is also, of course, the force of the word 'grounded.' The 'love' spoken of cannot be restricted, as some appear to think, to the love of Christians for each other; nor is it the love of Christ, or of the Father, for us. It must be that love which is the characteristic element of spiritual life, that love which (Col. 3:14) "is the bond of perfectness," that which (1 Cor. 13:13) is "greatest" of the three, and which is comprehensive of all the objects of true spiritual affection.

18 May be able to comprehend with all saints what is the breadth, and length, and depth, and height;
19 And to know the love of Christ, which passeth knowledge, that ye might be filled with all the fulness of God.

18 love, may be strong to apprehend with all the saints what is the breadth and length and height
19 and depth, and to know the love of Christ which passeth knowledge, that ye may be filled unto all the fulness of God.

18. May be able (*made strong*) **to comprehend with all saints.** If we take the rendering of the Revision in place of 'may be able,' the connection with what goes before is made clear. The 'strengthening with might by his Spirit in the inner man' is that 'Christ may dwell in your hearts by faith,' through the spiritual receptiveness of the renewed nature, and that in the operation of the gracious principle of 'love' 'ye may be made strong to comprehend.' Such comprehension of spiritual things as is here spoken of is not measured by intellectual capacity, as is often seen; is not in any way a natural gift. It is a spiritual endowment. 'Love' is the inspiration of it, and 'faith' its instrument. The 'comprehend' must be rightly understood. It does not mean comprehend in the sense of a complete and full understanding, as is clearly implied in words used below. The "apprehend" of the Revision expresses the sense more exactly. The Greek word means "to lay hold of, so as to make," what is spoken of "one's own." (Thayer.) If, as Dr. Riddell thinks, this word is "perhaps too weak, since more is meant than intellectual apprehension," the word 'comprehend' might mislead in another direction. There is spiritual apprehension, as well as intellectual, and both seem to be here meant. In the clause 'with all saints.' the apostle simply places these Gentile Christians in association with Christians everywhere and always, as needing, and permitted to ask for and hope for, this which he is asking for them. **What is the breadth, and length, and depth, and height.** The order of the last three words, 'depth and height,' changed in the Revision to 'height and depth,' is of course not material. The Sinaitic manuscript authorizes the former, the Vatican the latter, while other authorities differ in a similar way. Ellicott thinks, and apparently with reason, that the change to the more natural order is the one more likely to have been made. As to *what* is to be thus apprehended writers differ. Many far-fetched meanings may be dismissed at once, as that the divine nature is intended, or, as De Wette, the divine wisdom; also that one which Eadie approves, the spiritual temple described in the previous chapter. There is no occasion for departing from the connection of the passage, which makes it clear that these terms of measurement are tropically used of that which is mentioned in the verse next following, "the love of Christ." The apostle simply changes the form of expression for that which he began to say, which seems to be this: "That ye may be made strong to apprehend with all saints what is the breadth, and length, and depth, and height of the love of Christ which passeth knowledge." Before completing the sentence, however, he changes the form to what we find in the verse next following.

19. And to know the love of Christ, which passeth knowledge. It may be that the word 'apprehend' fell short of the idea he wished to convey, and that he changes to the word 'know' as fuller in its meaning. We can hardly say then that ver. 19 is epexegetical of ver. 18. Yet the former is certainly a more ample and a more satisfactory expression of thought, than the latter. There is no reason why difficulty should be found in the paradoxical form of expression, 'know the love of Christ which passeth knowledge.' Some, imagining such difficulty, have sought to overcome it by supposing the apostle to speak of two kinds of knowledge—one, that which is given in the ministry of the Spirit, and the other mere unaided human knowledge. The difficulty, however, even in this interpretation, still remains. 'The love of Christ' surely passes even that knowledge which we have through the Spirit, and the paradox is still substantially the same. The better interpretation is that adopted by the more judicious commentators, and which supposes Paul to speak of knowledge as *experimental* in the one case, and as *absolute* and complete in the other. In this sphere of knowledge, as in so many others, we may know by actual contact and experience what answers all the ends of a present need, while lying beyond is that to which we are to attain as knowledge grows.

20 Now unto him that is able to do exceeding abundantly above all that we ask or think, according to the power that worketh in us,
21 Unto him *be* glory in the church by Christ Jesus throughout all ages, world without end. Amen.

20 Now unto him that is able to do exceeding abundantly above all that we ask or think, according to 21 the power that worketh in us, unto him *be* the glory in the church and in Christ Jesus unto [1] all generations for ever and ever. Amen.

1 Gr. *all the generations of the age of the ages.*

This latter may be infinite in its nature, and so may pass all actual knowledge, whatever the measure of our attainment; such must be the perfections of the divine nature, and such 'the love of Christ.' **That ye might be filled with all the fulness of God.** "Unto" all the fullness of God, the preposition (εἰς) having, according to some, that meaning in this place. The difficulty of the passage is also somewhat relieved in this better translation. Dr. Boise's version is: "in order that ye [entering] into all the fullness of God [and thus being surrounded with it on all sides] may be made full." This gives to the Greek preposition its other meaning of "into." Either of these renderings—that of Dr. Boise or that of the Revision—disposes of the very serious difficulty found in that of the Common Version. To be 'filled *with* the fulness of God,' seems an impossibility, in whatever way the words be interpreted. This word 'fullness' has occurred once before in our Epistle (1:23), where the church, as the body of Christ, is spoken of as "the fulness of him that filleth all in all." Both there and here the allusion must be to the amplitude of the divine perfections, which, in the one case, are viewed as imparted for a complete spiritual endowment of the church as a spiritual body, and in the other as that standard of attainment toward which each individual believer may aspire. Another apostle (John 1:16) seems to have the same thought in mind, although the expression of it is there Johannean, while here it is Pauline. "Of his fulness have all we received," says John; "filled unto all the fulness of God," says Paul.

20-21. A Doxology.

20. Now unto him. Here that section of the Epistle which we may perhaps characterize as setting forth the doctrine of redemption, closes in an ascription of praise which most fittingly consummates and crowns the magnificent view which has been presented of this redemption, so wonderful in itself, so world-wide in its provision and scope. **That is able to do exceeding abundantly above all that we ask or think.** The terms employed, intense in their meaning, can only be viewed as expressing intense emotion. Dwelling as he has done upon what is contemplated in all this work of redemption which has been his theme thus far, and perhaps mindful of the "high calling" which he has set before those to whom he writes, he now calls upon them to adore with him the all-sufficiency of him from whom all human sufficiency must come. We are not to measure that sufficiency even by our own conscious need, nor to imagine that the imperfect petition will measure the gift. 'Above all that we ask or think,' he 'is able.' **According to the power that worketh in us.** We have present experience of this 'power.' We have proof of its reality, and by what it has done for us may know what it may yet do. "He that began a good work in you will perfect it until the day of Jesus Christ." (Phil. 1:6, Rev. Ver.)

21. Unto him be the glory in the church by Christ Jesus. "In the church *and* in Christ Jesus," as in the Revision. "The first member" of the clause "denoting the outward province, the second the inward and spiritual sphere in which God was to be praised." **Throughout all ages, world without end. Amen.** Literally, '*to all the generations of the age of the ages.*' It is a peculiar form of expression. Harless, as quoted by Ellicott, calls attention to the difference between the more common phrase, "ages of the ages" (αἰῶνες τῶν αἰώνων) and "age of the ages" (αἰὼν τῶν αἰώνων). Both alike imply the element of meaning in eternity, and are properly rendered, as in the Revision, "forever and ever." Harless makes the distinction in the two phrases to be that the former is more *extensive*, the latter more *intensive*—"an age of the ages which contains all ages in itself." Ellicott himself thinks this "ingenious," but "of doubtful application," and prefers to view the two forms of expression as practically identical.

SUMMARY OF THE EXPOSITION.

To some extent this chapter is a *resumé* of

CHAPTER IV.

1 THEREFORE, the prisoner of the Lord, beseech you that ye walk worthy of the vocation wherewith ye are called,

the former one. Having completed the view just taken of the comprehensiveness of that salvation of which he writes, and having shown these Ephesian brethren how much all this means for *them*, he has in his heart a prayer in their behalf, that they may be able to enter into the meaning of the great truth so presented, in some good degree comprehend it, and feel its mighty inspiration. He begins with an allusion to his own present condition; and, that the assurance of his prayer in their behalf may have more force with them, he dwells upon this; yet, as in a former instance, is carried away by this interposing thought into an extended parenthesis, the original purpose being for the moment dropped. He recurs to that period in his own life when this of which he has been writing to them was to him wholly "the revelation of a mystery." He was then made to understand, not only that the Jesus whom he persecuted was the Redeemer of men, the Messiah of his people, but also that he was a Redeemer for *all* men. More than this, it was then assigned to him, as his peculiar mission, that he should be in an especial manner the messenger and minister of this world-wide redemption. This he views, not as a ministry merely, but as a "grace," a mercy of God, a peculiar privilege, as undeserved as it is great. So he would have his brethren understand it, and along with him to accept the "tribulations" inseparable from it as cause of rejoicing, not of complaint.

In this way he may be almost said to bring those to whom he writes into those very surroundings amidst which he offers his prayer for them. It is as if they also, with him, were bowing the knee to the universal Father, while he prays for them that they may come to know, as he knows it, as "all saints" are permitted to know it, that love of Christ which is at once so wonderful and so unsearchable, and may be filled with the fullness of all richest spiritual experience. As he closes his prayer he bursts forth in a doxology of praise, as if the mean "hired house" of his Roman imprisonment had become "the gate of heaven," and the guarding soldier his angel of deliverance.

1 I therefore, the prisoner in the Lord, beseech you to walk worthily of the calling wherewith ye were

Ch. 4 : 1-16. THE DOCTRINE OF THE CHURCH.

Thus far we have been occupied with the doctrine of redemption, considered (1), as an eternal purpose in the mind of God; (2), as an election of grace, by which the redeemed of all ages were "chosen" in Christ "before the foundation of the world"; (3), as announced in the types, predictions, and promises of that Dispensation in which, as depositaries of the covenant, God's ancient people were set apart from the rest of mankind; (4), as consummated in the advent, ministry, death, and mediation of Jesus Christ; (5), as made in the gospel a world-wide redemption, all former limitations being done away; (6), as having in view for its ultimate result the salvation and glorification with Christ of a mighty host, made one in their common Redeemer and Lord, in whom to illustrate in the view of all intelligences "the manifold wisdom of God" and "the riches of the glory of his inheritance in the saints." The great subject so presented is treated discursively, not under any formal arrangement, yet so as to constitute a distinct division of the Epistle, with the special topics just indicated made prominent not so much in their logical order as in that which best answered the purpose of the apostle in writing. A second division of the Epistle is now reached, which may be viewed as briefly introductory to a third, in which it is shown how the subjects of this redemption may, and should, "walk worthy of" their "calling." This second division we may characterize as the doctrine of the church, as the first may in like manner be defined as the doctrine of redemption.

1. I therefore, the prisoner of [*in*] the Lord. As to what the word 'therefore' logically refers, commentators are not entirely agreed. Some, with Meyer, connect with what immediately precedes in the closing verses of the previous chapter; others, as Alford, with the whole previous chapter; Ellicott with so much of that chapter as relates "to the spiritual privileges and calling of the Ephesians." It may at least be assumed that

2 With all lowliness and meekness, with longsuffering, forbearing one another in love; | 2 called, with all lowliness and meekness, with longsuffing-

it is these last which the apostle would emphasize, in proceeding to those practical lessons found in the great theme so far treated. Paul here styles himself 'prisoner in the Lord' in much the same sense as he has already (ch. 3:1) named himself 'prisoner of Christ Jesus,' with this difference, however, that, as Ellicott says, having in view the force of the preposition in each case: "In the latter the captivity is referred immediately to Christ as its Author and Originator; in the former, to union with him and devotion to his service." In both instances it is to be noted at what a thoroughly *Christian* point of view the apostle regards that which it would be so natural to consider a calamity merely. **Beseech you.** Giving the words something of the emphatic form they have in the Greek, we may translate: "I therefore beseech you—I, the prisoner of the Lord." He would have his exhortation gain force and effect from the circumstances amidst which it is spoken. "Exhort you," "call upon you," are alternative renderings. **That ye walk worthy.** The word for 'walk' is the same as in ch. 2:2, "Wherein in time past ye walked"; that is, "in trespasses and sins." It means to "walk about." Thayer renders, "to regulate one's life," "to conduct one's self." There may be no intentional suggestion that in this new way of walking they should be as intent and earnest as in that old one; in the use we ourselves make of the passage, however, this parallelism may be permitted. **Of the vocation wherewith ye are called.** 'Vocation' has now a meaning unlike that which the apostle clearly has in mind. The Christian life is certainly not to be viewed as a pursuit, with an object to gain. Even the word "calling," used in the Revision, has a certain inadequacy. *Of the calling wherewith ye were called,* is, however, the best translation that can be made. The latter part of the clause explains the former part. It indicates that these Christians had been 'called' in the high Christian sense. The word for "calling," Thayer speaks of as "everywhere in the New Testament, in a technical sense," used for "the divine invitation to embrace salvation in the kingdom of God, which is made especially through the preaching of the gospel." To this should be added that element in the "call" which makes it so much more than a mere invitation; that efficiency of the Spirit of truth, in the word and operating through it, which makes it effectual. The appeal which the apostle makes in this and subsequent verses is grounded on what is more than an invitation merely; besides this, in that gracious exertion of divine power in which hardness was melted, indifference overcome, and the heart made "willing." The invitation alone were much; this special grace of God in their salvation was unspeakably more. A 'walk,' a character and manner of life 'worthy' of such a 'calling,' while it is the true Christian aspiration, implies, as the apostle proceeds to show, some of the truest types of human excellence.

2. **With all lowliness and meekness, with long-suffering.** In these ways they were to 'walk worthily.' 'Lowliness, and meekness, and long-suffering' have a certain relation to each other, with marked resemblance, yet to be carefully distinguished in the present case. 'Lowliness' may be termed that fundamental Christian characteristic on which all others, in a certain way, depend. It is as Trench, quoted by Ellicott, defines it, "the thinking truly, and because truly, therefore lowlily of ourselves." In all relations of the Christian life this just self-estimation is fundamentally essential. 'Meekness' is that attitude in which, under the prompting of this due self-estimation, we place ourselves toward God and toward men. It is the opposite of the exacting, overbearing, self-exalting spirit. 'Long-suffering,' while it connects itself immediately with what follows, is in relation also with the 'lowliness' and the 'meekness.' Ellicott calls the Greek for 'long-suffering' (μακροθυμία), "a fine word," and with Trench speaks of it as the antithesis of the Greek word (ὀξυθυμία), meaning "sudden anger." James (1:19) exhorts his brethren to be "slow to wrath," a phrase which expresses the meaning of the word 'long-suffering,' here considered. Hence the force of what immediately follows —**forbearing one another in love.** The literal meaning, in this place, of the word translated 'forbearing,' is "holding one's self

3 Endeavouring to keep the unity of the Spirit in the bond of peace.
4 There is one body, and one Spirit, even as ye are called in one hope of your calling;

3 fering, forbearing one another in love; giving diligence to keep the unity of the Spirit in the bond of
4 peace. There is one body, and one Spirit, even as also

up," a forcible way of expressing what is meant by 'patience,' 'endurance.' The word assumes that in the relations of Christians with each other occasions of difference, even of threatened alienation, are sure to arise. They are to 'forbear one another' in an exercise of Christian self-control, with 'slowness to wrath,' or with 'long-suffering,' exercising 'meekness,' and with proper estimate, not *exaggerated* estimate, of what is due to themselves. It is all, especially the 'forbearing,' to be 'in love,' which is, indeed, the indispensable and all-originating element in that gracious state which the apostle describes.

3. **Endeavouring to keep.** Davies translates the word for 'keep,' "to keep by giving heed to." The word for 'endeavoring' means seeking or endeavoring with diligence. Giving to the words their full meaning, therefore, we may read *diligently endeavoring to watchfully keep*. The form of the expression shows at once of how great moment is this which the apostle enjoins, and at the same time with what watchful earnestness it must be sought. **The unity of the Spirit.** By 'the Spirit' is meant the Divine Spirit, the promised Comforter, "Helper." The Greek genitive here, says Ellicott, is "the genitive of the originating cause." The 'unity' spoken of is, therefore, that unity which the Spirit produces. Keeping this in mind, we realize better the earnest injunction to watchfulness and diligence in preserving this 'unity.' The clear allusion is to Christians in their relation with each other, as the verse immediately following shows. This relation must be so sustained in the exercise of 'lowliness' of mind, 'meekness,' and 'long suffering,' as that the presence and ministry of the Spirit, as the source of all true 'unity,' may be a permanent divine abiding. **In the bond of peace.** An ancient interpretation, old as the time of Origen, seems to have been that 'peace' itself is 'the bond' binding Christians together. So Bengel would make peace equivalent to love, and this passage parallel with Col. 3: 14, 15, where love is spoken of as "the bond of perfectness." Ellicott, however, prefers to take the genitive here as "the genitive of *identity* or *apposi*tion." He accordingly understands 'the bond' —the "binding together"—'of peace,' as "the element in which the unity is to be kept and manifested." With this agree Meyer, Olshausen, Alford, Eadie, and many others. 'Peace' in this place is a comprehensive word. It implies that in each individual of those sustaining the relation held in view which fulfills in them, each and personally, the gracious assurance, "Peace I leave with you, my peace I give unto you" (John 14:27), and which at the same time becomes for them an element of tranquillity amid shocks and collisions of whatever kind.

4. **There is one body, and one Spirit.** The words 'there is' are not in the Greek. Taken literally, we should begin the verse with a certain abruptness. 'One body, one Spirit.' It is a question if the sense of the passage is really helped by supplying the words 'there is,' either in the Common Version or in the Revision. What we have in this verse is, as Ellicott says, "designed to illustrate and enhance the foregoing exhortation." He adds that "the very unconnectedness" of what is here said with what goes before "adds weight and impressiveness, and seems designed to convey an echo of the former warning." It would seem that we must understand the 'one body' consistently with that conception of the church as the body of Christ which pervades this Epistle. While what is said of the church in this broad sense is in the main true of it also in the sense of the local Christian community, we cannot in this way wholly localize the conception, nor even make this the primary intention. The New Testament view of that whole body of Christians which at any time makes up what we are wont to mean by "Christendom," is not that of division into what we are so accustomed to as *many*, but that of *oneness*. It is unnecessary to enter into any question of causes as to existing division, or to make any attempt at locating responsibility. What we are concerned with here is the important fact that the apostle in this place views that "church" through which "the manifold wisdom of God" is to be made known "to principalities and powers

EPHESIANS. 61

5 One Lord, one faith, one baptism,
6 One God and Father of all, who is above all, and through all, and in you all.
7 But unto every one of us is given grace according to the measure of the gift of Christ.

5 ye were called in one hope of your calling; one
6 Lord, one faith, one baptism, one God and Father of all, who is over all, and through all, and in all.
7 But unto each one of us was the grace given, accord-

in the heavenly places," not as *many*, but as *one*; that is to say, not as sects, nor even as local communities, but as one body of Christ. Possibly, we may say, though certainly we must be careful not to make too much of the concession, that, even while many, it is as one, through the indwelling of the 'one Spirit.' **Even as ye are called in one hope of your calling.** The call is one; the hope is one. Various as may be all that which is incidental in Christian experience, there are elements of such experience in all cases of true conversion which are identical. The gospel addresses each subject of the "call" in the same invitation, whatever the language in which it is expressed. The motive is always the same, the "hope set before" the soul always embracing the same objects of desire and centering in the same realities; while it is the one Spirit by whom invitation and motive, and all means of persuasion and of the later growth in grace, are made effectual. Herein is that essential 'unity' which does really prevail over the much in human nature and in the conditions of gospel propagation that makes for division; prevails so far, at all events, as to secure among real Christians of all names and times a measure, at least, of essential unity. The 'calling,' and the 'one hope' of the calling under the ministry of the 'one Spirit,' are the uniting principle of the 'one body.'

5. One Lord, one faith, one baptism. By the 'one Lord,' he must be meant to whom Christian allegiance is directly due. By the 'one faith' must be meant the faith essential to salvation. The truth upon which this faith fixes, and which it holds *as* truth, must also itself be 'one,' since truth in any one of those forms in which it addresses itself to human faith has an identity which it always preserves. But especially is the faith itself one; it finds in the truth as received that essential thing which makes the faith efficacious, above all the one Person there revealed, who is the all in all. We may say, therefore, that however various the accompanying incidents and conditions, the 'faith' by which men are saved is 'one.' The mention of the 'one baptism' in this connection is a striking indication of the significance belonging to this act of Christian obedience. Among all the many things required, this is selected for express mention. Of the two ordinances enjoined for perpetual observance, this one is named. The reason must be that while baptism is once for all in a Christian's life, it is that act of obedience in which he binds himself in terms of lasting allegiance to the 'one Lord,' in a profession of the 'one faith.' Its symbolism, besides, imparts to this act of outward profession a peculiar significance; and just because of this symbolism the 'baptism' must be in the form and manner of it, 'one.' It can never be made to appear that simply the use of water in any preferred way is baptism; because that symbolism (compare Rom. 6:4; Col. 2:12) in which all the significance of the action lies, requires the use of water in a certain way, while failure in this invalidates the whole. There are not many baptisms, but 'one baptism.'

6. One God and Father of all. "Climactic reference," as Ellicott says, "to the eternal Father, in whom unity finds its highest exemplification." **Who is above (*over*) all, and through all, and in you all.** Not in 'you' all, but 'in all.' We seem to have here three characteristics of that manifestation in which God makes himself known to men. The first is sovereignty 'over all'; the second providence, 'through all'; the third pervasive energy, 'in all.' Each of these is true of him in a spiritual as well as in a natural sense. So that the thought in this verse comes into true relation with that in the verses immediately preceding. The ultimate source of that unity of which the writer speaks, is in God, whose sovereignty controls all, whose gracious interpositions direct all, and whose divine indwelling pervades and animates all. Just in proportion as all this is true of Christians throughout the world, they are 'one body and one spirit.'

7. But unto every one of us is given grace. In this unity there is, after all, diversity. The verb for 'given' is in a past tense, and must be rendered *was given*. We cannot therefore take the meaning as altogether the

8 Wherefore he saith, When he ascended up on high, he led captivity captive, and gave gifts unto men.

same as in those many other places in the New Testament which promise present supplies of 'grace' for every present "time of need." The word 'grace,' besides, must be understood in the light of what is said below of our Lord's ascension 'gifts.' Some allusion may also be in the word to that which the apostle has already said of himself (3:8), speaking of the grace given to him that he "should preach among the Gentiles the unsearchable riches of Christ." The privilege of service and the endowment *for* service are alike to be viewed as 'grace' shown by our Lord to his people, and thus not simply in incidental ways, but in accordance with methods of dispensation, of which particulars appear in verses below, especially ver. 11 and 12. **According to the measure of the gift of Christ.** "The gift is measured," says Eadie, "and while each individual receives, he receives according to the will of the Sovereign Distributer." The language used, in its applications to those assignments of service which the various needs of the one service as a whole require, makes it impossible for us to view calling, or position, or the diverse conditions of the service as incidental things, or even as matters of independent choice. As appears in what is said below, the ordering of all that should concern administration and service in the spiritual kingdom of our Lord was committed to him in his ascension, and this he through the Spirit distributes "to every man severally as he will." (1 Cor. 12:11.)

8. Wherefore he saith. No subject appears in the Greek for the verb (λέγει) translated 'saith.' Some difference of opinion exists, in consequence, as to the word which should be supplied; whether "God" (ὁ θεός) or "the Scripture" (ἡ γραφή). The opinion of most recent commentators that the context appears to require the former is probably correct, and will make the phrase mean simply that the words used in the quotation which follows are words divinely inspired. **When he ascended up on high, he led captivity captive, and gave gifts unto men.** It is agreed that the quotation is from Psalm 68:18, which in the Revision, as preferred by the American Company of Revisers, is as follows:

"Thou hast ascended on high, thou hast led away captives,
Thou hast received gifts among men."

Prof. C. H. Toy's translation is: "Thou didst go up on high, thou didst lead captives captive, thou didst receive gifts among men." Prof. C. A. Briggs ("Messianic Prophecy," p. 434) translates:

"Thou hast gone up on high, thou hast led captives captive,
Thou hast taken gifts of men."

The authorities we consult, with the exception of the American Company of Revisers, preserve in the translation of the Hebrew the peculiar expresion in our present text, or its equivalent, 'led captivity captive.' In the Greek, according to Ellicott, the word for "captivity" (αἰχμαλωσίαν) is used for that denoting "those taken captive" (αἰχμαλώτους); so the Greek, like the Hebrew, will mean "led captives captive," not 'captivity' in any abstract sense. The expression is thus made in some degree more intense. Boise would more freely render, "took captive a company of captives." These "captives," in our present passage, it is now substantially agreed, are those hostile powers to subdue whom was so much the purpose of our Lord's mission; namely, sin, Satan with all his host, and death itself. It is simply, as will be seen below, a Messianic picture of the triumph won in Redemption.

The use made by the apostle of the passage which he quotes suggests some points of criticism upon which writers are by no means agreed. These are principally three: (1) The historical setting of the words quoted; (2) that the 'captivity' in the one case is so unlike that in the other; (3) the fact that while the passage in the Psalms reads "received gifts," as quoted by the apostle, it is made to read 'gave gifts.' As to the first of these, Dr. Briggs ("Messianic Prophecy," p. 428) places the date of the Psalm at the time of the restoration of Israel under Cyrus. This, of course, denies its Davidic authorship. Dr. Toy ("Quo-

9 (Now that e ascended, what is it but that he also descended first into the lower parts of the earth?

9 (Now this, He ascended, what is it but that he also

tations in the New Testament," p. 197) views the Psalm as "apparently written for some temple celebration; describing in its first half the march of Yahwe before Israel into Canaan, from Sinai to Mount Zion, which God chose in preference to other hills, as the place in which he would dwell forever." These two views may be taken as the latest conclusions of the "higher criticism." "Very many expositors," says Eadie, "among them Stier and Hofmann, have adopted the view that it [the Psalm] was composed on occasion of the removal of the ark to Mount Zion, and the view of Alford is the same. But the frequent introduction of martial imagery forbids such a hypothesis. What the campaign was at the issue of which this pæan was composed, we cannot ascertain." Ellicott thinks that "with high probability" the Psalm "may be deemed a hymn of victory in honor of Jehovah, the God of battles, of high originality, and composed by David on the taking of Rabbah," at the close of the Ammonite war. (2 Sam. 12: 26.) In this he follows Hengstenberg, and it is probably as nearly a positive ascertainment of the date as can now be reached. (2) The leading of 'captivity captive' simply recognizes the Messianic element in that ancient song of victory. "Our position is," says Eadie, "that the same God is revealed as Redeemer both under the Old and the New Testament, that the Jehovah of the one is the Jesus of the other, that Psalm 68 is filled with imagery which was naturally based on incidents in Jewish history, and that the inspired poet, while describing the interposition of Jehovah, has used language which was fully realized only in the victory and exaltation of Christ. Not," he says, "that there is a double sense; but the Jehovah of the theocracy was he who, in the fullness of time, assumed humanity, and what he did among his people prior to the incarnation was anticipative of nobler achievements in the nature of man." (3) Perhaps the most serious difficulty of all is the change made in the quotation of "received gifts among men" to 'gave gifts to men.' Meyer, in the explanation he proposes, calls attention to the fact that the Hebrew word translated "received" has often "a proleptic signification,"

in which, besides the action of receiving or taking, an act of giving is implied by anticipation; "taking"—that is, in order to "give." Gesenius notes, as an example of this, the place in Gen. 34: 4, where we read, "he took a wife for his son"—that is, says Gesenius, "the father gave his son a wife." As Hengstenberg puts it, "the giving in our passage presupposes the taking; the taking is succeeded by the giving as its consequence." Eadie evidently approves of this. "Such," he says, "is the idiomatic usage of the verb, and the apostle, as it specially suited his purpose, seizes the latter portion of the sense, and renders the word 'gave' (ἔδωκε). Ellicott is less satisfied with this solution of the difficulty, partly in view of "the nature of the gifts, which in one case were reluctant, in the other spontaneous." He thinks we should admit, "frankly and freely, the verbal difference, but remembering that the apostle wrote under the inspiration of the Holy Ghost, recognize . . . simply the fact that the Psalm, and especially ver. 18, had a Messianic reference, and bore within it a further, fuller, and deeper meaning. This meaning the inspired apostle, by a slight change of the language and substitution of the Greek for 'gave' for the more dubious Hebrew word for 'take,' succinctly, suggestively, and authoritatively unfolds." This would seem to be, upon the whole, the more judicious conclusion.

9. Now that he ascended, what is it but that he also descended first. The word for 'first' is now omitted by the best authorities, not being found either in the Sinaitic or the Alexandrian manuscript. It is believed to have been inserted as an explanatory gloss. The parenthetical argument in this and the following verse seems intended as an identification of Christ as fulfilling the conditions of the Messianic passage just quoted— Christ, not simply as one divine, but as one who had taken upon himself humanity. Such an ascension could not be declared of any mere man. The very fact of such ascension implies, as going before, what could be nothing less than the descent from the same heavenly region of one having pre-existence, and accordingly a higher nature than that of hu-

| 10 He that descended is the same also that ascended up far above all heavens, that he might fill all things.) | 10 descended ¹ into the lower parts of the earth? He that descended is the same also that ascended far above all the heavens, that he might fill all things.) |

1 Some ancient authorities insert *first*.

manity. This is what we know to be true of our Lord, and authorizes us to see in him one in whom the Messianic conditions are fulfilled. But neither could such ascension be affirmed of God, whose omnipresence makes such a statement inconsistent. The ascension could be true only of one who, originally in heaven, had in the fulfillment of some purpose, 'descended' to earth, and, the purpose accomplished, had ascended "up where he was before." (John 6:62.) All this we find in the divine-human "Son of Man," the Messiah and Redeemer. **Into the lower parts of the earth.** That the word 'parts' should appear in the translation is agreed, although some critics, like Ellicott, seem to think the corresponding Greek word (μέρη) to have been inserted in the original manuscript as "explanatory." As it is approved, however, by such very ancient authority as manuscripts א A B C, there seems no good reason for rejecting it in the text. Considerable difference exists as to the meaning that should be given to the words 'lower parts of the earth.' Commentators of the Church of England, influenced evidently by the traditional belief in that body as represented in the Prayer Book and in the "Apostle's Creed," regarding our Lord's "descent into hell," would view this as, by implication at least, a proof-text on that point. Some ancient writers, like Tertullian, Irenaeus, Jerome, and others, influenced by similar beliefs then current, give the same interpretation. Meyer, Alford, and Ellicott, among modern commentators, prefer this view of the passage. Such exposition assumes the Greek for 'of the earth' (τῆς γῆς) to be a partitive genitive, which Winer and Thayer do not admit, making it an appositional genitive—"to the lower parts, that is, of the earth, or which constitute the earth." (Winer 59 : 8, a.) Eadie names a long list of expositors, older and more recent, who give this simpler and far more likely interpretation of the words in question. Among these are Thomas Aquinas, Calvin, Grotius, Michaelis, Bengel, Harless, De Wette, and Hodge. With this view Eadie himself agrees. He thinks also, appu- rently, that the use of the comparative 'lower' (κατώτερα) may have reference to that condition of lowliness and humiliation in which our Lord was born, and especially the conditions under which his earthly life came to a close. "Reproach, scorn, and contumely followed him as a dark shadow. Persecution at length apprehended him, accused him, calumniated him, scourged him, mocked him, and doomed the 'man of sorrows' to an ignominious torture and a felon's death. His funeral was extemporized and hasty; nay, the grave he lay in was a borrowed one. He came truly to 'the lower parts of the earth.'" Whether this be accepted or not, two plain facts are to be kept in mind: (1) That the terms of contrast in this passage are evidently not "hades" and heaven, but the earth and heaven. As Thayer says : "Paul is endeavoring to show that the passage he has just before quoted must be understood of Christ, not God, because '*an ascent into heaven*' necessarily presupposes a descent to earth (which was made by Christ in the incarnation), whereas God does not leave his abode in heaven." Clearly there is no suggestion in the leading thought of the passage of any portion of the universe save earth and heaven. (2) It is a fact that, save in that passage of doubtful meaning in 1 Peter 3 : 19, there is nothing whatever in the New Testament to warrant or even suggest such a meaning as the one supposed in the words before us.

10. He that ascended is the same also that descended. "The man of sorrows" is he who has now become the Lord of glory. **Far above all heavens.** Bishop Pearson's paraphrase is : "Whatsoever heaven is higher than all the rest which are called heavens, into that place did he ascend." The Rabbinical notion of seven heavens cannot be alluded to. There may be a reference, however, to a usage in language common among the Greeks, by which "air" (ἀήρ) represented the lower atmosphere, "ether" (αἰθήρ) the upper, and "third heaven "(τρίτος οὐρανός) what was beyond. In another place this apostle speaks of "the third heaven," meaning, it would seem,

Cii. IV.]   EPHESIANS.   65

11 And he gave some, apostles; and some, prophets; and some, evangelists; and some, pastors and teachers;

11 And he gave some to be apostles; and some, prophets; and some, evangelists; and some, pastors and

the abode of the blessed, and possibly with reference to the usage just described. In this place, however, it is quite sufficient to understand him as meaning to say that "whatever regions are termed heavens, Jesus is exalted far above them, yea, to the heaven of heavens. The loftiest exaltation is predicated of him. As his humiliation was low, his exaltation is proportionately high." (Eadie.) **That he might fill all things.** The expression 'all things' is to be taken in its full import, not limiting it, as has been done, to what concerns the work of redemption; nor to the redeemed themselves, as Grotius; nor to the church of Jews and Gentiles. "The expression," says Ellicott, "is perfectly unrestricted, and refers, not only to the sustaining and ruling power, but also to the divine presence of Christ." The special meaning of the words looks back to what is said in ver. 7 and 8 above, as well as forward to what appears in ver. 11 and 12. Filling 'all things,' our Lord, out of his own divine fullness and in the 'gifts' bestowed on man, provides, as the apostle proceeds to show, for the equipment and endowment of his church.

11. And he gave. We must take the word 'gave' (ἔδωκε) in its strictness of meaning. It does not mean that he appointed, or set (ἔθετο), certain offices in the church. We are to keep in mind the "gift" (δωρεὰς) of ver. 6 and the "gifts" (δόματα) of ver. 8. These of which the apostle is now to speak are ascension 'gifts.' He "ascended far above all the heavens that he might *fill all things.*" And now, in equipping his church with the various ministries needful to it in the work it has to do in the world, and in supplying to these ministries all required endowment of grace and sufficiency, he exercises that high prerogative. The 'he' (αὐτὸς) is emphatic: *he himself—* this very ascended One. **Some, apostles.** '*Some to be apostles*' expresses the full meaning. The apostolic office had its own especial purpose, and its own limitation, as respects the persons chosen and the period during which it should continue. It was no part of the purpose of our Lord's own ministry, either to set in order the church as an institution, or to set forth fully and in an orderly manner the doctrines of his kingdom. What

he himself kept mainly in view was to make himself fully manifest and known among men as the sent of God, the Messiah and Redeemer. In some sense, we might say the purpose of his ministry as such was fully declared to the woman of Samaria: "I that speak unto thee am he." If we bear this in mind, we shall the better understand the nature, purpose, and function of the apostolical office. The proper and due setting forth of Christian doctrine, in a way authoritative and complete, and the ordering of that which was essential in the constitution of the church as organized, officered, and equipped for its work—this was left for the chosen men whom our Lord called, taught, and endowed for this precise service. The office they bore was for them alone. It was to continue in the church only until the special purpose of it had been fully accomplished, and was then to cease. Such a thing as an "apostolical succession," in the proper meaning of that phrase, never existed, never could exist. The following may be named as what Paul himself terms "the signs of an apostle" (2 Cor. 12:12): 1. The apostles held their commission immediately from Christ, without any human intervention whatsoever. This Paul declares of himself (Gal. 1:1), and evidently means to indicate by it the fundamental fact in the apostleship he claimed. 2. They were those who had been with Christ in his earthly ministry, and were prepared to bear personal testimony to his death, burial, and resurrection,—facts so essential in the authentication of their claim in his behalf,—or who had experienced what was equivalent to this. So we find Peter declaring (Acts 1:21, 22; 2:32); so Paul claims for himself (1 Cor. 9:1); and so we find the apostles interpreting their mission at the beginning of their ministry. (Acts 4:33.) 3. They were inspired men. In illustration of this those passages should be consulted, in the fourteenth, fifteenth, and sixteenth chapters of John's Gospel, in which this needful endowment is distinctly promised, it being borne in mind that what is thus assured to them is, in the specific terms of the promise itself, an extraordinary endowment for an extraordinary service. 4. They possessed and exercised miraculous powers. Paul specifies these (2 Cor. 12:12) in speaking with reference

E

to himself of the "signs of an apostle." In Heb. 2 : 4, the gospel first "spoken by the Lord" is declared to have been "confirmed unto us by them that heard him,"—a phrase which clearly indicates the apostolical function in this regard,—"God also bearing them witness, both with signs and wonders and with divers miracles, and gifts of the Holy Ghost, according to his own will." 5. They spoke and acted with the authority of Christ himself. No otherwise than this ought those words to be interpreted. (John 20 : 21-23.) "Then said Jesus to them again: Peace be unto you: as my Father hath sent me, even so send I you," etc. That the apostles themselves so interpreted their commission is clear from such passages as 1 Cor. 5 : 4, 5; 2 Cor. 10 : 8. Thus commissioned and thus endowed, the apostles must be understood to have completely set in order what things were to be practiced as Christian institutions, and what was to be believed and taught for Christian doctrine. They left no successors. The power delegated to them, the inspiration under which that power was exercised, the office they bore,—none of these have been possessed, or of right exercised by any save those who in the New Testament were accredited and recognized as "apostles." Their teaching, therefore, is the rule of faith for all succeeding times, and their institution and example the infallible guide in the order and administration of the churches. **And some** (*to be*), **prophets.** Inasmuch as we have upon record no such prophecies by the New Testament prophets as in the case of those of the Old Testament, it may be that there is some tendency to undervalue the importance of this office in the primitive church. Twice already in this Epistle (2 : 20; 3 : 5) we have had mention of 'apostles and prophets' in a way to show that the importance of the one office bore some considerable proportion to that of the other. The prediction of future events was by no means the sole, even it could be called the chief, function of the prophet. "The name," says Eadie, "has its origin in the peculiar usages of the Old Testament. The Hebrew term" for prophet (נָבִיא) "has reference, in its etymology, to the excitement and rhapsody which were so visible under the divine afflatus.... As the prophet's impulse came from God, and denoted close alliance with him, so any man who enjoyed special and repeated divine communications was called a prophet, as Abraham (Gen. 20 : 7.) ... While in the New Testament the Greek word (προφήτης) is sometimes used in its rigid sense of the prophets of the Old Testament, it is often employed in the general meaning of one acting under a divine commission. Foundation is thus laid for the appellation before us." We are to understand by 'prophets' in the verse now under consideration, persons acting and speaking under this extraordinary divine impulse and inspiration, whether in prediction or in teaching. Naturally, their service would accompany and supplement that of the apostles, and so be entitled to mention in the "foundation" then being laid. Like that of the apostle, the function of the prophet ceased to be necessary when that foundation had been securely laid, and has therefore not been a continuous one. As Eadie says, "these important functions were superseded when a written revelation became the instrument of the Spirit's operation upon the heart." In the opinion of this writer, "the prophets concerned themselves specially with the subjective side of Christianity—with its power and adaptations; they appealed to the consciousness, and showed the higher bearings and relations of those great facts which had already been learned on apostolical authority." In such ways their ministry was clearly of great advantage in applying and setting home the more formal teaching and testimony of the apostles, while their strictly prophetic utterance, whenever made, bore witness to the supernatural character of this new religion itself. **And some** (*to be*), **evangelists.** Ellicott quotes an ancient writer, Theodoret, who describes these as "persons who went about preaching"; and Chrysostom as qualifying this with "not going about everywhere." They seem to have acted under apostolical direction, and were the missionaries of the time. It would be a mistake to view the word here as applied to the authors of the gospels; and no less a mistake to view the class of laborers alluded to as represented, in any proper sense, by those in our own time who bear the same name. **And some** (*to be*), **pastors and teachers.** The form of the expression might seem to imply that the functions of 'pastor' and 'teacher' were united in the same person. Such may often have been

12 For the perfecting of the saints, for the work of the ministry, for the edifying of the body of Christ:

12 teachers; for the perfecting of the saints, unto the work of ministering, unto the building up of the

the case; the terms, however, seem meant to indicate distinct forms of service. The Greek word here translated 'pastors' means "shepherds." Ellicott, very justly, views it as designating the same office as "bishop" (overseer) and "elder." It points to those who are charged in an especial manner with the care of the flock. The verse in 1 Timothy (5 : 17), "Let the elders that rule well be counted worthy of double honour, especially they who labor in word and doctrine," seems to indicate quite clearly that some of the elders, or 'pastors,' were not 'teachers.' There is no evidence, however, that 'pastors and teachers' constituted distinct classes, or that the two offices were themselves necessarily distinct.

In summarizing now the teaching of this, very properly styled 'famous passage,' we may say: (1) That the two first named of these 'gifts' of the ascended Lord were clearly meant for the period during which Christianity should be receiving authentication in the supernatural endowments bestowed upon certain of its chief witnesses, and its doctrine and institutions put in order, once for all; (2) that in what was meant for permanency in the church we recognize three elements of service: (a) the distinctively evangelistic, the purpose of which should be preaching, in the strict meaning of that word, and in an itinerating way, with a view to carry the gospel where as yet it had not been heard; (b) the pastoral care of the flock, where churches had been gathered; with which was associated, (c) that ministerial function which consists in teaching, or the instruction of those already made converts, in the truths and duties of the new religion—these two being sometimes, though not always, united in the same person. (3) That there is in all this no appearance of an intention to institute "orders" in the Christian ministry, least of all anything to countenance, but much to condemn, as in utter conflict with the New Testament Christianity, the hierarchy of later times, whether Papal or Anglican.

12. For the perfecting of the saints, for the work of the ministry, for the edifying of the body of Christ. This rendering of the Common Version would make it appear that these three clauses in the verse are parallel clauses, indicating, each, a distinct purpose of those offices in the church which have just been named. This rendering, however, is shown to be incorrect by the fact that the preposition (πρὸς) translated "for" is not the same as that in the second and third, translated "for;" though the three clauses in the Common Version all commence with the preposition "for," the first in the Greek is not the same as that in the second and third. The first (πρὸς) is properly translated 'for'; that in the second and third (εἰς) should be rendered "unto." Westcott and Hort, with Tischendorf, omit the comma after the word for 'saints' (ἁγίων), which would give a translation indicating that the official functions assigned to certain in the church are intended for so instructing 'the saints,' or consecrated Christian believers, as that they shall be fully equipped for service. This, however, gives to the word (διακονίας) so often rendered "ministry" a wider meaning, and to some extent one unusual in the New Testament. Influenced by this consideration, it would seem, Ellicott prefers in the translation to change the order of the several clauses and paraphrase the sense as follows: "He gave apostles, etc., to fulfil the work of the ministry, and to build up the body of Christ, his object being to perfect his saints." In this Ellicott follows Meyer, and Alford approves. Eadie quotes Meier, Schott, Rückert, and Erasmus as of the opinion that the apostle means to say, "for the perfecting of the saints unto all that variety of service which is essential unto the edification of the church." This, Eadie tell us, he himself preferred in his first edition. Influenced, however, by Meyer's argument "that the Greek word (διακονία) in such a connection never signifies service in general, but official service," he "inclines now to concur" in the opinion of Meyer, Ellicott, and Alford, as also above. It may be doubted if the argument resting on the usual more "official" sense of the word (διακονία) is so conclusive as the writers named appear to think. Thayer, evidently, does not agree with them. He names this, along with 1 Cor. 12 : 5 and 2 Tim. 4 : 5, as passages where the word designates "the ministration or service of all who, endowed by God with powers of mind and heart peculiarly adapted to this

EPHESIANS. [Ch. IV.

13 Till we all come in the unity of the faith, and of the knowledge of the Son of God, unto a perfect man, unto the measure of the stature of the fulness of Christ:

end, endeavor zealously and laboriously to promote the cause of Christ among men, as apostles, prophets, evangelists, elders, etc."; intending, apparently, to indicate all forms of special Christian service, whether properly official or not. So the Revisers evidently view the passage, as shown in their translation. The alternative explanation preferred by Meyer, and the others quoted above, appears to be a forced one, while it is difficult to see what authority we can have for reading the several clauses of the verse otherwise than as the apostle himself chose to arrange them. We shall, therefore, take the verse as meaning that the purpose of that official provision and equipment described in ver. 11 is that "the saints," Christian believers, may be "perfected," fully prepared for that kind of "work" which consists in "service," and that so in the exercise of all Christian activities, "the body of Christ" may be "built up."

13. Till we all come in (*unto*, or, *to*) **the unity of the faith.** Dr. Boise prefers to translate the preposition (*εἰς*) more literally, "*into* the unity of the faith." It is agreed that the Greek word for "till" indicates the period during which the ministry provided and given to the church as described in ver. 11 shall last. Ver. 12 summarily indicates the nature of the service appointed, with especial reference to its object—the edifying, building up, perfecting of the body of Christ. Under this metaphor, in harmony with that idea of unity which so pervades this Epistle, is presented that which we mean by "the church," using the phrase in its largest sense. This is 'the body of Christ.' The promotion of all those spiritual ends which are contemplated in the church, especially as concerns its own up-building in all that can make it worthy of its name and office as the body of Christ—this is the work of the ministry Christ has 'given' to it; this, of course, comprehending all that work of ingathering which the growth of the church in numbers and in spiritual power necessarily implies. This ministry is to be performed, and in this behalf, 'till we all come to the unity of the faith.' It is, perhaps, not amiss to see in these words just quoted an implied foreshadowing of that

13 body of Christ: till we all attain unto the unity of the faith, and of the knowledge of the Son of God, unto a full-grown man, unto the measure of the

which has been the actual fact in Christian history; namely, the fact that 'unity of the faith' was not to characterize the body of Christ during all the periods of this history; that, in fact, it was something to be "arrived at,"—the meaning of the Greek word translated 'come to,'—and that this result was to come as the issue of a faithful ministry, whose service, perhaps, should run through many centuries and be characterized by immense vicissitudes. All this, at least, is what history records. Paul may have seen, in his own day, enough of foretokenings to suggest a degree of forewarning in the spirit of his words here. But what they expressly teach and what is of especial interest for us, is the fact so clearly implied further, that 'the body of Christ,' "the church of the living God," Christ's redeemed people, *are* to "arrive" at this 'unity of the faith.' It would be certainly a mistake to assume that division, and above all controversy, is the normal and necessary condition of the Christian world. Indeed, many things now show the contrary, and clearly indicate that the faithful ministry of so many centuries is beginning to bear fruit already in a substantial unity, destined to grow much farther yet toward ultimate perfection. **And of the knowledge of the Son of God.** Unity of such 'knowledge' is what is meant, and this a direct means toward unity of faith. In this sense, as in so many others, while the doctrine of the person of Christ must always be central in the general scheme of Christian truth, that conception of him which Christians have, serves among them as the efficient principle of spiritual unity. **Unto a perfect man.** The Revised Version renders, "A full-grown man." Commentators incline to regard the expression 'perfect,' or, 'full-grown man' in this verse, as in contrast with "children" in the verse which follows. In any case, the clause in immediate connection here explains the meaning. **Unto the measure of the stature of the fulness of Christ.** As to the meaning of the Greek word (ἡλικία) translated 'stature,' critics differ. Later writers, however, substantially agree that of the two meanings—"age" and "stature"—in which the word is used in the New Testament,

14 That we *henceforth* be no more children, tossed to and fro, and carried about with every wind of doctrine, by the sleight of men, and cunning craftiness, whereby they lie in wait to deceive;

14 stature of the fulness of Christ: that we may be no longer children, tossed to and fro and carried about with every wind of doctrine, by the sleight of men,

the latter is here the proper one. It corresponds to the epithet 'perfect,' or, 'full-grown' in the previous clause, and harmonizes more fully than 'age' does with the conception given us of the church as a 'body of Christ' growing up into perfection. When it reaches that perfection it will have 'the measure of the stature of the fulness of Christ'; his fullness as being wholly filled and possessed by his Spirit and as fully representing him in his own divine-human perfections.

14. That we henceforth be no more children. There is a question as to the connection, whether more immediately with ver. 14 or with ver. 11, 12. The thought seems to be that the ministry described in ver. 11 is given, in order that through those results of it, summarily set forth in ver. 12, the attainment of spiritual manhood described in ver. 13 may be realized, and so there be 'no longer' that spiritual childhood characterized as in ver. 14. Taking the view given as having respect, properly, to the growth of the whole body of believers, or the church regarded as the body of Christ, what the apostle has in mind must be that ultimate result of a faithful Christian ministry which is to appear when at last this ministry shall have fully realized the purpose of its appointment. What intervenes before that time arrives is a process of growth, succinctly set forth in ver. 15; but when the purpose of this ministry shall be fully attained, 'the measure of the stature of the fulness of Christ' will have come. We shall then be 'no more children.' **Tossed to and fro, and carried about.** The metaphor is taken from the tossing of the sea waves in a storm; not tossed *on* the waves, but tossed and driven about *like* the waves of a disturbed sea. (Ellicott and Thayer.) **With every wind of doctrine.** It is a graphic picture of a Christian condition, whether of the individual, the community, Christendom as a whole, or the church itself, in the successive long periods of its history, under the operation of those influences which arise out of various conflicting and ever-changing forms of doctrine or teaching. The word in the Greek (διδασκαλία) means "teaching," rather than 'doctrine,' in the sense commonly intended by that word. **By the sleight of men.** The word translated 'sleight' (κυβεία) in the Common Version and in the Revision means, literally, "dice-playing," with particular reference to the arts of the gamester, and as used here characterizes the 'teaching' (διδασκαλία) of which the apostle speaks. Ellicott and others think that the preposition 'with' should be 'in,' as suggesting "the *element*, the evil *atmosphere*, as it were, in which the varying currents of doctrine (teaching) exist and exert their force." **And cunning craftiness.** The translation is faulty, and should be changed as in the Revision, "in craftiness." **Whereby they lie in wait to deceive.** This is much more a paraphrase than a translation, and fails, at the same time, to represent the meaning truly. Precisely in what words to give that meaning it is not easy to see, and commentators differ. The Revision reads, "after the wiles of error." Ellicott's rendering seems almost as paraphrastic as that of the Common Version, "in craftiness tending to the deliberate system of error." Eadie would translate "in craft, with a view to a system of error." The difficulty centres mainly in the Greek word (μεθοδεία) rendered in the Revision "wiles," by Eadie "system," and by Ellicott "deliberate system." Thayer derives the word from a verb which means: "1, to follow up or investigate by method or settled plan; 2, to follow craftily, frame devices, deceive." Of the noun, as here employed, he says that it occurs "neither in the Old Testament nor in profane authors," and gives it the meaning, "cunning arts, deceit, craft, trickery." The word occurs again in 6:11 of this same Epistle, where, in connection with "devil" (διαβόλου), it is translated "wiles of the devil." It is doubtful if the idea of "system" is in the word at all as used in our present passage. The general thought in the verse makes "after the wiles of error" a correct representation of the meaning. The 'teaching,' then, by which immature and unstable souls are tossed and carried about, like sea billows in a storm, is that which error invents, with a view to mislead.

15 But speaking the truth in love, may grow up into him in all things, which is the head, even Christ;
16 From whom the whole body fitly joined together and compacted by that which every joint supplieth,

15 in craftiness, after the wiles of error; but ¹ speaking truth in love, may grow up in all things into him, 16 who is the head, even Christ; from whom all the body fitly framed and knit together ¹ through that which every joint supplieth, according to the work-

¹ Or, dealing truly......² Gr. through every joint of the supply.

15. But speaking the truth in love. The Revision follows the Common Version here, although it may be doubted if 'speaking the truth' represents all that is meant. Some, besides, would connect 'in love' with what follows rather than with this opening clause of the verse. The verb whose participle occurs here, translated 'speaking the truth,' occurs also in Gal. 4: 16, "Am I therefore become your enemy because I tell you the truth?" (ἀληθεύων ὑμῖν.) In both passages the Revision places in the margin the alternative translation, "deal truly." Eadie's rendering, "imbued with truth," does not seem lexically warranted. Ellicott thinks that we should recognize a meaning antithetical to "wiles of error," and accordingly would render "walking in truth" or "holding the truth." Boise says that the "full meaning" of the Greek verb (ἀληθεύω) is, "to be true, whether in word or act." It may be difficult to find an English expression that will completely represent the Greek. 'Speaking the truth' represents only one side of its meaning. If such a phrase as "truthing it" might be allowed, that would perhaps concisely express what the apostle would say. As to the connection of 'in love,' the reasons given for making the order different from the accepted one do not seem to be conclusive. **May grow up into him in all things.** "May in love grow up into him" is the alternative reading proposed. Meyer, Eadie, and Ellicott adopt it. Alford, with De Wette, Calvin, Erasmus, and others, prefers to connect 'in love' with 'speaking the truth,' and this seems the more natural order. **Which is the head, even Christ.** We must keep in mind the representation, throughout this entire passage, of the church as the body of Christ, the body of which he himself is 'the head.' For the church as his body to grow up into him, is to grow up into living relation with him as the body with the head. 'In all things,' as Meyer says, is "in all the elements of our growth."

16. From whom. From Christ, the head of the body. "It is not wholly uninteresting," says Ellicott, "to remark that the force of the metaphor is enhanced by the *apparent* physiological truth that the energy of vital power varies with the distance from the head." **The whole body fitly joined together and compacted.** "Fitly framed and knit together," as in the Revision, is better. Some writers object to the rendering 'knit together' as inapplicable to the unity of parts in the human body. "Brought together," however, or "put together," hardly seems strong enough to represent that firm and vital connection which is seen to exist. 'Compacted,' upon the other hand, expresses too much. The body is not 'compacted,' but it *is* 'knit together' in its various parts in many marvelous ways. **By that which every joint supplieth.** A part of the verse not easy to explain. There is again a question as to connection. Meyer would place a comma after 'knit together,' and connect the words immediately following with "maketh increase of the body," further on. Alford, Stier, and Bengel approve this arrangement. Eadie and Ellicott, however, decline to accept it, and with good reason. The construction is a harsh one, and not called for by any real exigency of interpretation. The chief difficulty in this part of the verse is in the word 'joint' (ἁφῆς). The more literal translation, and possibly the more correct one, is that which appears in the margin of the Revision, "through every joint of the supply" (διὰ πάσης ἁφῆς ἐπιχορηγίας). Canon Barry translates, somewhat freely, "by every contact with the supply"; that is, "from the head." The word rendered 'joint' is from a verb (ἅπτω) meaning "to fasten together, to fit." It also means to "touch"; not mere touch, but one that implies connection and adhesion. It is the word having much the meaning of "handle" or "examine," in what our Lord says to Mary Magdalene. (John 20: 17.) The meaning seems to be that the fitly framing and knitting together are in this way effected. Two ideas appear to be expressed in the words used: (1) that sort of contact and joining by which the parts of the according to the effectual working in the measure of every part, maketh increase of the body unto the edifying of itself in love.

17 This I say therefore, and testify in the Lord, that ye henceforth walk not as other Gentiles walk, in the vanity of their mind,

body are 'framed' and 'knit together'; and (2) a 'supply' of that vital sufficiency to this end, which is the really active force. This supply is from 'the head,' which is Christ (ἐξ οὗ, 'from whom'). Its action is **according to the effectual working in the measure of every part**—or, as in the Revision, "according to the working in due measure of each several part," and its effect is that it **maketh increase of the body unto the edifying of itself in love.** More correctly, in the Revision, "maketh the increase of the body unto the building up of itself in love." The spiritual body of Christ, which is the church, is thus described as deriving its life from Christ, who is the head, all its several parts, in the operation of that life, being framed and wrought together in perfect symmetry, like the parts of man's physical body, and so growing, making increase of itself, up to 'the measure of the stature of the fulness of Christ,' all this being 'in love,' as the element in which all spiritual life lives. The analogy of the spiritual and the physical body of which the apostle makes use must not be too literally pressed. It seems clear, however, that in that part of the whole representation in which all writers upon the passage find so much difficulty, he avails himself, for purposes of illustration, of that in the human body which serves not only to connect, but to *vitally* connect, all the several parts of this amazing mechanism. The difficulty is in finding a representation in English of the precise idea expressed in the Greek. Taking the words literally, they read "through every joint of the supply." To translate 'by that which every joint supplieth' is to make of the Greek noun, meaning 'supply,' a verb, and to fail, after all, in expressing the sense correctly. For it is not the 'joint' which supplies this spiritual vitality whose 'working in due measure' is in "each several part." That 'supply' is the life itself, derived from Christ, and pervading the whole body. But, then, mere "contact with the supply" (as Hofmann and Barry), or "perception of supply" (as Meyer), seems to leave

ing in *due* measure of each several part, maketh the increase of the body unto the building up of itself in love.

17 This I say therefore, and testify in the Lord, that ye no longer walk as the Gentiles also walk, in the

out another important element in the meaning, that which corresponds to the fitly framing and knitting together of the several parts. It may be that the rendering in the margin of the Revision, "through every joint of the supply," which is the most literal one, at the same time, though itself inadequate, comes nearest to a full and proper expression of the idea.

17-24. THE RENEWED NATURE AND THE NEW LIFE.

17. This I say therefore. The practical injunctions which follow are to be viewed as growing out of that which has gone before. These are not precepts of a mere morality. They belong to that 'higher law' of the Christian life whose origin and whose motive are found in the new relation into which redeemed men are brought. Hence the force of the 'therefore.' **And testify in the Lord.** This is to be taken, not as an adjuration. "Paul speaks," says Dr. Hodge, "as one who had access to the mind of Christ, knew his will, and could therefore speak in his name." His words are those of one inspired and authorized to make known the will of 'the Lord' in the matters now to be treated of. **That ye henceforth walk not as other Gentiles walk.** The Revision properly substitutes "no longer" for 'henceforth.' The changed form is a more distinct allusion to that condition in which redeeming grace had found these Gentile Christians, and emphasizes more strongly the appeal based upon the mercy and the divine kindness thus shown to them. The text of Westcott and Hort, followed by the Revision, omits the word for 'other,' in accordance with the reading in the three oldest manuscripts, with several others. It is, however, found in numerous later ones, also in the Greek Fathers and the Syriac Version. Ellicott, Eadie, and Tischendorf think it should be retained; "and we can imagine," says Eadie, "a finical reason for its being left out by early copyists, as the Ephesian Christians seem by 'other' (λοιπά) to be reckoned among Gentiles yet." As this Epistle dwells so much, in the portions of it already com-

18 Having the understanding darkened, being alienated from the life of God through the ignorance that is in them, because of the blindness of their heart:
19 Who being past feeling have given themselves over unto lasciviousness, to work all uncleanness with greediness.

18 vanity of their mind, being darkened in their understanding, alienated from the life of God because of the ignorance that is in them, because of the hardening of their heart; who being past feeling gave themselves up to lasciviousness, [2] to

[2] Or, to make a trade of.

mented on, upon the favor shown to the Gentiles, the Gentile element in the Ephesian Church being thus especially appealed to, the expression 'other Gentiles' seems in this place not only a natural one, but even necessary, as marking a distinction between the converted Gentile and the unconverted. The change in the Revision, in view of these considerations, does not appear to be well judged.[1] The force of the word 'walk' has before been noticed, as denoting the habitual manner of life. **In the vanity of their mind.** Thayer defines the word for 'mind' (νοῦς) in this place as "the faculty of perceiving divine things, of recognizing goodness, and of hating evil." His more general definition, given earlier, is probably to be preferred: "The mind, comprising alike the faculties of perceiving and understanding, and those of feeling, judging, and determining." What the apostle seems to have in mind is that whole deteriorated condition, intellectual and moral, into which their heathenism had brought them. The words that follow in the next verse may then be taken as particularizing this general condition. The verb with which the word translated 'vanity' stands related, means "to make empty," and the word itself may be taken, as by Hodge, to mean "moral and intellectual worthlessness and fatuity."
18. Having the understanding darkened. "Being darkened in their understanding" is a better rendering. The word here for 'understanding' (διανοία) is a less comprehensive one than the word for 'mind' in the previous verse. The reference in this place is more to intellectual apprehension; that intellectual effect, however, being included which is a result of moral depravation. **Being alienated from the life of God through** (or, *because of*) **the ignorance that is**

in them. In order to get the whole idea correctly, the words which follow should be put in connection with these—**because of the blindness** (that is, *the hardening*) **of their hearts.** Their alienation from the life of God is due to two causes: ignorance, a result of 'having the understanding darkened,' and their 'hardness (or, "*callousness*") of heart,' heathen ignorance and heathen depravity. In speaking here of 'the life of God,' the apostle points to that which is the sole element of true life to man; that which unfallen man had in the intimacy of his communion with God, and which redeemed man possesses again. From this the heathen Gentile was alienated: living apart from it, and, as a consequence, 'walking' in darkness, in ignorance, and that depraved moral condition indicated as a heart, or moral nature, "calloused" by indulgence in evil, and resistance of all good impulses.
19. Who being past feeling. The inevitable effect of what is already said of them. Ellicott speaks of the translation as an "admirable" one. **Have given themselves over unto lasciviousness.** Wholly surrendered themselves, as if this were the real purpose and the real good of living. Such is the natural result of unchecked habit of sin. **To work all uncleanness with greediness.** The word here translated 'greediness' is the one so frequently in the New Testament rendered "covetousness." Its strict meaning is, as given by Thayer, "greedy desire to have more." Taken in connection with what is meant by 'uncleanness,'—indulgence of vile and brutal passions,—it points emphatically to the universal result of such indulgence, the desire for which "grows by that it feeds on."
Of the truth of this whole description of that Gentile world to which so many of these

[1 The eighth edition of Tischendorf omits λοιπά, as do the critical editions of Lachmann, and Westcott and Hort. The MSS. ℵ* A B D* F G O⁶, with a number of cursives, and the Vulgate, Egyptian, Æthiopic Versions omit the word. The uncials that contain it are of decidedly inferior authority; namely, ℵ° D⁵, etc., E K L

P, but it is represented in the following Versions, both the Syriac, the Gothic, and the Armenian. Accordingly, it seems to me that the evidence *against* is stronger than the evidence *for* its insertion; and that it is more likely to have been added than to have been omitted by transcribers.—A. H.]

20 But ye have not so learned Christ;
21 If so be that ye have heard him, and have been taught by him, as the truth is in Jesus:
22 That ye put off concerning the former conversation the old man, which is corrupt according to the deceitful lusts;

20 work all uncleanness with ¹ greediness. But ye did
21 not so learn Christ; if so be that ye heard him, and
22 were taught in him, even as truth is in Jesus: that ye put away, as concerning your former manner of life, the old man, who waxeth corrupt after the

1 Or, covetousness.

Ephesian Christians so lately belonged, they had, as Paul well knew, example and illustration all about them. As the metropolis of a large and rich Roman province, and a great centre of idolatrous worship, Ephesus was also the centre of those influences by which heathen society was most corrupted. Of the brutal fury of the Ephesian populace, Paul himself, and they with him, had had full experience; while of those aspects of heathen depravity which came less into the light, they and he were alike well aware.

20. But ye have not so learned Christ; better, *did not so learn Christ*. The expression 'learn Christ' is peculiar and unique," without example." (Hodge.) It would seem that any other form of expression failed to satisfy the apostle's conception. Christ is, in the view he here takes, not the medium, but the object of that knowledge to which a Christian, in becoming a Christian, attains. He knows more than the doctrine about Christ, more than other doctrines through what Christ teaches. He knows *Christ*, in that apprehension of his personality which includes all this, and that *much more than this* which constitutes the ineffable relation existing between "the saint and his Saviour."

21. If so be that ye have heard him, or, *that ye heard him*. The 'if so be,' or *if indeed*, is not to be understood as expressing doubt. Another form of expressing the same in English would be, "if, as I take for granted." 'Heard him,' we should here notice, is not 'heard *of* him.' It implies a conception kindred with that in 'learned Christ.' The allusion is to that intimate spiritual experience in communion with Christ, in which we come into close personal relation with him, so that we are as if personally taught and led by him. Herein is the spring of that new life which, as the apostle is showing, so contrasts that which is Christian with that which these converted Gentiles saw in the unconverted Gentile world around them. **And have been** (*were*) **taught by** (*in*) **him.** 'Taught in him,' the correct translation, is not the same as "taught by

him." As Eadie explains: "One with him in spirit, they were fitted to become one with him in mind." **As the truth** (better, *even as truth*) **is in Jesus.** The omission of the article before the word for 'truth' is to be noticed. The expression of the thought is thus made more general. The change of name, 'Jesus' instead of 'Christ' as used before, is also particularly noticeable. The purpose seems to be to fix the thought upon Jesus in his especially personal and human manifestation; that in which he comes nearest to us, and through which he is most easily and perfectly apprehended by us. The close and vital relation of the true believer with him is still kept in mind. That which in this relation they 'heard' and 'were taught' is that 'truth' of which he was the embodiment, and so is truth 'in' him. Truth as in Jesus is truth in such form as the Gentile world never knew, and such as only those can know who have 'learned Christ,' have 'heard' him, and have been 'taught in him.' What the truth specially intended by the writer in a present application of his words is, appears by what follows.

22. That ye put off concerning the former conversation the old man. The change in the Revision should be noticed. The verb (ἀποθέσθαι), rendered in the Common Version 'put off' and in the Revision 'put away,' would be, apart from the connection, correctly translated in either way. (Compare Thayer.) As, however, the antithetical idea a little further on is expressed by 'put on,' it is a question if the change made in the Revision is a desirable one. "The obvious allusion is," says Hodge, "to a change of clothing. To put off is to renounce, to remove from us, as garments which are laid aside." So likewise Ellicott, Alford, Eadie, and others. The change of 'conversation' to "manner of life" substitutes for an obsolete form one that is in accordance with present usage, 'In the old man.' The figure employed, as also in Col. 3:9, in Rom. 6:6, and in other places, is a very striking one. It has reference to that opposition of 'the flesh' and 'the spirit,' of

74 EPHESIANS. [Ch. IV.

23 And be renewed in the spirit of your mind;
24 And that ye put on the new man, which after God is created in righteousness and true holiness.
25 Wherefore putting away lying, speak every man truth with his neighbour: for we are members one of another.

23 lusts of deceit; and that ye be renewed in the spirit
24 of your mind, and put on the new man ¹ who after God hath been created in righteousness and holiness of truth.
25 Wherefore, putting away falsehood, speak ye truth each one with his neighbour: for we are members

1 Or, *who is after God created, etc.*

which mention is found in other writings of this apostle, and of which every renewed person is conscious. The resistance, the subduing, the absolute overcoming of those sinful propensities and habits, and the abandoning of those sinful acts which are so contrary to the new principle of spiritual life begotten in us in our regeneration, is the putting off of the old man; represented here under the figure of the laying aside of an uncomely garment, that another and better may be put on. **Which is corrupt according to the deceitful lusts;** or, *waxeth corrupt after the lusts of deceit.* The rendering of the last clause in the Common Version misses the striking antithesis in 'lusts of deceit' here, and "holiness of truth," as in the Revised Version, at the end of ver. 24, which two renderings, besides, are in accordance with the Greek. The expression 'lusts of deceit' reminds us of "deceitfulness of sin." (Hebrews 3:13.) There is almost a personification, as if this 'deceitful' element in all sin were some insidious evil spirit, misleading and betraying. That the old nature 'waxes corrupt,' tends to go ever from bad to worse, is one of the commonest and saddest of all human experiences.

23. And be renewed in the spirit of your mind. Some question has arisen among critics as to whether the Greek verb here (ἀνανεοῦσθαι) shall be taken as in the middle voice ("renew yourselves"), or in the passive ("be renewed"). Upon this Ellicott says: "The active [of this verb] is certainly rare; still, as Harless satisfactorily shows, the middle, both in its simple and metaphorical sense, is so completely devoid of any reflexive force, and is practically so purely active in meaning, that no other form than the passive can possibly harmonize with the context. There is, therefore, a very important distinction to be noticed between the 'put off the old man' in ver. 22 and this 'be renewed' in ver. 23. In

the former we are active; it is the overcoming and crushing out of what remains of sinful propensity and habit; in the latter we are the subject of that divine renewal of which the apostle speaks in the next verse. Whether "spirit" (πνεύματι) shall in this place be understood as the Holy Spirit (Ellicott), or as "the governing spirit of the mind" (De Wette, Eadie, Hodge, Meyer, in his later edition), would now perhaps not be much debated among commentators. The meaning clearly is that governing principle in man by which alike his inner life and his outer life are ruled and shaped.

24. And that ye put on the new man. Denoting that active attention to all which concerns growth in grace, which conditions gifts of the Spirit in the process of spiritual renewal. **Which after God.** In the likeness of God, in a restoration of that "image" which in such a high and important sense was lost in the fall. To that effect Ellicott quotes Irenæus with approval.¹ **Is created in righteousness and true holiness**—or, as in the Revised Version, "in righteousness and holiness of truth." The use of the strong word 'created' is here to be noticed, as showing how truly and entirely this work of renewal, as such, is of God. 'In holiness of truth' is a phrase antithetical to 'lusts of deceit' above. It is truth in the inward parts, truth in its deepest and largest meaning, as distinguished from that 'deceit' of which is born not only error and unbelief and falsehood, but the whole brood of what is most hateful to God and ruinous to man.

4 : 25–5 : 2. LAW OF THE NEW LIFE IN SPECIFIC PRECEPTS.

25. Wherefore putting away lying, speak every man truth with his neighbour. Compare Zech. 8 : 16. What remains, to the end of the chapter, is the practical conclusion drawn, in the form of specific precept,

¹ "*Ut quod perdideramus in Adam, id est, secundum imaginem et similitudinem esse Dei, hoc in Christo Jesu reciperemus.*" "That what we lost in Adam—that is, to be in the image and likeness of God—in Christ Jesus we might recover."

26 Be ye angry, and sin not; let not the sun go down upon your wrath;
27 Neither give place to the devil.
28 Let him that stole steal no more; but rather let

26 one of another. Be ye angry, and sin not: let not
27 the sun go down upon your ¹wrath: neither give
28 place to the devil. Let him that stole steal no more:

¹ Gr. *provocation*.

from what has just been said. In the way described these Ephesian Christians have 'learned Christ'; they have been 'taught in him, even as truth is in Jesus'; their renewal 'in righteousness and holiness of truth' is assumed. These that follow are the things thenceforth not to be considered possible for them. The precepts given are not simply parts of a moral code. They are the logical outcome of Christianity itself. This is implied in the very first of the precepts given, if we take the participle in its past tense, as it would seem we should—*having put away*; it is assumed that that of which mention is made, and which was a characteristic of the 'old man,' has now been put away. These renewed persons are now viewed as walking 'in holiness of truth.' The 'lying,' according to Ellicott and the Revision, should be "falsehood," that principle of falseness out of which every manner of 'lying' proceeds. Thus 'speaking every man truth with his neighbour' will mean more than barely telling the truth as occasion calls. It means that each member of this Christian community shall deal with every other in absolute truthfulness in all respects. Hence the force of the reason given—**for we are members one of another.** Members of the one body of Christ, we are in a like relation each with the other, and should be true to each other, in every best meaning of the word.

26. Be ye angry, and sin not. Compare Ps. 4 : 4. Critics are not agreed how to treat these two closely connected imperatives. Winer holds the meaning of the words to be "unquestionably this," "We should not let anger lead us into sin." He makes the first imperative "permissive," and the second "jussive." Meyer, upon the other hand, as quoted by Winer, though with disapprobation, "holds that of two closely connected imperatives, the one cannot denote a permission and the other a command." Against this, Winer quotes an example of such usage in the saying: "Go (I give you leave), but do not stay above an hour." Ellicott thinks this plausible, but not wholly satisfactory as regards New Testament usage. Ellicott's own view is: "Both imperatives are jussive [that is, in the nature of a command]; as, however, the second imperative is used with" '*not* (μή)' "its jussive force is thereby enhanced, while the affirmative command is, by juxtaposition, so much obscured as to be *in effect* little more than a participial member, though its intrinsic jussive force is not to be denied." The meaning of the injunction then would be, in effect, "being angry, sin not"; or, perhaps, "shun sinful anger." This would imply that there is a kind of anger or indignation which is not sinful, and this is no doubt true. **Let not the sun go down upon your wrath.** A difference is to be recognized between "anger" (ὀργή) and "wrath" (παροργισμός). The latter means more a sudden ebullition of temper, such as arises under provocation of some sort. What the apostle enjoins is that this be at once brought under control and subdued. "Anger" (ὀργή) may be that just revolt of the mind against what is sinful, or unjust, or shameful, which, while proper in itself, and in certain circumstances even a duty, must still be so exercised by us that in it we shall not 'sin.'

27. Neither give place to the devil. The connection with the previous injunction is very close, especially with the concluding words of the previous verse. The indulgence of exasperated feeling gives place, opportunity, for temptation and the Tempter. There ought not to be any doubt as to the personal character of the allusion in 'the devil' (διαβόλος), not "accuser," "calumniator." No such jejune conception is in the apostle's mind. He uses the word in its "constant and regular meaning in the New Testament" (Ellicott), for "the devil." It is "a name," says the same writer, "derived from the fearful nature and, so to say, *office* of the Evil One," as man's "accuser." Satan is the more personal appellation.

28. Let him that stole (or, *the stealer*) **steal no more.** It may seem singular that an injunction of this nature should be necessary in a letter to a Christian Church. It is to be him labour, working with *his* hands the thing which is good, that he may have to give to him that needeth.

29 Let no corrupt communication proceed out of your mouth, but that which is good to the use of edifying, that it may minister grace unto the hearers.

30 And grieve not the Holy Spirit of God, whereby ye are sealed unto the day of redemption

but rather let him labour, working with his hands the thing that is good, that he may have whereof
29 to give to him that hath need. Let no corrupt speech proceed out of your mouth, but such as is good for edifying as the need may be, that it may give grace
30 to them that hear. And grieve not the Holy Spirit of God, in whom ye were sealed unto the day of

1 Or, *the building up of the need.*

---

borne in mind, however, how venial an offense ordinary thieving was in the eye of Pagan morality. It may be, too, that the reference is mainly to that which had been, in their unconverted state, the habit of certain members of the Ephesian Church. The injunction would then be in effect the indication of one important particular in which the life of the Christian and the life of the Pagan must differ. What a Christian must do, instead of living as the thief does by the labor of others, he shows in what follows. **But rather let him labour, working with his hands the thing which is good.** Honest industry, occupation in a worthy calling, is a part of Christianity. **That he may have to give to him that needeth.** An appropriate and needful suggestion that our labor is not to be regarded for our own good alone, but that there may be means for doing good to others.

29. Let no corrupt communication (Rev. Ver., *speech*) **proceed out of your mouth.** The word here rendered 'corrupt' (σαπρός) occurs also in Luke 6:43, and the parallel passage in Matt. 12:33; reading, as in Luke: "For a good tree bringeth not forth corrupt fruit; neither doth a corrupt tree bring forth good fruit." In such a connection the word means "worthless," as also in Matt. 13:48, where the application is to fishes. The stricter meaning seems to be that which has become putrid, and thus unfit for use. Of course, in the passage now before us, the use made of the word is figurative, and means along with what is positively bad, that also—as what follows clearly implies—which is either in any way hurtful, or even not in some way useful. **But that which is good, to the use of edifying.** The rendering in the Revision, "for edifying as the need may be," is the more correct. The principle of conduct involved is simply this: That Christians should guard their speech as they guard their actions; aim to have their conversation, not only not either disgraceful or frivolous, but positively suited in some way to benefit those with whom they converse. This does not forbid cheerfulness of intercourse, nor those genialities which lend grace to society; nor does it require that conversation shall be always on grave subjects. But it requires that there shall be a curb upon the tendency to carry a harmless gayety into frivolity, and especially condemns everything whatever that partakes of the shameful or the vile. **That it may minister grace to the hearer.** Give *grace* is the more literal translation. It is grace, however, in the sense of "benefit."

30. And grieve not the Holy Spirit of God. Some commentators (as Harless) would make this verse independent of connection with what goes before, giving it the force of a general precept. The connecting particle 'and' (καὶ) makes it necessary to recognize the relation of what is said here to what appears in ver. 25-29. The implication is that by conduct, and even by conversation, such as those addressed are warned against, one may 'grieve' the Holy Spirit. This language, as applied to 'the Holy Spirit of God,' distinctly recognizes his personality. Such a word could not be in any proper use of terms even figuratively applied to an "operation," or an "influence." As thus used of the personal Spirit, it teaches us that the ministry of that gracious Divine Person may be repelled and driven from us, if not finally, yet so as to occasion great spiritual loss; the representation of this effect by the word 'grieve,' however, more than hints at the fact that this ministry is one which expresses toward the subject of it a real divine interest, an interest susceptible of tender concern in our behalf. **Whereby ye are sealed.** *In whom* is a more correct rendering, and, besides, expresses the thought with far greater exactness. Sealed *by* the Spirit might imply something mechanical. Sealed *in* the Spirit expresses the fact of a relation to him such as that he becomes the element, so to speak, of our spiritual life. Thus the sealing is that gracious effect of life in this element which appears in growth in

31 Let all bitterness, and wrath, and anger, and clamour, and evil speaking, be put away from you, with all malice:
32 And be ye kind one to another, tenderhearted, forgiving one another, even as God for Christ's sake hath forgiven you.

31 redemption. Let all bitterness, and wrath, and anger, and clamour, and railing, be put away from you, with all malice: and be ye kind one to another, 32 tenderhearted, forgiving each other, even as God also in Christ forgave [1] you.

[1] Many ancient authorities read *us*.

grace and enlarged Christian experience. **Unto the day of redemption,** then, points to that ultimate result of all, in which the final victories of grace for each one are achieved. There seems to be, in the language used, a suggestion of that which we mean by the doctrine of the saint's perseverance; and also as to that in which such experience consists. It is life in the Spirit of God as in a divine element, which promotes in us more and more, unto a final perfection in glory, the work of saving grace.

31. Let all bitterness, and wrath, and anger, and clamour, and evil speaking, be put away from you. A comprehensive prohibition, having reference to violences of temper of every sort, and withal, the cherishing of that 'bitterness' which is the expressly evil spirit in such. **With all malice.** That lurking animosity, often cherished almost without consciousness till something occurs to bring it forth, like a wild beast from his cage. The apostle particularizes thus, no doubt, with a view to fix attention specifically upon those liabilities against which Christians, even in their relations with each other, need to be on their guard.

32. And be kind one to another. *Become* kind is a more recent rendering of the Greek (γίνεσθε), suggesting that the substitution of a spirit wholly Christian for these things of which he has been speaking, may be a matter of growth and attainment, as, indeed, with possibly every one it must be. The Greek for 'kind' (χρηστός) is a word having much fullness of meaning—"full of benign courtesy," says Eadie, "distinguished by mutual attachment, the bland and generous interchange of good deeds, and the earnest desire to confer reciprocal obligations." **Tender-hearted, forgiving one another.** Ellicott quotes Origen as calling attention to the fact that the apostle uses the reflexive pronoun (ἑαυτοῖς) for 'one another,' almost as if he had said "forgiving yourselves." The use of this pronoun in the plural in the sense of the reciprocal one (ἀλλήλοις), is not uncommon. It occurs in Col. 3: 13, where we have the same expression as here, "forgiving one another," and in ver. 16 of the same chapter, "teaching and admonishing one another." Origen's view seems to have been that what was thus done to one another was done to themselves; and Eadie appears to think that in such connections as this the form used may have an "emphatic significance" of this nature. "Forgiving yourselves," "admonishing yourselves," if allowed as alternative renderings, would certainly seem to suggest, at this interesting point of view, the *oneness* of that relation into which Christians are supposed to be brought in their conversion and their organic union in the church. **Even as God, for Christ's sake** (or, as *God in Christ*) **hath forgiven you.** The change in the translation should here again be noticed. The apostle does not mean "for Christ's sake," and it is doubtful if that form of expression is strictly Scriptural. What he says here is "as God in Christ," revealed, acting, speaking in him. In Christ we see the forgiving grace of God manifested and offered; while in the acceptance of Christ by faith, that forgiving grace becomes an experience and a possession. Christians, in that relation with each other upon which the apostle has been dwelling in these last verses of the chapter, have had experience of this grace. As God in Christ forgave them they should forgive; be 'kind one to another, tenderhearted,' finding in the exceeding kindness of God in Christ toward them an example and a model.

SUMMARY OF THE EXPOSITION.

Paul's conception of the church, in this chapter, and indeed throughout the Epistle, differs in one respect from that which we find to be common with him. Usually, where this is his topic, he has in view circumstances as connected with the church or the person addressed, which give him occasion for treating of those things which concern the Christian organization strictly as such, or the officials of the organization, with particular reference to their required character and assigned duties. It suits the general purpose of this Epistle that the church should be viewed, not with reference to organization, but with reference to spiritual unity. He accordingly does not, in this chapter, where we speak of him as setting forth the doctrine of the "church," make use of that term itself at all, although in the fifth chapter (ver. 23, 27, 32) we find him using the term, and in this same large sense. Here it is 'the body of Christ'—a spiritual unity, comprehensive of all the redeemed. (Ver. 3-6.)

A like view is presented of that official provision, in which the needs of the church, in this large sense, in fulfillment of its mission, are anticipated. (Ver. 7-12.) Apostles, prophets, evangelists, pastors, and teachers are, as here considered, not persons assigned to these spheres of service by choice of their brethren, and so are not treated of in any individual capacity, but are simply 'gifts' of Christ to his church. In his ascension to that headship over his church, as in its spiritual unity 'his body,' he 'received' these 'gifts.' In other words, it belonged to him in the exercise of this headship to provide in this way for the exigencies and the various conditions of that mission which his church in the ages of its earthly career was to fulfill.

In this view of the church and its ministry, there seems to be anticipation of much that is now history. As we find it here, we can scarcely speak of it as prophecy; yet the apostle, as even a knowledge of human nature and the usual course of human events might suggest, much more when enlightened and directed by the Spirit of inspiration, seems to forecast those vicissitudes which now are matter of record, and yet to foresee a time when the spiritual unity of the body of Christ, the church purchased with his blood, should be a unity in fact, and not alone in conception.

(Ver. 13-16.) To effect this is great part of the purpose of that ministry which the Lord appointed, while it is to be, in every age, the aspiration and the hope of those who have "the mind of Christ."

It is as belonging to this high spiritual fellowship that Paul would have these to whom he writes view themselves, and of this 'vocation' he would have them be 'worthy.' They are to see themselves in even a more sacred relation than that of their visible church fellowship. They are of that communion into which their redeeming Lord has brought himself, in vital and holy relations. They are of that spiritual 'body' of which he is the spiritual Head. Their life is in their union with that body. Separation from it must be death. It is through their regeneration that they have come to be of this body. It is only 'the new man' that can be in harmony with that relation. 'The old man' is wholly discordant, and by as much as it still exists and prevails, is dishonoring and unworthy. Hence, that high motive which the apostle urges for purity of character and holiness of life. (Ver. 17-32.)

In the conception of the church here found there is nothing of the strictly formal and the organic, save as these may compose a part of that practical law of the Christian life which the apostle hence deduces. It will simply follow that in all their organic relations with each other Christians should seek after that unity of faith and that fidelity in all Christian observance which are implied in the high spiritual ideal set before them. Neither is there in this conception of the church any possible element of the hierarchical. The ministry described is a ministry purely, a *service*. The unity toward which it serves is a 'unity of faith,' not of rule upon the one side and of subservience on the other. The whole conception is in eminent harmony with that saying of the Lord himself: "One is your Master, even Christ, and all ye are brethren."

CHAPTER V.

BE ye therefore followers of God, as dear children; 2 And walk in love, as Christ also hath loved us, and hath given himself for us an offering and a sacrifice to God for a sweetsmelling savour.

1 Be ye therefore imitators of God, as beloved children; and walk in love, even as Christ also loved you, and gave himself up for ¹ us, an offering and a

¹ Some ancient authorities read you.

Ch. 5: 1. Be (or, *become*) **ye therefore followers** (or, *imitators*) **of God.** The division by chapters is often in a degree misleading as respects the connection of the thought. If we read the last verse of the previous chapter and the first verse of the present one together, the proper connection will be fully apparent: 'Be ye kind one to another, tender-hearted, forgiving one another, even as God for Christ's sake (*God in Christ*) hath forgiven you. Be ye therefore followers (or, *imitators*) of God as dear children (or, *children beloved*), and walk in love,' etc. God's kindness, forbearance, perhaps we may even say 'tender-heartedness,' in forgiving us, suggests a rule of conduct for ourselves in the mutual relations of our Christian fellowship. We should again notice, in view of the 'imitation' here spoken of, and referring to the more correct rendering of 4: 32, that it is 'as God *in Christ* hath forgiven,' not 'for Christ's sake.' There is, therefore, an express and definite form of the example. The model to be followed is seen in a divine-human personality, in which God's exceeding kindness is manifested, while every expression of loving compassion seen in Christ, his person, his words, his acts, his sufferings, expresses really the loving kindness of God. When, accordingly, our Lord is taken as the model of that which Christians should be in their relations with one another, it is not alone as the model of a perfect humanity, but also as the model of such a humanity, expressing what is divine in utmost tenderness, compassion, and love. It should be observed that we give as the proper rendering: '*Become* ye therefore imitators of God.' The Revision follows the Common Version here, but Ellicott and Eadie take the Greek word (γίνεσθε) in its proper force. So used it seems to express better the Christian attainment in the particular named as the *ideal* one. **As dear children** (or, '*as children beloved*'). Not only are those who are beloved under obligation to the exercise of love in return, but the fact of being beloved and the consciousness of it supply a moral force in that same direction. In the thought itself of God's love for his people, much more in the personal consciousness of that love as an experience, there is what resembles the atmosphere of mutual tenderness in which the members of a united and affectionate household live from day to day. It is not love begotten of a sense of duty, but spontaneous mutual interchange. So would the apostle have his brethren be, as God's 'beloved children.'

2. And walk in love. This would be the natural effect of what is named in the previous verse. In such circumstances as those described, Christian love becomes the proper element of the Christian life—the love toward one another of those who are God's beloved children, and whose mutual love has in that common relation with the loving Father its original and perennial source. **As Christ also hath loved us.** It is 'God *in Christ*' whose 'beloved children' we are. Hence the propriety of this more specific reference to him. Indeed, whether such specific reference be to the Father or to the Son, it is equally appropriate, since in essence, as well as in the form of manifestation here alluded to, these two "are one." **And given himself for us, an offering and a sacrifice to God.** The word here used is not simply (δίδωμι) 'give,' but (παραδίδωμι) 'surrender,' as to deliver into custody, or surrender one for punishment. (Thayer.) Taken with the reflexive pronoun (ἑαυτόν), it means giving one's self up with a view to some specific purpose. Hence the more correct force of the rendering in the Revision, "gave himself *up* for us." The force of the preposition (ὑπέρ) "for" should also be noticed. With the genitive, as here, Thayer gives it as meaning, in New Testament usage, for the "safety" or the "advantage" of another. The primary meaning, with the genitive, he states as "over," "above," "across." The secondary meaning, which is that of the word in its New Testament use, is, he adds, in allusion to the fact that "one who does a thing *for* another is conceived of as standing 'over' the one whom he would shield or defend." In this sense and in this way Christ 'gave himself up for us.' 'An offering and a sacrifice to God.' He gave himself up *to* God, and *for* us. The vicarious nature of this self-surrender seems to be thus made most plainly evident. The purpose of the vicarious self-offering is further very distinctly implied in the words, 'offering and sacrifice.' These words seem to carry their distinction of meaning in the proper sense of each. 'Offering' is the more general term, 'sacrifice' the more specific one. Many things may be spoken of as offerings which are not sacrifice. That which is offered in sacrifice is offered in a special way—one which is implied in the word for 'sacrifice' (θυσία). It is the word occurring at 1 Cor. 10 : 18, "Have not they which eat the sacrifices (θυσίας) communion with the altar?" where the reference is, as the connection shows, to victims offered in sacrifice. The sense of the word meaning 'offering' in general (προσφοράν) might be satisfied by that view of our Lord which regards him as consecrated in general to some mission of mercy in behalf of men. As a 'sacrifice,' he is seen as a victim upon the altar. And he is thus made a victim 'for us' and 'to God.' The idea of expiation is so distinctly implied that it seems surprising it should ever have been questioned. **For a sweetsmelling savour.** "For an odor of sweet smell," in the Revison; "a savour of sweet smell." (Ellicott.) The words express the *acceptableness* of the sacrifice so made. "The burning of spices," says Eadie, "or incense, so fragrant to the Oriental senses, is applied to God." The same writer points to the "radical idea of sacrifice" as being "violent and vicarious suffering and death." He cannot, therefore, approve the view of those who "place the value of Christ's sufferings, not in their substitutionary nature, but in the moral excellence of him who endured them." Neither does it satisfy the meaning of this passage to say that the redemptive efficacy of Christ's sufferings was in the expression by means of them of the divine love. The efficacy lay in the 'sacrifice' itself, not in anything incidental to it, nor even in the motive by which it was prompted. It is the *sacrifice* which was 'for a savour of sweet smell,' that in which the element of acceptableness and efficacy appeared. This is not because God has pleasure in the sight of suffering. It is because the expiation thus made was so complete and ample, opening the way for an expression so free and so full of his own compassionate kindness toward men.

3-21. THE LAW OF THE NEW LIFE, WITH REFERENCE TO FORMS OF BESETTING SIN.

3. But fornication, and all uncleanness, or covetousness. We observe now a change to the prohibitive manner of address. The writer has, for the most part, in preceding verses occupied himself with the things which ought to characterize the Christian. These which follow are things which ought not to be found in any one bearing the Christian name. It is, perhaps, not amiss to assume that in pointing so emphatically to these forms of sin, the apostle has in mind the social surroundings of the Ephesian believers, aiming his prohibition at those which were the besetting sins of Pagan society, and to which even these Christians might still, in some degree, be liable. Ellicott calls attention to this apostle's constant and emphatic condemnation of 'fornication' (πορνεία) as one of the things which the old Pagan world deemed "indifferent" (αδιάφορα). By 'all uncleanness' must be meant every kind of moral impurity. The mention of 'covetousness' in connection with the sins just mentioned, is notable, although the use of the disjunctive 'or' indicates that it is to be viewed as belonging to a different class of such. As in the case of these others, this present one is by no means the only place in the writings of Paul where the sin of 'covetousness' is pointedly condemned. **Let it not be once named among you.** Let absence of each of these sins be so entire that there shall be no occasion to even mention it, much less let it ever be the theme of careless mention, as if of light account. **As becometh saints.** In these things, very especially, there should be marked contrast with that old condition out of which they have come. They are now

4 Neither filthiness, nor foolish talking, nor jesting, which are not convenient; but rather giving of thanks.
5 For this ye know, that no whoremonger, nor unclean person, nor covetous man, who is an idolater, hath any inheritance in the kingdom of Christ and of God.

4 saints; nor filthiness, nor foolish talking, or jesting, which are not befitting: but rather giving of thanks.
5 For this ye know of a surety, that no fornicator, nor unclean person, nor covetous man, who is an idolater, hath any inheritance in the kingdom

consecrated persons, chosen that they might be holy, dedicated to lives of purity and to virtue in a higher sense than heathen moralist ever knew. Let their manner of life in the particulars named be such as in these circumstances is becoming.

4. Neither (*Nor*) filthiness, nor foolish talking, nor (*or*) jesting. These words, though having a mutual resemblance in meaning, do not express the same thing. The first does not mean filthiness in words alone. "The noun," in the Greek, as Eadie says, "denotes indecency, obscenity, or wantonness; whatever—not merely in speech, but in anything—is opposed to purity." The word in the Greek for 'foolish talking' might perhaps be rendered, *talking like a fool*. It includes, with gossip and tattle of every sort, that senseless kind of talk which is such a palpable abuse of the power of speech. The question may arise, how far the prohibition of 'jesting' may extend. The Greek (εὐτραπελία), from two words which mean to "turn easily," refers, in its more literal sense, to that kind of humorous talk which consists in a nimble "turning" of words and phrases so as to excite laughter. In this sense, Thayer gives the meaning to be "pleasantry," "humor," "facetiousness." But the word is also used in a bad sense, denoting "scurrility," "ribaldry," "low jesting," though with some element of wit retained. It is no doubt in this sense that the word is here employed. **Which are not convenient** (*not befitting*). **But rather giving of thanks.** The apostle seems to have in mind proper ways for the manifestation among Christians of a cheerful, joyous state of mind. He forbids what is boisterous, unseemly, mere levity, and, above all, what is in any way shameful or scurrilous. In this way the ungodly world sometimes gives expressions to its hilarious moods. He would have the Christian be still a Christian, even at such times as these. His great occasions of cheerfulness and a joyous mood of mind are those which come to him in gifts and mercies of the good God. Of this he would have him conscious, so that there shall be an element of gratitude in his joy, and that he shall be devout even in his gladness.

5. For this ye know. "Know of a surety," in the Revision. "This ye know, being aware." (Ellicott.) The connection in which all these prohibitions stand quite clearly indicates that the things specified are not viewed in any of those characteristics which make them innocent, but those in which they are wrong. **That no whoremonger, nor unclean person, nor covetous man, who is an idolater.** The specifications before mentioned standing in this connection are to be understood, whatever milder meaning they might have when otherwise used, as indicating what belongs to the same class as the things here named. The sins before specified are to be avoided; *for* it is so surely well known that things of which what is now named is representative, are wholly opposed to all that can be meant by the kingdom of God. 'This,' says Paul, 'ye know' (ἴστε γινώσκοντες). One of the sins named is given a place by itself—the 'covetous man, who is an idolater.' How true this is the conduct of every 'covetous man' makes fully evident. No worship is more absorbing or more exacting than that which the covetous man pays to his possessions. Truly may he say, when these are lost, and with a despair hardest of all to control, "Ye have taken away my gods."[1] **Hath any inheritance in the kingdom of Christ and of God.** "A weighty present," says Ellicott, alluding to the form of the verb, "involving an indirect reference to the eternal and enduring principles by which God governs the world—not so much "'*has* no inheritance,' and *shall* have none,' but 'has no inheritance, and *can* have none.'" We should read, as in the Revision, not 'of Christ and of God,' but *of Christ and God*, the word for 'God' being without the article. Whether there is any polemical value in the form of the phrase is doubtful. Other places occur in the New

[1] "What does it avail (*Qu' importe, en effet*)," says a French writer quoted by Eadie, "that one does not worship idols of gold or silver, if he worships gold and silver themselves?"

6 Let no man deceive you with vain words: for because of these things cometh the wrath of God upon the children of disobedience.
7 Be not ye therefore partakers with them.
8 For ye were sometime darkness, but now *are ye* light in the Lord: walk as children of light;
9 (For the fruit of the spirit *is* in all goodness and righteousness and truth;)

6 of Christ and God. Let no man deceive you with empty words: for because of these things cometh the wrath of God upon the sons of disobedience.
7 Be not ye therefore partakers with them; for we 8 were once darkness, but are now light in the Lord: 9 walk as children of light (for the fruit of the light is in all goodness and righteousness and truth),

Testament where the same form appears. The utmost that can be said, perhaps, is that Christ and God are thus named in a way to indicate, as Ellicott says, "a single conception," yet not so as to imply any intention to speak of the two as one. By 'the kingdom of Christ and God' [literally, "of the Christ and God."—A. H.] must be meant that kingdom of grace which comprehends all the saved. Persons having the character described, and retaining it, are shut out from all hope of salvation.

6. Let no man deceive you with vain (*empty*) words. The sins named are those for which men are only too ready to find excuse, or even justification. All such pleas are 'empty words.' No serious and thoughtful person should be 'deceived' by them. **For because of these things cometh the wrath of God upon the children (*sons*) of disobedience.** Some specific reference may be intended to the manner in which the moral condition of the Pagan world was characterized by such sins as those in question. It amazes one, often, to see how lightly such things were regarded even by the best and wisest of Pagan teachers. Eadie, for example, quotes even Cicero as follows: "He that blames young men for their meretricious amours does what is repugnant to the customs and concessions of our ancestors, for when was not this done? when was it not permitted?" Paul may intend to imply that in these ways especially the Pagan world brought itself into condemnation under the divine displeasure. But what he says has a wider meaning still. Participants in such sins, in whatever age of the world, in heathen or in Christian lands, are under the wrath of God on account of them, and while they thus remain can therefore have no inheritance in the 'kingdom of Christ and of God.'

7. Be not ye therefore partakers with them. A somewhat different meaning, and perhaps a more correct one, is given to the verse if, as in the first verse of the chapter, we read *become* instead of 'be.' What will be then intended is a warning "against allowing themselves to *lapse* into any of the prevailing sins and depravities." (Ellicott, with whom Eadie agrees.)

8. For ye were sometimes (*once*) darkness. A strong expression, meaning more than simply being *in* darkness. They were, in that old heathen state, as if transformed into the very nature of the element in which they lived. **But now are ye light in the Lord.** Where (in Matt. 5: 14) Christians are called "the light of the world," more is meant than simply that they are light-*bearers*. In themselves they are, if such as their Lord would have them be, lights. Regenerated character and the new life have a radiance in themselves. But it is 'light in the Lord.' He is not only the source of it, but the very illuminating principle is their life *in him*. **Walk as children of light.** The 'walk' is again that figurative way of indicating the notion of a life in the world, already used, as in ch. 2: 3 and elsewhere in this Epistle. Without applying the figure too literally in the present case, we may understand by it that living and acting in many relations, which is more or less true of every one. In all this we should be such as 'children of light' necessarily will be. Having spoken first of these Ephesian Christians as, in their former state, 'darkness,' partaking of the very nature of the element they lived in, now he describes their contrasted condition as 'light.' It is a new element; they are 'in the Lord'; they partake now of *this* element; they are 'light in the Lord,' who is "*the* light," and so are 'children of light.' Surely they should 'walk' as such; and they will if truly what they seem to be.

9. For the fruit of the Spirit. It is now well agreed among critics that the reading of the three oldest manuscripts, א A B, should be adopted here—'light' instead of 'Spirit.' The latter appears to be, as Ellicott thinks, "clearly a gloss from Gal. 5: 23." To certain ancient copyists, 'fruit of the light' appears to have seemed obscure, and accordingly, assuming an error in the text, they are believed to have

10 Proving what is acceptable unto the Lord.
11 And have no fellowship with the unfruitful works of darkness, but rather reprove *them*.
12 For it is a shame even to speak of those things which are done of them in secret.
13 But all things that are reproved are made manifest by the light: for whatsoever doth make manifest is light.

10 proving what is well-pleasing unto the Lord; and
11 have no fellowship with the unfruitful works of darkness, but rather even ¹ reprove them; for the
12 things which are done by them in secret it is a shame
13 even to speak of. But all things when they are ² reproved are made manifest by the light: for every thing that is made manifest is light. Wherefore he

¹ Or, *convict*......² Or, *convicted*.

adopted one instead, which this apostle uses elsewhere. The word for 'fruit,' however (καρπὸς), is not in the Greek so restricted in meaning as the corresponding English word is. It means also, in general, an effect or result, as where our Lord sends his disciples that they may "bring forth fruit" (John 15:8,16); with other places where we read of "the fruit of righteousness" (James 3:18), and fruits of "the kingdom of God." (Matt. 21:43.) 'The fruit of light' may seem a singular expression, yet is quite similar in general to those just quoted, and means simply that result of a life in this new element of which we at once read. **Is in all goodness and righteousness and truth.** Meyer's remark is eminently just, that the whole of Christian morality is presented under these three aspects, the good, the right, the true.

10. Proving what is acceptable unto the Lord. Particular attention should be given to the word 'proving' in this place. The verb in the Greek means "to test, to try, to examine, to scrutinize." To ascertain that which 'is acceptable unto the Lord' is viewed as a matter of most serious concern. It may often supply an occasion for earnest and prayerful inquiry. By as much as it is important to *do* that which is acceptable, it is important first to *know* it. This injunction comes fitly, therefore, in connection with the foregoing earnest exhortation, as to the kind of living suitable to those who are 'light in the Lord.'

11. And have no fellowship with the unfruitful works of darkness. De Wette would have the meaning to be, "take no part in." Ellicott thinks the rendering in the Common English Version, as here, "a good and accurate translation." Having 'fellowship with' implies more than taking part in, and is a more correct rendering of the Greek. Paul would have his brethren do more than simply abstain; he would have them be in temper and spirit utterly averse to and out of fellowship with, all 'works of darkness.' And truly,

"what communion (or, *fellowship*) hath light with darkness?" (2 Cor. 6:14.) The use of the epithet 'unfruitful' is to be marked. It is in the English version as in the Greek, strictly antithetical to the expression 'fruit of light' in a previous verse, just as 'light' and 'darkness' are also in contrast. Works of darkness have their 'fruit' in the consequences sure to follow them. In all that is to be desired or sought, however, they are 'unfruitful' (ἀκάρποις). **But rather reprove them.** Above all, 'reprove them' in the example of a godly character and a pure life.

12. For it is a shame even to speak of those things which are done of them in secret. How can they be 'reproved,' if not spoken of? The 'for' must, it should seem, refer to what is said in the first part of the previous verse. That the sins done in secret are so bad and shameful as that it is impossible even 'to speak of them,' enforces the injunction not to fellowship them in any way. We have nothing to do with such things save to 'reprove them.'

13. But all things that are reproved (*when they are reproved*) **are made manifest by the light.** This verse is in some degree a difficult one. Ellicott does not translate the Greek words (τὰ δὲ πάντα) 'all things,' but "they all," referring directly to the 'things done in secret' of the previous verse. The meaning appears to be a reason why these 'things done in secret,' though so bad that 'it is a shame even to speak of' them, must still be reproved. Their secrecy affords them a certain immunity. When they are brought to the light their infamy is exposed. The writer is not so much stating a general proposition as showing how and why certain forms of wickedness are to be dealt with. We are not to leave them unreproved because they are done in secret, nor because 'it is a shame even to speak of them'; but they must at least be in such a manner reproved as that the darkness amidst which they are done shall no longer shield

14 Wherefore he saith, Awake thou that sleepest, and arise from the dead, and Christ shall give thee light.
15 See then that ye walk circumspectly, not as fools, but as wise,

14 saith, Awake, thou that sleepest, and arise from the dead, and Christ shall shine upon thee.
15 Look therefore carefully how ye walk, not as unwise,

them. **For whatsoever doth make manifest is light.** The change in the Revision is noticeable. Not all the critics would accept the change so made. The Common Version is certainly more clear in its meaning. The Greek, however, does not have the active form for 'make manifest.' It is the passive participle (φανερούμενον), and it is difficult to see how it can be rendered otherwise than "being made manifest," or "when it is made manifest." Eadie, though admitting what Meyer claims,—that this participle is always passive,—still urges that it has sometimes, in the New Testament, a reflexive signification, partaking the force of the middle voice. The passages to which he refers (Mark 16:12; John 1:31; 9:3; 2 Cor. 4:10, 11) scarcely bear him out in this. He quotes several of the older commentators, among them Beza, Calvin, and Grotius, as supporting the rendering he would give; namely, "whatever makes manifest is light." Were such rendering allowed, the meaning of this part of the verse would be much more evident. That in the Revision, it should seem, is the only one grammatically allowable. We must then understand the apostle as still using the word 'light' in a tropical way. When that which is secret has been made manifest, it is no longer darkness; it has become 'light,' and may be seen for what it really is.

14. **Wherefore he saith.** God 'saith'; a method of quotation not unusual with Paul. Compare 4:8. As to the passage cited, much difference of opinion exists, and partly for the reason that the citation is not exact. Perhaps the best view is that which selects Isa. 60:1, seq., as the passage which the writer has in mind and which he uses in a way of free quotation. **Awake, thou that sleepest, and arise from the dead, and Christ shall give thee light** (*shall shine upon thee*). The 'wherefore' at the beginning of the verse refers to the general exhortation addressed to the Ephesian brethren in previous verses; and this verse, taken as a whole, must be viewed as in some sort a summary of what has gone before. Bengel and others (so, likewise, the Revision) take the words 'Christ shall give thee light' as equivalent to "Christ shall shine upon thee," as the sun illumines the world when night is past ("*illucescet tanquam sol*"). In a summarizing way, the two conditions before described are now put in contrast. That old Pagan darkness was as the night, the very darkness of spiritual death. What they have now experienced is as when the night is gone and the sun has risen: is, in fact, as life from the dead. In his use of a Messianic passage in the Old Testament, illustrating this,— whether the one mentioned above, or some other,—Paul employs it simply in its general sense and with accommodation to his present purpose.

15. **See, then, that ye walk circumspectly.** We do not find any of our authorities approving the change here made in the Revision. The Greek word (ἀκριβῶς) translated 'carefully,' the Revisers connect, evidently, with the words 'look therefore' (βλέπετε οὖν). Alford, Eadie, Ellicott, Davies, Hodge, Meyer, Bengel, all connect the word in question with 'how ye walk' (πῶς περιπατεῖτε). It would appear to be—in part, at least—the occurrence here of the 'how' (πῶς) which occasions the rendering in the Revision, and the apparent objection to such a reading as "Take heed how ye walk carefully," or "correctly," which is the more exact rendering. Ellicott, however, finds no difficulty in such a translation, while Alford and others see in the word 'how' (πῶς) a double meaning, as if the apostle would say, "Take heed, not only that your walk be exact, strict, but also of *what sort* that strictness is—not only that you *have* a rule and *keep to it*, but that the rule be the *best* one." **Not as fools, but as wise.** The Revised Version gives, "*Not as unwise* (ἄσοφοι), *but as wise* (σοφοί)." This clause of the verse so far explains the meaning of the former one. The tenor of it may have suggested the rendering, in the Revision, of the words at the beginning; the walking 'as wise' being understood to imply the 'looking carefully.' The same implication, however, appears to be no less in the 'how ye walk correctly,' or "strictly." This latter rendering suggests a purpose in the writer to enjoin something more than carefulness in the manner of life;

16 Redeeming the time, because the days are evil.
17 Wherefore be ye not unwise, but understanding what the will of the Lord is.
18 And be not drunk with wine, wherein is excess; but be filled the Spirit;
19 Speaking to yourselves in psalms and hymns and spiritual songs, singing and making melody in your heart to the Lord :
20 Giving thanks always for all things unto God and the Father in the name of our Lord Jesus Christ;
21 Submitting yourselves one to another in the fear of God.

16 wise, but as wise ; [1] redeeming the time, because the
17 days are evil. Wherefore be ye not foolish, but
18 understand what the will of the Lord is. And be not drunken with wine, wherein is riot, but be filled
19 [2] with the Spirit ; speaking [3] one to another in psalms and hymns and spiritual songs, singing and making
20 melody with your heart to the Lord ; giving thanks always for all things in the name of our Lord Jesus
21 Christ to [4] God, even the Father; subjecting yourselves one to another in the fear of Christ.

1 Or. buying up the opportunity..... .2 Or, in spirit......3 Or. to yourselves.......4 Gr. the God and Father.

in addition to this, a strictness which should save them from weak compromises, or from assuming things to be indifferent which are not positively criminal.

16. Redeeming the time. The expression in the Greek is remarkable, the participle employed having the meaning to "buy up," or to "buy for one's own use." It is also used in the sense of "ransom" or "redeem." The better rendering of the word for "time" (καιρόν) is "opportunity." Ellicott, accordingly, translates: "Buying up for yourselves (or, *making your own*) the opportunity, the fitting season." It is a highly forcible way of setting forth the *value* of "opportunity," and the importance of making it our own. And this the more **because the days are evil.** True for those to whom he especially wrote; true always, since temptation and 'evil' are permanent conditions of man's life in this world.

17. Wherefore be (or, *become*) **ye not unwise.** A different word occurs here (ἄφρωνες), meaning "foolish," "senseless," "stupid," instead of the word used in ver. 15, 'unwise' (ἄσοφοι). Hence the more emphatic force in what follows—**but understanding what the will of the Lord is.** "Be not foolish, but understand"—the imperative of the verb, not the participle, so the text of Westcott and Hort. Other critics prefer the participle. The point is not a material one. The state of mind enjoined is the opposite of that "senseless" one in which there is neither knowledge, nor effort after knowledge, of 'what the will of the Lord is.'

18. And be not drunk with wine, wherein is excess (*riot*). It is the intoxication with wine which is forbidden, and this because of the 'excess,' the "riot," the "dissoluteness" to which it leads. **But be filled with the Spirit.** "To the Christian," says Hodge, "the source of strength and joy is not wine, but the Spirit."

19. Speaking to yourselves (or, *one to another*) **in psalms and hymns and spiritual songs.** We have here another example of the use of 'yourselves' (ἑαυτοῖς) for "one another" (ἀλλήλοις), as in 4 : 32. But how shall we distinguish between 'psalms, hymns, and spiritual songs'? It is perhaps unnecessary to make exact distinctions in this case. The 'psalm' may be understood in general as "a sacred song chanted to the accompaniment of instrumental music," as in the ritual of the ancient sanctuary, although a freer use of the word seems to occur at 1 Cor. 14 : 26. By 'hymns' may be intended a form of sacred song coming into use especially among Gentile Christians, such as in time became so general in the service of public praise. 'Spiritual songs' may represent those more impromptu effusions to which the glow of Christian feeling gives birth. **Singing and making melody in** (*with*) **your heart to the Lord.** In this way should Christians give expression to joyful feeling, and not in any of those customary in the Gentile world around them.

20. Giving thanks always for all things unto God and the Father. Meyer would limit the 'all things' to blessings. Is such limitation required? Surely, if "all things work together for good to them that love God," the thankful mood of mind is one for which there will always, and in all circumstances, be occasion. **In the name of our Lord Jesus Christ.** The medium of our approach to God, whether we come with prayer or with thanksgiving.

21. Submitting (*subjecting*) **yourselves one to another in the fear of God.** The connection with what goes before is not clearly apparent. Hodge, on this account, and because of the relation to what follows, would begin "a new paragraph" here. The verse does, indeed, appear to enjoin in general what

22 Wives, submit yourselves unto your own husbands, as unto the Lord.
23 For the husband is the head of the wife, even as Christ is the head of the church: and he is the Saviour of the body.
24 Therefore as the church is subject unto Christ, so *let* the wives *be* to their own husbands in every thing.

22 Wives *be in subjection* unto your own husbands, 23 as unto the Lord. For the husband is the head of the wife, as Christ also is the head of the church, 24 *being* himself the saviour of the body. But as the church is subject to Christ, [1] so *let* the wives also *be* to

[1] Or, *so are the wives also*.

is more specifically required in the remainder of the chapter. At the same time, the use of the participle suggests a like close connection with what goes before. The verse seems to present in general a spirit in the mutual relations of the Christian life which is in harmony with that spirit of devotion as toward God, of which he had just been speaking.

22-23. LAW OF THE NEW LIFE IN SPECIFIC RELATIONS.

22. Wives, submit yourselves unto your own husbands. There is no verb here in the Greek, so that one must be supplied. Grammatically, it may be made to read, either "Wives, be in subjection," or "Let wives be in subjection." When, however, the writer comes, in ver. 25, to speak of the duty of husbands, it is the imperative in the second person, and not in the third. This may suggest a like form of the verb to be supplied here. Besides, the connection with the immediately preceding verses would make this the more likely. The verb there has the form of a direct address, and naturally might have the same form here. The Sinaitic and Alexandrian manuscripts, however, with the Greek text of the Common Version, have the verb expressed, and give it in the third person, so that Tischendorf's marginal rendering is: "Let the wives submit themselves unto their own husbands." Westcott and Hort do not approve this reading, and we observe that other critics, as Alford, Eadie, Ellicott, reject it, as probably a "gloss." **As unto the Lord.** It is to be observed how, in this as in respect to those relations named subsequently,—parents and children, masters and servants,—the injunctions given have direct reference to such relations seen in their Christian aspect. It is as Christian wives and husbands, children and parents, servants and masters, that he addresses them. This may sufficiently explain the words immediately in hand. They do not imply that the husband is to the wife in place of 'the Lord'; neither do they imply any reference to that analogy between the relation of the husband with the wife and that existing between Christ and the church, of which mention is made in the verse following. What they appear to mean is simply that the wife shall observe this rule as a matter of Christian obligation.

23. For the husband is the head of the wife, even as Christ is the head of the church. The purpose of this is evidently to show how thoroughly Christian is the marriage relation as it exists between those who themselves are Christian. They are to see an analogy and illustration in the relation existing between Christ and his church, and to understand that sacred as is this relation in which they stand to each other under the original ordinance of marriage, it gains fresh sacredness from that consecration which it receives under the law of the new life in Christ. **And he is the Saviour of the body.** Literally, '*himself Saviour of the body*'—of that 'body' which is 'the church.'

24. Therefore as the church is subject to Christ, so let the wives be to their own husbands in every thing. This verse contains in summary what the apostle would enjoin as touching one of the parties to this relation of marriage. It is altogether a misapprehension of his meaning to interpret what is said as implying anything inconsistent with the dignity and personal freedom of the wife, or with the equality of the sexes properly viewed. What the apostle requires is simply that which every Christian wife yields, while holding her husband in due estimation as to his relation in the family, properly sensible of her dependence upon his superior ability to face and to bear the heavier burdens of life, and honoring in him those qualities which characterize and adorn the Christian manhood. The 'subjection' required implies nothing servile, nor anything more, in any way, than the true wife spontaneously yields to the husband whom she honors and loves. The

25 Husbands, love your wives, even as Christ also loved the church, and gave himself for it;
26 That he might sanctify and cleanse it with the washing of water by the word,
27 That he might present it to himself a glorious church, not having spot, or wrinkle, or any such thing; but that it should be holy and without blemish.
28 So ought men to love their wives as their own bodies. He that loveth his wife loveth himself.

25 their husbands in every thing. Husbands, love your wives, even as Christ also loved the church, and gave himself up for it; that he might sanctify it, having cleansed it by the ¹ washing of water with 27 the word, that he might present the church to himself a glorious *church*, not having spot or wrinkle or any such thing; but that it should be holy and without blemish. Even so ought husbands to love their own wives as their own bodies. He that love-

¹ Gr. *laver.*

---

expression '*her own* husband,' used in ver. 22 and here again in ver. 24, may be intended simply to suggest the closeness and the *exclusiveness* of that tie in which husband and wife are united in the marriage relation.

25. Husbands, love your wives. 'Subjection' on the one side and 'love' upon the other are not to be interpreted so as to imply inequality of position or privilege in this relation. The 'subjection' itself of the wife is such as love not only warrants, but prompts, while the 'love' of the husband involves a certain answering subjection on his own part. The husband who truly loves his wife holds her in a degree of reverence and honor which, if it differ from that enjoined upon the wife, only so differs in accordance with what belongs to the nature and position of the woman upon the one side, and of the man upon the other. **Even as Christ also loved the church, and gave himself for it.** 'Gave himself *up* for it,' as in the Revised Version, is a stronger expression, implying what is taught as to Christ's self-offering in our behalf. The simile here is to be understood *as a* simile and illustration, though implying, also, the force of an example.

26. That he might sanctify and cleanse it with (*sanctify it, having cleansed it by*) **the washing of water by** (*with*) **the word.** One of the principal meanings of the verb here translated 'sanctify' is "to render, or declare, holy, or to consecrate." The corresponding noun is that which in various parts of this Epistle is translated "saints," with the meaning "consecrated persons." The participle translated 'having cleansed' implies as actually done what the washing symbolizes. The verse, then, should be taken as meaning that those who, through the instrumentality of 'the word,' the gospel, have been 'cleansed,' made free from guilt, and in a process of which baptism is the symbol, Christ dedicates, consecrates, sets apart to himself, and with a view to the ultimate purpose set forth in the verse next following. "The meaning is," says Eadie, "that having purified her [the church] he might consecrate her to himself; this idea being suspended till it is brought out with special emphasis in the following verse." Davies understands 'the washing of water' to refer to "the bath which it was the custom for the bride to take as one of the ceremonies preceding marriage." And he further explains: "The church in every place was formed by the preaching of the word. The word was the message of forgiveness and reconciliation through Christ. Those who received this message and yielded to the call came out from the world, were baptized, and became members of a holy or consecrated community. Christ, then, gave himself up, in order that he might proclaim peace effectually to men, and so might fashion for himself a pure church." Critics have discussed the passage at great length, finding in it, we cannot but think, quite needless difficulty. The above appears to be its meaning, as taken apart from all attempts to use the passage for polemical purposes.

27. That he might present it to himself a glorious church—or, *he himself might present to himself.* Ellicott says: "Christ permits neither attendants nor paranymphs to present his Bride: he alone presents; he alone receives." The change of order in the words in the Revision will be noticed. **Not having spot, or wrinkle, or any such thing.** Terms denoting physical perfection are used to express that which is spiritual. **But that it should be holy and without blemish.** Such is his ultimate purpose as regards his redeemed people.

28. So ought men (*husbands*) **to love their wives as their own bodies.** The thought here is a comparison of the love which a husband should have for his wife with the love of Christ for his church. It resumes what has already been expressed in ver. 25: 'Even as (καθὼς) Christ.' . . . 'Even

29 For no man ever yet hated his own flesh; but nourisheth and cherisheth it, even as the Lord the church;
30 For we are members of his body, of his flesh, and of his bones.
31 For this cause shall a man leave his father and mother, and shall be joined unto his wife, and they two shall be one flesh.
32 This is a great mystery: but I speak concerning Christ and the church.

29 eth his own wife loveth himself; for no man ever hated his own flesh; but nourisheth and cherisheth
30 it, even as Christ also the church; because we are
31 members of his body. For this cause shall a man leave his father and mother, and shall cleave to his wife; and the twain shall become one flesh.
32 This mystery is great; but I speak in regard of

so' (οὕτως). The thought, then, is not that as a man loves own body he should love his wife, but that as Christ loves his body, the church, so a husband should love his wife, who by virtue of the closeness of the relation, as described in verses following, is "his own flesh." In this view such writers as Hodge, Ellicott, and others agree, although Alford would have the "so" (οὕτως) connect with the "as" (ὡς) in the same verse, implying that as a man loves his own body, so he should love his wife. The former view seems to us far more in harmony with the general thought of the apostle in this place; the close mystical relation of Christ with the church being in the entire passage the constant term of comparison. He that **loveth his** (or, *his own*) **wife loveth himself.** The reason for this appears in what follows.

29. For no man ever yet hated his own flesh. The argument urged is strengthened by being shown to consist with a law in man's own nature. **But nourisheth it and cherisheth it, even as the Lord** (or, *as Christ*) **the church.** The change of 'the Lord' to 'Christ' is required by manuscript authority. The verbs in the Greek translated 'nourish' and 'cherish,' mean, literally, to supply nutriment and to warm. They describe graphically the way in which the body, in due regard for health and life, is cared for. In the application of the comparison, they suggest with what tender and watchful care, upon the one hand, Christ watches over his church, which is *his* body, and, upon the other, the husband should 'cherish' his wife.

30. For we are members of his body, of his flesh, and of his bones. It will be noticed that the Revision omits the words 'of his flesh, and of his bones.' This is according to the text of Westcott and Hort, and is sus-

tained by such ancient authorities as the Sinaitic, the Vatican, and the Alexandrian manuscripts. Tischendorf at first opposed the omission, though in his seventh edition he inserts the words.[1] Most manuscripts and versions contain them, while in the passage as used by Irenæus, Chrysostom, Jerome, and many others, they are retained. Ellicott thinks that in the manuscripts first named, א A B, there occurred an accidental omission "from the transcriber's eye having fallen upon the third pronoun 'his' (αὐτοῦ) instead of the first." He urges, also, "internal considerations." Eadie and Alford also retain them. If the critical judgment be accepted, as perhaps it ought, the reference to Gen. 2 : 23 becomes more evident and striking. Adam there says of his wife: "This is now bone of my bone and flesh of my flesh"; and the apostle makes use of the same strong expression, in illustrating alike the unity implied in the marriage tie, and the oneness of Christ with the church.

31. For this cause shall a man leave father and mother, and shall be joined (or, *shall cleave*) **unto his wife, and they two shall be one flesh.** This is clearly a citation of Gen. 2 : 24; with what special sense may best be considered in a study of the verse which follows.

32. This is a great mystery. Various explanations are given of the word 'mystery' in this place. We can scarcely suppose that the apostle means to speak thus of the marriage relation in itself. He began, indeed, to treat of this relation as it exists in the human compact, but in enforcing the truth of its sacredness, especially of that unity into which the parties to it are brought, he makes use of that high spiritual relation subsisting between

---

[1] [But he omits them in his eighth edition, as do Lachmann, Westcott and Hort, and the Revision. Is it not more probable that the words were written on the margin from Gen. 2 : 23, and introduced by a copyist into the text, than that, being so striking, emphatic, and familiar, they were dropped from the text? It seems to me that the weight of evidence against their genuineness is really greater than that in favor of it. A. H.]

33 Nevertheless, let every one of you in particular so love his wife even as himself; and the wife see that she reverence *her* husband.

33 Christ and of the church. Nevertheless do ye also severally love each one his own wife even as himself; and *let* the wife *see* that she fear her husband.

Christ and his church. Looking back, then, to the original institution of marriage, he finds in the terms of it what strikingly sets forth the thought he has in mind. He sees in words from Genesis, quoted in ver. 31, an application to the human relation of marriage, and to that spiritual wedlock in which Christ and his church are one. There is here, he then says, a deeper meaning than appears upon the surface—a 'mystery' in such analogies which he does not attempt to explore. **But I speak concerning Christ and the church.** The 'mystery' does not relate to marriage in itself considered, but to that spiritual union of Christ with his church, of which, in some sense, we might view marriage as a symbol. Whether in the institution of marriage there was any looking forward to this spiritual relationship between our Lord and his redeemed people, he does not authorize us to say. The most we can safely infer is the lesson which the apostle himself evidently aims to impress—that marriage has in it a sacredness which Christian husbands and wives should recognize, a sacredness due to the closeness of this union as divinely appointed, and due also to the fact that it is used under the guidance of inspiration to represent that other union, so high and holy, of Christ with his church. If marriage were, in itself, what human folly and wickedness so often conceive it to be, we should never find it bearing a part in analogies such as this.

33. Nevertheless, let every one of you in particular (or, *severally*) **so love his wife even as himself; and the wife see that she reverence** (*fear*) **her husband.** The 'nevertheless' has reference to what is said of the 'mystery.' Notwithstanding all that may be mystically implied in this human relationship,—perhaps more than at present we are prepared to understand,—there is this plain, mutual duty: that the husband 'love' his wife,' that the wife 'fear' her husband. He enjoins it as an individual duty ('*every* one of you in particular,' or *severally*). He is not stating an abstract proposition, but enjoining *personal* duty. We quote here the comment of Dr. Hodge: "The word translated 'fear' (φοβέω) may express the emotion of fear in all its modifications, and in all its degrees, from simple respect, through reverence, up to adoration, according to its object. It is, however, in all its degrees, an acknowledgment of superiority. The sentiments, therefore, which lie at the foundation of the marriage relation, which arise out of the constitution of nature, which are required by the command of God, and are essential to the happiness and well-being of the parties, are, on the part of the husband, that form of love which leads him to cherish and protect his wife as being himself; and, on the part of the woman, that sense of his superiority out of which trust and obedience voluntarily flow."

SUMMARY OF THE EXPOSITION.

The first and second verses of this chapter really belong with that which precedes. The teaching of the apostle in this connection has (1) a positive, and (2) a negative aspect. Under the first he sets forth that ideal of character and life toward which the Christian should aspire; under the second he presents to view that contrasted character and conduct which is on every account to be avoided. The approved character is *regenerate* character, 'the new man'; the approved life that which is in harmony with the principle and impulse of this new nature. Contrasted with this is all that which these Ephesian Christians knew of themselves in their former heathen condition, and which they see to be characteristic of the heathen society in the midst of which it is their lot still to live. With ver. 3 of chapter 5 the former of these two aspects of the general theme changes to the latter, and we have set forth in plain and pointed prohibition those forms of outbreaking sin to which these converted Gentiles had perhaps been more or less addicted, but which must no more be even 'named' among them 'as becometh saints.' (ver. 3-21.)

Turning to the more positive aspects of this moral teaching, it is to be again noticed how much more elevated is the point of view of the Christian morality than that which rests purely in any law of human relations, or in considerations of either private or public utility. The Christian, by the single fact of becoming a

CHAPTER VI.

1 Children, obey your parents in the Lord; for this is right. Honour thy father and mother (which is
2 commandments with promise;

Christian, is in a sphere wholly new. There is a new law of life within, and a new law of life without. The principles by which he tests character and conduct are found in the essential nature of that new life within, and in those relations into which in becoming a Christian he is brought. What 'becometh saints' is a much higher rule of life than that which concerns personal reputation, social decency, or even social obligation. 'The will of the Lord'—this is what most of all needs to be 'understood.' The things 'acceptable unto the Lord' are the things to be ascertained, chosen, and done. They are to be Christian, even in their joyousness. (ver. 18-20.) Their religion is a religion of cheerfulness, and they can have no need of a resort to worldly sources of enjoyment, or worldly ways of expressing their happier moods.

It is with good reason that the apostle in this chapter dwells at such length and with such emphasis upon the subject of marriage, at the Christian point of view. (Ver. 22-33.) At this point those so lately converted from heathenism needed especially to be placed upon their guard. Scarcely any two things could be more in contrast than the heathen and the Christian idea of marriage; at the same time, as this relation is the basis of all human relations, right conceptions of it and right action under it were peculiarly important. Perhaps, too, we ought to say that in this Christian law of marriage certain things are assumed. The parties to it are themselves assumed to be Christian, and each of these parties such in character as that the 'love' upon the one side, and the 'reverence' upon the other shall be possible. Indeed, it is one essential element in this Christian law of marriage that each party to the relation so indicated shall on his or her own part recognize a duty back of all others, which is the duty of cultivating a personal character *worthy* alike of the 'love' and the 'reverence' enjoined.

But beyond this, we should find implied in the Christian law of marriage a general law that must be in force among those who are not Christians equally as with those who are. This relation among Christians is simply the original institution redeemed from the abuses and the degradation to which the folly and wickedness of men have subjected it. Such as is here described it was meant that marriage should always be, and they who refuse to see it in that light, or who make these ideal conditions of it impossible, are guilty of a double wrong: they contemn the divine authority in the institution, and they dishonor the institution itself by perversion and abuse.

Ch. 6 : 1-9. LAW OF THE NEW LIFE IN OTHER SPECIFIC RELATIONS.

1. Children, obey your parents in the Lord. The words 'in the Lord' are wanting in four ancient manuscripts; and one critic, Lachmann, thinks they should be omitted. Most manuscripts have them, including ℵ and A; and the Greek Fathers treat them as authentic. They are therefore retained by nearly all modern commentators. Quite in keeping with what has gone before in these teachings of Christian morality, they enjoin the duty of children to parents as at the Christian point of view. This duty of obedience to parents is a Christian duty, and is to be rendered, like all others, in recognition of the Lord's will and in obedience to it. That will is always supreme, and both enjoins and regulates the obedience required. **For this is right.** The Greek word does not mean "fit," "becoming" (πρέπον), but "just" (δίκαιον), in accordance with natural law. Obedience to parents is thus shown to be, not an arbitrary rule, but as belonging to the very relation of parent and child.

2. Honour thy father and thy mother. The apostle here points back to the fifth commandment of the Decalogue, like all the ten commandments grounded in natural right, and so brings to this which he now enjoins the sanction of that ancient statute. **Which is the first commandment with promise.** In what sense this fifth commandment is 'the

3 That it may be well with thee, and thou mayest live long on the earth.
4 And, ye fathers, provoke not your children to wrath: but bring them up in the nurture and admonition of the Lord.
5 Servants, be obedient to them that are *your* masters according to the flesh, with fear and trembling, in singleness of your heart, as unto Christ;

3 the first commandment with promise) that it may be well with thee, and thou [1]mayest live long
4 on the [2]earth. And, ye fathers, provoke not your children to wrath: but nurture them in the chastening and admonition of the Lord.
5 [3]Servants, be obedient unto them that according to the flesh are your [4]masters, with fear and trembling,

1 Or, *shalt*......2 Or, *land*......3 Gr. *Bondservants*......4 Gr. *Lords*.

first commandment with promise' has been thought not altogether clear. Some have interpreted the *second* commandment as being 'with promise,' since Jehovah there describes himself as "showing mercy unto thousands of them that love him and keep his commandments." This is, however, more in the form of a general statement, and applies as much to each of the following commandments as to this one. The fifth seems certainly first of the ten with a promise specifically attached— "that thy days may be long upon the land which the Lord thy God giveth thee." Then, a further difficulty is supposed to be in the fact that so far as the ten commandments are concerned, this is not only the first, but the *only* one 'with promise.' Perhaps it is unnecessary to hold the writer of this Epistle to such exactitude of expression. If we must do so, then it may be sufficient to say that this fifth commandment is first of all which distinctly appear in the Sinaitic legislation with a definite and express promise attached. The connection of a promise with the command lends to it unusual emphasis.

3. **That it may be well with thee, and that thou mayst live long on the earth.** The apostle here, as is common with writers of the New Testament, quotes from the Septuagint, instead of the Hebrew. He also omits the words "which the Lord thy God giveth thee." There is, therefore, an adaptation of the ancient promise to his own especial purpose. The general purport of the promise, however, as originally given, warrants him in this. This general purport is that, connected with the observance of this duty, there shall be the blessing of long life as a result. Along with the especial divine approval and blessing vouchsafed to obedience in the particular named, there is that which is the natural consequence of addiction to this virtue, and to those by which it is so apt to be accompanied. A well-regulated life, under the general order of divine providence, will, as the rule, be a long life; untimely death being so often due, in some way, to violation or neglect of those laws which assign conditions both of health and of life. Disregard of such laws, and reckless living in general, commonly begin with violations of this fifth commandment, breaking this law of God and law of nature leading on swiftly to general lawlessness, perhaps to crime and a death of shame. Even heathen moralists, like Confucius, have seen this, and so have placed this duty of reverence for parents at the very foundation of all virtue, personal and social.

4. **And ye fathers, provoke not your children to wrath.** Fathers are addressed, because authority in the household is primarily lodged with them, and by them, perhaps, most apt to be exercised with harshness. The injunction here requires that judicious exercise of such authority which takes due account of whatever may be peculiar in the disposition of the child, or in circumstances of the case calling for admonition, and so appeals to a sense of justice, instead of exciting that feeling of rebellion and 'wrath' which a sense of wrong suffered is so sure to cause. **But bring them up in the nurture and admonition of the Lord.** Here again we find ourselves at the Christian point of view. While the child may rightfully expect of the parent what is more than mere control,—may expect 'nurture,'—and while 'admonition' will always be necessary, these should be 'in the Lord': nurture, education, discipline, in knowledge of the Lord's will, and a disposition conforming thereto, and 'admonition,' grounded, not in mere parental authority, but in that higher law of a divine commandment. The general sense of the injunction would cover the whole sphere of a nurture and training that should be thoroughly Christian in spirit, and aim, and result.

5. **Servants, be obedient to them that are your masters according to the flesh.** The word for 'servants' (δοῦλοι) means, of

6 Not with eyeservice, as menpleasers; but as the servants of Christ, doing the will of God from the heart;
7 With good will doing service, as to the Lord, and not to men:
8 Knowing that whatsoever good thing any man doeth, the same shall he receive of the Lord, whether he be bond or free.

6 in singleness of your heart, as unto Christ: not in the way of eyeservice, as men-pleasers; but as ¹servants of Christ, doing the will of God from the 7 ²heart; with good will doing service, as unto the 8 Lord, and not unto men: knowing that whatsoever good thing each one doeth, the same shall he receive again from the Lord, whether he be bond or

---

1 Gr. *Bondservants*......2 Gr. *soul*.

---

course, *bondservants*; and the precept given must be understood as addressed to those who were in this unfortunate situation, the number of whom in every great ancient city, like Ephesus, was very large. Very many of this class became Christians. This new faith of theirs, however, had nothing in it which would warrant a turbulent spirit, or conduct of any kind inconsistent with the relations of that condition of life in which their Christian faith and hope had found them. Obedience to these 'masters' (κυρίοις) was the immediate duty, whether the relation were one of servitude in its harsher or its milder form.[1] **With fear and trembling.** Ellicott rightly understands this as referring "to the 'anxious solicitude' they ought to feel about the faithful performance of their duty." Other places where the same expression occurs, are 1 Cor. 2:3; 2 Cor. 7:15; Phil. 2:12. Reference to these places will show that the phrase implies nothing servile, but only that natural and proper solicitude which a sense of responsibility occasions. **In singleness of your heart, as unto Christ.** The commanding motive to such obedience should be always the Christian one.

6. Not with eye-service, as men-pleasers. Ellicott regards the word for "eye-service" (ὀφθαλμοδουλείαν) as "coined by St. Paul." It occurs only in this place and at Col. 3:22. There is great significance in the advice here given. The natural tendency of servitude, in which the motives that ordinarily influence men are so much absent, is toward those of which the apostle here speaks. Even here, as he implies, the Christian sense of higher obligation than that of mere task-work may have room, and may lift into a certain dignity even the most servile occupation. **But as the servants of Christ.** The most menial and unwelcome forms of service may be rendered with this high motive, and so may become tolerable, even to those who naturally most revolt at them. **Doing the will of God from the heart.** The marginal rendering in the Revision, "soul" for 'heart,' is preferred by Eadie, Ellicott, Alford, and others; the last-named, however, connecting the words 'from the soul' with the next verse, following, in this, the text of Knapp and Lachmann, and such commentators as Bengel, Harless, De Wette, and Stier. The Syriac Version also connects in this way, so as to read in translation, "and serve them with all your soul." Eadie objects to this as an apparent tautology, when 'from the heart,' or '*soul*' becomes connected with the following verse.

7. With good will doing service, as to the Lord, and not to men. "It is no good will," says Eadie, "which the slave often bears to his master, his common feeling being the torment of his master's presence and the terror of his lash."

8. Knowing that whatsoever good thing any man doeth, the same shall he receive of the Lord. It is noticeable how Paul dwells upon this advice to 'servants,' who if literal "bondmen," "slaves," so much needed, not only comfort in their hard lot, but guidance also in the ordering of their new life in Christ under such harsh conditions. His advice to them certainly meets, in the only possibly effectual way, the necessities of their case. A spirit of comparative acquiescence in their condition, and, above all, a new and elevating motive, making them, in some sense, superior to that which they must endure, was

---

[1] The use of κύριος instead of δεσπότης ought, perhaps, to be noticed. The latter, as Thayer explains, is "more strictly the correlative of δοῦλος, 'slave.'" Since the writer here employs the former word, with its "wider meaning, applicable to the various ranks and relations of life, and not suggestive, either of property or of absolutism," the interpretation of the passage should be made to cover the relation of master and servant in all forms of it, although especially applying to servitude in the form it had amongst those to whom this Epistle is immediately addressed.

9 And, ye masters, do the same things unto them, forbearing threatening: knowing that your Master also is in heaven: neither is there respect of persons with him.

9 free. And, ye ¹ masters, do the same things unto them, and forbear threatening; knowing that he who is both their master and yours is in heaven, and there is no respect of persons with him.

¹ Gr. Lords.

the only availing help for them. When they should come to make the service they rendered a service for Christ, and their obedience to the master a doing of the will of God, and their service as done 'to the Lord, and not to men,' with confidence that in the Lord's best way, whatsoever good in these ways they should do, the same they should 'receive of the Lord,' the darkness of their lot would be relieved with a genuine radiance, and the burden and the humiliation of it become at last tolerable. The verb for 'receive' ("receive again," in the Revision) is in the middle voice (κομίσεται). Thayer explains thus: "Since in the rewards and punishments of deeds, the deeds themselves are as if requited and so given back to their authors, the meaning is obvious when one is said to "receive again" (κομίζεσθαι) *that which he has done*—that is, "either the reward or the punishment of the deed." "The word refers," says Ellicott, "to the receiving back of a *deposit*." The doctrine implied is that constant doctrine of the New Testament, that while, as is said below, "there is no respect of persons" with God, there *is* respect of character; so that while all present favor, and, above all, the final salvation, is of grace, and "not of works, lest any man should boast" (2 : 9), it is by no means forgotten, either now or in the final apportionment of destiny, what the life has been. **Whether he be bond or free.** The real point of what is said is perhaps in these words. The Christian bond servant is entitled to feel that in all that concerns his relations with God he is upon the same footing as the free man. He should, therefore, view himself as addressed by precisely the same motive, as regards the conduct of his life. If a free man, he would expect, in all relations, to have regard supremely to the will of God, and do all things 'as unto Christ.' Let him do the same now, realizing that in no respect will the divine dealing with him be made to differ because of his present condition, however much one of humiliating servitude it may be.

9. And ye, masters, do the same things unto them. The principle just stated with regard to servants is here applied to masters. There is one law of Christian intercourse for all classes of men. **Forbearing threatening.** The word for 'threatening' has the article (τὴν ἀπειλήν), and is therefore made more specific than either the Common Version or the Revision would indicate. It means the threatening common with 'masters,' the harsh, rude, contumelious way in which the "hard master" has always been wont to treat especially the slave. In the relations of the Christian master and slave all this is to be changed. **Knowing that your Master also is in heaven.** The Greek (καὶ αὐτῶν καὶ ὑμῶν ὁ κύριος) means, *both their Master and yours*. The American Revisers would read, "he who is both their Master and yours." The thought is that in the common relation of master and servant with him who is in heaven, the difference of condition disappears; for, **neither is there respect of persons with him.** Thayer explains the Greek word translated 'respect of persons' as indicating "the fault of one who, when called on to requite or to give judgment, has respect to the outward circumstances of men, and not to their intrinsic merits, and so prefers, as the more worthy, one who is rich, high-born, or powerful, to one who is destitute of such gifts." There is none of this with that Master of us all who is in heaven. It is impossible that the human distinctions which are often of such importance to us should be of equal importance to him, or, indeed, of any importance at all, save as "to whom much is given, of him shall much be required." (Luke 12 : 48.)

It is to be noticed that, although these principles and precepts of Christian morals are addressed to those who are themselves Christian, and so have an immediate application to them, they are so grounded in fundamental principles of right and justice as to be equally in force for all classes and conditions of men. The Christian law of right in human relations is the natural law of right, set forth with a special divine sanction, and addressed to motives originating in the new nature of one who

10 Finally, my brethren, be strong in the Lord, and in the power of his might.
11 Put on the whole armour of God, that ye may be able to stand against the wiles of the devil.
12 For we wrestle not against flesh and blood, but against principalities, against powers, against the rulers of the darkness of this world, against spiritual wickedness in high *places*.

10 ¹Finally, ¹be strong in the Lord, and in the
11 strength of his might. Put on the whole armour of God, that ye may be able to stand against the
12 wiles of the devil. For our wrestling is not against flesh and blood, but against the principalities, against the powers against the world-rulers of this darkness, against the spiritual *hosts* of wickedness in

1 Or, *from henceforth*......2 Gr. *be made powerful.*

---

has been born again. These motives, even, are, however, such as every one should be capable of; so that it can by no means be claimed that what is here taught and enjoined, though addressed in the first instance to Christians, is for Christians only. The law of the new life is of universal obligation, and they whose spiritual condition makes them insensible to its claim are just so much the more in fault.

10-20. THE NEW LIFE AS A CONFLICT.

10. Finally, my brethren. One manuscript (A) omits the word for 'my.' Four others, ℵ B D E, omit both words, and read simply, 'Finally.' This text the Revision and most modern critics adopt, **Be strong in the Lord.** The verb has a more intense meaning than simply 'be strong.' It means "*be strengthened.*" Having set forth with such fullness as we see the doctrine of redemption; having shown what provision has been made for making the redeeming purpose effectual in a regenerate people, saved through the grace that is in Christ Jesus; having presented to view the new life, with the law that is to rule it and the virtues that are to adorn it, the apostle comes now to the admonitory truth that there are many adversaries, and these the Christian believer must be prepared to meet. For this, strength is needful. Hence his exhortation, 'Be strengthened in the Lord.' **And in the power of his might.** This does not mean 'in' or *by* "his mighty power." As Ellicott says, we are to "preserve the proper force of each substantive." What the Christian, preparing for conflict, needs is 'power.' The armor he is to wear is described in verses which follow; but first there must be the 'power,' as otherwise armor, whether defensive or offensive, is little availing. This power the believer must receive in communications of that 'might' which he finds in fellowship with his Lord and in answer to prayer.

11. Put on the whole armour of God. There is one word in the Greek for 'whole armour' (πανοπλίαν), from which comes our word "panoply." The emphasis is upon this word, not upon "God" (θεοῦ). In subsequent verses this 'panoply' is described. What the apostle would urge is that *all* of it, 'the whole armour,' be 'put on.' The Christian believer, since he is also a Christian warrior, should seek a complete equipment of that which has been provided him, undervaluing nothing, omitting nothing. How can he know at what unguarded point the subtle foe he has to meet may aim his "fiery dart"? **That ye may be able to stand.** The word for 'stand' (στῆναι) is a military term. It means the firm and prepared attitude of the true soldier confronting his enemy. **Against the wiles of the devil.** As will be seen further on, the passage we are considering recognizes distinctly the existence of malignant spirits of evil, with whom men have to deal. The chief of these seems to be here intended. It is held by judicious commentators that alike here and in ver. 16 below—"the fiery darts of the wicked" .,*one*"—Satan himself is meant. Not that to this chief of the evil spirits anything like omnipresence is to be attributed, but that, as the leader of that dreaded host, he acts by his instruments, whether fallen angels or wicked men; while especially the 'wiles' against which we are to be always on guard are of his devising. 'Wiles' may as well mean "stratagems," and refer to those many and subtle and dangerous ways in which evil assails men, and the Christian by no means least of all.

12. For we wrestle not against flesh and blood. What we have in the verses which follow deals with matter of deepest concern to all men, and yet of which all too few are willing to be convinced. That form of skepticism which finds in "the unseen" a presumption of non-existence is especially slow to admit that men, even in their moral conflicts, have more to contend with than that of whose existence they are directly conscious. What the apostle here says is that man's real 'wrestle,' that upon which the alternatives of destiny most depend, is not with the seen, but with the unseen. But **against principalities, against powers.** Like terms with these have been before used in this Epistle, although in quite a contrasted application. We read in 3 : 10 of 'principalities and powers in the heavenly places,' by which are clearly meant, as the connection there shows, good angels, in the several orders of dignity and administration. The analogy between that passage and the present one makes the meaning here no less clear. It is one of those places in Scripture where allusion is made to facts in the spiritual world of which we know but little, yet of which so much as this is made certain—that the evil of the universe is not a vague, impersonal "possibility," but an organized force, represented in personalities as real as those in which the opposite principle of good becomes embodied and active. The language of Paul in this place implies further, that there is order and administration among evil spirits, as among good spirits, while the warfare of humanity with the one of these is as real and as much to be dreaded as the help in this warfare to be sought and expected from the other. **Against the rulers of the darkness of this world.** It is agreed among critics that the Greek term for 'world' (αἰῶνος) does not belong to the true text. It is not found in the three oldest manuscripts, א, A, B, and is omitted in many of the versions and by many of the Fathers. The word for 'rulers' (κοσμοκράτορας), besides, expresses more than the translation would imply. It means, as the Revision reads, "world-rulers." These 'principalities and powers,' therefore, are 'world-rulers'; their sway is world wide, and they are rulers of 'this darkness'—the moral darkness pervading humanity. This is alike the element and the kingdom of these evil 'powers' and 'principalities.' **Against spiritual wickedness in high places** (*heavenly places*). The changed translation in the Revision will be noticed. The word for 'spiritual' (πνευματικά) is (like ἱππικόν, "cavalry," and λῃστρικά, "robber-hordes") an adjective used as a substantive. It does not qualify the word for 'wickedness,' but governs it in the genitive. "*Spiritual hosts of wickedness*" is therefore the correct translation. 'Spiritual hosts of wickedness in the heavenly places' (τοῖς ἐπουρανίοις), however, is difficult of explanation. This phrase, 'heavenly places,' has occurred repeatedly before in this Epistle,—in 1 : 3, 20; 2 : 6; and 3 : 10,—in each case in a connection very different from this. It has not seemed to us, in commenting upon those passages, that its meaning should be wholly localized, as if denoting heaven merely, but as embracing that whole sphere of higher reality in human experience which has its centre in heaven, is pervaded by heavenly influences and enriched by heavenly ministries. It seems also to us a mistaken exegesis to give to the phrase in this present passage a meaning so essentially different from what it manifestly has in the earlier ones, as some have proposed; either as meaning by 'heavenly' the lower regions of the atmosphere, once supposed to be the haunt of evil spirits,—although this view has a formidable array of distinguished names in its support,—or any of the more fanciful ones anciently preferred. We suggest the following points as perhaps helpful toward a solution: 1. That the thought in this verse seems in some degree to move toward a climax. The 'wrestle' of the Christian is *not* 'against' such comparatively feeble opponents as 'flesh and blood'; it *is* against 'principalities and powers,' at first vaguely mentioned, which, however, become more a reality as dwelling in and ruling the world's moral 'darkness,' and then are brought face to face with us as 'spiritual hosts of wickedness in the' very 'heavenly places' themselves. It seems to us a material letting down of the whole thought when from such a conception as 'world-rulers of the darkness' we drop to that of haunting spirits in the atmosphere around us. 2. It would seem a thing to be expected, that the apostle in the view here to be given of the malignant activity of evil spirits, would in an especial manner show how this activity immediately concerns the Christian. The first two points of description in the verse are general, and describe the agency of such spirits as it affects humanity everywhere. His especial theme, however, is the spiritual conflict of the Christian believer. May it not be his intention to touch upon this in the part of the verse now under consideration? 3. We know for a fact that short of heaven itself there is no sphere of Christian life that is secure against

13 Wherefore take unto you the whole armour of God, that ye may be able to withs.and in the evil day, and having done all, to stand.
14 Staud therefore, having your loins girt about with truth, and having on the breastplate of righteousness.

13 the heavenly *places*. Wherefore take up the whole armour of God, that ye may be able to withstand in
14 the evil day, and, having done all, to stand. Stand therefore, having girded your loins with truth, and

the invasions of evil in its manifold forms. The closest and dearest fellowships, the most sacred spiritual associations, the inner spiritual life itself of the Christian, even those experiences of his which have in them most of heaven may be, and sometimes—too often, indeed!—are intruded upon by that sinister power whose ministry is always evil. 4. As before intimated, it would be most consistent with a correct exegesis to understand this repeatedly recurring phrase in a like way throughout the Epistle. "There are," as Eadie says, "beyond a doubt, 'heavenly places' on earth. The gospel, or the Mediatorial reign, is 'the kingdom of heaven.' That kingdom or reign of God is 'in us,' or among us. Heaven is brought near to us through Christ Jesus. Those spiritual blessings conferred on us create heaven within us, and the scenes of divine benefaction are 'heavenly places.'" As the same writer implies, the church itself may be included in the representation. Into all these spheres and relations 'the spiritual hosts of wickedness' are known to intrude, and here especially Christian men and women need to be prepared for the encounter.

13. **Wherefore take unto you** (*take up*) **the whole armour of God.** According to Thayer, the rendering 'take unto you,' in the Common Version, would be correct as a secondary meaning of the word ἀναλάβετε, although 'take up' is the primary meaning; of course 'take up' with a view to use. This last rendering, in the present case is, perhaps, the more graphic. The repetition of the counsel given emphasizes its importance. The armor in question is the 'armour of God.' The language used distinguishes it from all manner of merely human precautions, defenses, or disciplines. It is a special provision for the Christian believer in response to his prayerful trust in God. **That ye may be able to withstand in the evil day.** *To stand against* (ἀντιστῆναι). The 'evil day' is the day of temptation. Not always realized as such, by any means, since evil rarely presents itself to men as the evil thing it is. All the same, that day is an 'evil' one in which a foe so subtle must be encountered, and dangers so fearful faced and overcome. It is limiting too much the meaning of the phrase 'evil day,' to understand by it the day of death, as some have interpreted, or, as Meyer, "some future and terrible outbreak of Satan before the expected advent of Christ." (Eadie.) Upon the other hand, we should not with others, characterize every day as 'evil' in the sense here intended. The reference is to those special seasons and circumstances of spiritual or moral exposure which may come at any time, and for which it is important to be always prepared. **And having done all, to stand.** The 'having done all' is a specific reference to the counsel given in the passage, as a whole. Its meaning, however, is somewhat broader than simply "having made full preparation" for the encounter. It includes all that may be needful, alike in preparing for the encounter and *in* it. "To be in condition for warring a good warfare"—this seems to be what is had in view. Some commentators, as Olshausen, Conybeare, De Wette, would understand by 'having done all,' having fought the battle and won it. We shall do better to keep in our interpretation to that which the apostle evidently has distinctly in view throughout the passage, namely, *preparation*.

14. **Stand, therefore.** For the third time in the same immediate connection the word 'stand' is employed, suggesting how momentous, in Paul's conception, is that attitude of the Christian soldier which the word implies. The true soldier intends to conquer. His whole attitude and bearing mean this. Too often temptation finds men already half conquered. They are inadequately armed, if armed at all, and the purpose to resist can scarcely be termed a purpose. This is not to 'stand.' **Having your loins girt about with truth.** The article is omitted in the Greek as in the translation. It is not *the* truth which the apostle means, but 'truth,' *inward* truth, genuineness, the *reality* of that which seems; with all else that may be intended, implying a genuine and resolute *purpose*.

15 And your feet shod with the preparation of the gospel of peace;
16 Above all, taking the shield of faith, wherewith ye shall be able to quench all the fiery darts of the wicked.

15 having put on the breastplate of righteousness, and having shod your feet with the preparation of the
16 gospel of peace; withal taking up the shield of faith, wherewith ye shall be able to quench all the ..

The girdle of the Roman soldier, says Ellicott, was "the first and most necessary part of the equipment... Independently of serving to keep the armor in its proper place, it appears also... to have been used to support the sword." The girdle of the soldier was often highly ornamented, but it is not to this that the writer here refers, but to its serviceableness, its indispensableness for the fully equipped soldier. **And having** (*having put on*) **the breastplate of righteousness.** Commentators differ as to the exact import of the term 'righteousness' (τῆς δικαιοσύνης) in this place. Some, as Harless, De Wette, Eadie, incline to understand by it, in the language of the last named, "the righteousness of God, or of faith, or as 'justification by the blood of the cross,' three Scriptural phrases, meaning in general one and the same thing"; being influenced in this view, evidently, by the presence of the article. Elliott, with Meyer, Olshausen, and others, would understand, "Christian moral rectitude, or, more correctly speaking, the righteousness which is the result of the renovation of the heart by the Holy Spirit." We do not find ourselves quite clear as to which of these interpretations is the preferable one. As this equipment, throughout, appears to be that which the Christian soldier has *in himself*, however much it may be 'the gift of God,' it is, perhaps, safer to accept the second of the two views named above. It would, too, be perhaps in better keeping with the imagery of the 'breastplate.' This last is an important part of the soldier's *defensive* armor, and as a matter of fact, that in the Christian which *resists*, and in some sense *defends*, is not "imputed righteousness," but the new man within, which refuses to entertain the evil suggestion.

15. And your feet shod (or, *having shod your feet*) **with the preparation of the gospel of peace.** The word 'preparation,' though retained in the Revision, scarcely expresses the full idea. "Readiness" (ἑτοιμασία), "preparedness," is what seems meant. Special attention appears to have been given, anciently, to the soldier's footwear. As his fighting was so much hand to hand, a firm footing was exceedingly important to him. His sandals, or *caligae*, were accordingly not only bound firmly to the foot and ankle, but were, as we are told, "thickly studded with hobnails." The Christian soldier's 'preparedness,' in this regard, he is to find in 'the gospel of peace,' It is this gospel of peace as realized in experience. It is that principle of steadfastness which has its origin in a sense of oneness with God, and so of divine aid equal to any extremity. It is not the gospel of peace as given him for proclamation to others, but the gospel of peace is an experience in himself.

16. Above all, taking the shield of faith. The Greek phrase in the Revision is rendered "withal" (ἐν πᾶσιν). The 'above all' of the Common Version is in any case incorrect. The text of the Revisers has the warrant of the Sinaitic and Vatican manuscripts (א and B). The phrase in the Alexandrine (ἐπὶ πᾶσιν) Ellicott prefers, translating "in addition to all." The sense is much the same, in either case. 'Above all,' besides not being warranted by the Greek text, conveys a wrong impression. The apostle does not mean to say that the most important part of the equipment is this which he now mentions. He simply describes a part of the soldier's armament differing from those before mentioned; one to be not attached to the body, but borne upon the arm or hand so as to be shifted about as need may require. It is 'the shield of faith,' or, '*faith as a shield*,' the genitive being that of apposition. The Christian believer's 'faith' serves him in his need, as his shield does the soldier. **Wherewith ye shall be able to quench all the fiery darts of the wicked.** There is general consent among commentators, with whom Thayer, in his Lexicon, agrees, that by the term rendered 'the wicked' in the Common Version, 'the evil one' in the Revision, is meant Satan, the devil; "either," says Eadie, "in proper person, or as leader and representative of the foes so vividly described in ver. 12." To make the term descriptive, simply, of evil as impersonal would be inconsistent with the *personal* character

98 EPHESIANS. [CH. VI.

17 And take the helmet of salvation, and the sword of the Spirit, which is the word of God:
18 Praying always with all prayer and supplication in the Spirit and watching thereunto with all perseverance and supplication for all saints:
19 And for me, that utterance may be given unto me, that I may open my mouth boldly, to make known the mystery of the gospel,

17 fiery darts of the evil one. And take the helmet of salvation and the sword of the Spirit, which is the word of God; with all prayer and supplication praying at all seasons in the Spirit, and watching thereunto in all perseverance and supplication for
19 all the saints, and on my behalf, that utterance may be given unto me [1] in opening my mouth, to make known with boldness the mystery of the gos-

1 Or, *in opening my mouth with boldness, to make known.*

---

of the representation throughout. Perhaps where, in ver. 12, the apostle tells us that 'we wrestle not against flesh and blood, but against principalities, against powers,' etc., he intends, in part at least, to indicate the fact that it is not tendencies toward evil, in ourselves or others, against which we are to contend, but against evil itself in personal forms. This personal element in the representation is preserved throughout, and cannot, in the place now considered, be set aside without violence done to the laws of good exegesis. The larger shields of the soldiers, anciently, we are told, "which for lightness were made of wood, were covered with hides and similar material, designed to prevent the full effect of the 'fiery darts.'" (Ellicott, who refers to Arrian, ii., 18.) Arrows tipped with some inflammable substance were used, we are also told, in sieges or under certain circumstances against the enemy in the field. This was true alike of the Romans, the Greeks, and the Hebrews. It was evidently the most dangerous form of that kind of missile. The imagery here, accordingly, is used to enforce the thought that against Satan's worst form of attack 'the shield of faith' will avail.

17. And take the helmet of salvation—literally, "receive, take with the hand (δέξασθε), the helmet of salvation," since it is "the gift of God." Not, here, "*the hope* of salvation," as in 1 Thess. 5 : 8, but 'salvation' itself. It is making "our calling and election sure." (2 Peter 1 : 10.) **And the sword of the Spirit, which is the word of God.** "The only offensive weapon," says Eadie, "which the Christian soldier is to assume." Says Hodge: "In opposition to all error, to all false philosophy, to all false principles in morals, to all the sophistries of vice, to all the suggestions of the devil, the sole, simple, and sufficient answer is the word of God." The particular reference here appears to be to personal experiences of the Christian believer himself; since with this as his main topic the writer is deal-

ing throughout. Yet the broader view just suggested may be admissible as a remoter application of the words. It is, then, a question of serious practical import, whether, in his personal warfare with evil or his general encounter with the error and evil of the world, the Christian or the Christian teacher makes supreme account of this 'sword of the Spirit' in the full meaning of what is here said.

18. Praying always with all prayer and supplication in the Spirit. The rendering in the Revision, "at all seasons" for 'always,' will be noticed. By 'all prayer and supplication' is implied prayer adjusted to varying conditions of need; and by 'at all sensons' that constant prayerful frame of mind which becomes uttered and pleading 'supplication' as for such supplication occasions arise. However well equipped the Christian soldier may be, his sufficiency is still 'of God.' **And watching thereunto.** Watching *with reference to this* (εἰς αὐτό), or, *for this,* that is the prayer and supplication; exercising care not to become remiss, or to fall into habits of neglecting what is so essential always as prayer, and most of all in those spiritual conflicts so inevitable for Christians in this world. **With all perseverance and supplication for all saints.** "No soldier," says Hodge, "entering battle prays for himself alone, but for all his fellow-soldiers also. They form one army, and the success of one is the success of all."

19. And for me that utterance may be given unto me. A different preposition (ὑπέρ) is used here, 'for me,' from that employed above (περί), 'for all saints.' Eadie would find some significance in this change of the preposition, supposing the former (ὑπέρ) to have more intensity of meaning, as if the apostle would desire some special fervency of prayer in his own behalf. Ellicott thinks this scarcely warranted, while Alford, though he sees "something in it," regards Eadie as pressing it too far. In making this request the apostle doubtless has reference, in part at least, to his cir-

20 For which I am an ambassador in bonds; that therein I may speak boldly, as I ought to speak.
21 But that ye also may know my affairs, *and* how I do, Tychicus, a beloved brother and faithful minister in the Lord, shall make known to you all things:
22 Whom I have sent unto you for the same purpose, that ye might know our affairs, and *that* he might comfort your hearts.

20 pel, for which I am an ambassador in ¹chains: that in it I may speak boldly, as I ought to speak.
21 But that ye also may know my affairs, how I do, Tychicus, the beloved brother and faithful minister in the Lord, shall make known to you all things: 22 whom I have sent unto you for this very purpose, that ye may know our state, and that he may comfort your hearts.

¹ Gr. *a chain.*

cumstances at the time of writing. It is noticeable that his mind is evidently intent upon his work, for which some opportunity was afforded him even as a prisoner. Of all opportunity for such service it was his especial desire that he might be enabled to make the best use, alike as he now is and in his general ministry. **That I may open my mouth boldly**—or, *in opening my mouth boldly.* In this way he desired that utterance might be 'given.' Whatever he should be able to do, especially in such circumstances, he felt would be through divine help given in answer to prayer. **To make known the mystery of the gospel.** The gospel itself is viewed as a 'mystery,' a matter of revelation, making known what could become matter of either knowledge or of faith only as thus revealed.

20. **For which I am an ambassador in bonds;** or, *in a chain,* the Greek word being in the singular. It is not simply that he still is an 'ambassador' though bound with a chain, but that while an ambassador, an ambassador in behalf of the gospel, an "ambassador for God," and "in Christ's stead," he yet is bound thus with a chain, as any felon might be. **That therein** (or, *in it*) **I may speak boldly, as I ought to speak.** He is still to fulfill his office, even under these conditions, and as opportunity serves is required to 'speak boldly.' In this behalf he desires that there may be remembrance of him in the prayers of those in Ephesus who under his ministry have come to know what prayer is.

21-24. A MESSAGE AND A BENEDICTION.
21. **But that ye may know my state, and how I do.** We come, now, to the closing words. They take the form, as so often is the case with this apostle, of personal address, with allusions to the writer's own present circumstances. There is a nice question, here, with reference to the force of the particle translated 'also' (καὶ). Some, as Eadie and others, would make it simply a "particle of transition," putting what is now to be said in relation with that which has gone before. Ellicott, however, regards this transition as already made by the particle 'but' (δὲ). He accordingly translates, "But in order that ye also may know," instead of "that also ye may know," or, "in order also that ye may know." He holds that the particle (καὶ), as so understood, makes the passage "indisputably refer to others besides the Ephesians," though admitting that "who they were cannot be satisfactorily determined." If the Epistle to the Colossians was written first of the two, he thinks the reference may be to them. We do not see that the point can be made really so indisputable as to supply basis for any theory as to this, or any other of the collateral questions supposably involved. **Tychicus, a beloved brother and faithful minister in the Lord, shall make known to you all things.** In Acts 20: 4, and in Col. 4: 7, Tychicus is mentioned: in the latter place as bearer, also, of the letter to the Colossian Church. Where, in 2 Tim. 4: 12, Paul says, "Tychicus have I sent to Ephesus," it is supposed reference may be made to his commission as bearer of this present Epistle. In such a case, it may be allowable to draw from the circumstance proof of our Epistle having been, at least, first of all intended for the Ephesian Church. As so sent, Tychicus would be a messenger direct from the apostle himself, and could make known to these brethren, whose solicitude in this behalf may be inferred from the scene of the parting at Troas (Acts 20: 17-38), all particulars of his life in this Roman captivity.

22. **Whom I have sent unto you for the same purpose** (or, *for this very purpose*) **that ye might know our affairs, and that he might comfort your hearts.** In 3: 13, of this Epistle, Paul has entreated his brethren not to 'faint at' his 'tribulations for' them. He now assures them that the special purpose of his message by Tychicus is that 'he might comfort' their 'hearts.' The emphatic words, 'for this very purpose,' shows how tenderly

23 Peace be to the brethren, and love with faith, from God the Father and the Lord Jesus Christ. 24 Grace be with all them that love our Lord Jesus Christ in sincerity. Amen.

23 Peace be to the brethren, and love with faith, from God the Father and the Lord Jesus Christ. 24 Grace be with all them that love our Lord Jesus Christ in uncorruptness.

he thinks of those to whom this message is sent, and how warmly desirous he is that their solicitude concerning him may be relieved.

23. Peace be to the brethren, and love with faith. It is 'peace' in the broad meaning of the word; not simply peace amongst themselves; the 'peace of God.' (Phil. 4:7.) 'Love with faith' means more than love and faith; it means these two in simultaneous exercise. They are kindred graces, and live together in the same regenerate heart. **From God the Father and the Lord Jesus Christ.** From whom all right spiritual affections proceed.

24. Grace be with all them that love our Lord Jesus Christ in sincerity. Amen. A second benediction, comprehensive of all who love Jesus Christ—all who are truly his; that in the preceding verse being addressed especially to those at Ephesus. The use by the Revisers of 'uncorruptness' for 'sincerity,' is to be noticed. The Greek word (ἀφθαρσία) is the word found at 1 Cor. 15:42, "it is raised in incorruption," where the thought is, *no longer subject to death.* The underlying idea is that of imperishableness. The 'love' here mentioned is the love that *endures.* It may not be allowable to trace in the word as so employed any doctrinal intention; yet since the word clearly means more than simple 'sincerity' it must point to a 'love' such in its nature as that, while sincere it is perpetual, and so an element in that new life which, begotten in regeneration, fulfills those words of the Lord himself, "I give unto them eternal life." (John 10:28.)

SUMMARY OF THE EXPOSITION.

In this concluding portion of the Epistle (5:22-6:9), in which the writer treats the subject of Christian morals, human relations are viewed in three aspects: (1) That of husband and wife (5:22-33); (2) parent and child (6:1-4); (3) master and servant (6:5-9). These are fundamental relations. Of Christian morals in their more general aspect (4:25-32; 5:3-13), he has treated before. Both these and here we notice, as has already been mentioned, that the morality enjoined is as seen at the distinctively *Christian* point of view. Practical Christianity, even where it deals specifically with conduct, takes higher ground than mere morality ever does. ·Its life is fed, also, at sources more profound and more pure. What is first of all, what goes before precept of every kind, is that of which we read in 4: 22-24: 'the old man' put off, 'the new man' put on. Practical Christianity thus becomes a *power* as well as a *precept.* Its reformation begins with transformation. It is thus a new life within, and it is under the law of that new life that the Christian comes. All things implying duty are thenceforth to be seen in their relation to that which this law of the new life enjoins, which is, that all obedience shall be 'as unto Christ'—all morality 'doing the will of God from the heart.' (6:5,6.) It were easy to show, alike from reason, from experience, and from history, that the deep-seated and incorrigible evil of the world can in no other way be radically reached and cured. The emphasis which Paul, in these later portions of the Epistle, places upon the domestic relations, is quite consistent with the importance of these relations, as fundamental to all others, and as so essential in determining alike the formation of character and conduct of life.

There may be reason for the suggestion sometimes made, that the vivid imagery under which the apostle sets forth Christian conflict and *preparation* for conflict (6:10-20), may have been prompted by the constant presence with him of the armed Roman soldier. We can conceive this 'panoply' of the armed man as made thus a subject of study, perhaps of conversation, in a way for which opportunity may never before have been afforded. He may have heard much, too, from his armed attendant, of what befalls the soldier on the march, in the ambuscade, and on the field of battle—all being turned to account in the interest of the one engrossing theme. Thus become palpable to him the analogies of truth for the girdle of the Christian soldier, righteousness his breastplate, the gospel of peace his shoes of preparation, faith as his shield, salvation his helmet, and the word of God as the "sharp, two-edged sword." (Heb. 4:12.)

What is said as to the real nature of spiritual conflict (6:10-13) should be especially remarked. Much of the peril of humanity in the moral issues of its destiny arises out of a deluding misapprehension as to what these issues imply. It is one thing to wrestle with 'flesh and blood,' quite another with principalities, with powers, with world rulers of the moral darkness, with spiritual hosts of wickedness in the very heavenly places themselves. It is this startling truth which men are so unwilling to face, or to deal with it honestly and truly. Evil, not merely as a possibility, nor merely as a fact; but evil as an organized, actual, and, so far as human experience is concerned, omnipresent force; evil in spiritual embodiment, with order, administration, with malignant purpose and intelligent method. Of the reality of this, how earnestly does inspired Scripture seek to impress the mind of man!

The closing words of the Epistle (6:21-24), as so often in these writings of Paul, reveal to us the tender, sympathetic, and loyal heart, whose interest in the welfare of those addressed has dictated all that went before. From his Roman captivity he looks forth upon the fields of former labor, and for each one of those whom he has seen brought to saving knowledge of the truth under his ministry,—specially, now, all such in the city where three eventful years of that ministry were spent,— he is mindful and thoughtful and prayerful. His Christian sympathy, indeed, embraces '*all* them that love our Lord Jesus Christ in uncorruptness.' He closes his letter with a benediction upon all such, of whatever race, or nation, or age.

www.ingramcontent.com/pod-product-compliance
Lightning Source LLC
Chambersburg PA
CBHW020155170426
43199CB00010B/1057